METAPHYSICAL PERSPECTIVES

METAPHYSICAL

PERSPECTIVES

NICHOLAS RESCHER

University of Notre Dame Press
Notre Dame, Indiana

University of Notre Dame Press
Notre Dame, Indiana 46556
undpress.nd.edu

Published in the United States of America

Library of Congress Cataloging-in-Publication Data

Names: Rescher, Nicholas, author.
Title: Metaphysical perspectives / Nicholas Rescher.
Description: Notre Dame : University of Notre Dame Press, 2017. |
    Includes bibliographical references and index. |
Identifiers: LCCN 2017030359 (print) | LCCN 2017034712 (ebook) |
    ISBN 9780268102913 (pdf) | ISBN 9780268102920 (epub) |
    ISBN 9780268102890 (hardcover : alk. paper) |
    ISBN 0268102899 (hardcover : alk. paper)
Subjects: LCSH: Metaphysics.
Classification: LCC BD111 (ebook) | LCC BD111.R3195   2017 (print) |
    DDC 110—dc23
LC record available at https://lccn.loc.gov/2017030359

∞ *This paper meets the requirements of ANSI/NISO Z39.48-1992*
(Permanence of Paper).

For Gereon Wolters
in cordial friendship

CONTENTS

Preface   ix

Introduction: On the Mission of Philosophy   1

One   Ultimate Questions   9

Two   World Views   22

Three   Terminological Contextuality   31

Four   On Contingency and Necessity   41

Five   Randomness and Reason   53

Six   Issues of Self-Reference and Paradox   60

Seven   Explanation and the Principle of Sufficient Reason   69

Eight   Intelligent Design Revisited in the Light of Evolutionary Neoplatonism   82

Nine   What If Things Were Different?   95

Ten   On the Improvability of the World   112

Eleven   Consciousness   133

Twelve   Control   146

Thirteen   Free Will in the Light of Process Theory   159

Fourteen   Personhood   172

Fifteen   The Metaphysics of Moral Obligation   188

Sixteen   Empathy, Shared Experience, and Other Minds   197

Seventeen   Philosophy as an Inexact Science   210

Eighteen   Philosophy's Involvement with Transcendental Issues   220

Nineteen   Religious Variation and the Rationale of Belief   230

Notes   236
Bibliography   249
Index of Names   256

PREFACE

Metaphysics is the study of existence at the highest level of generality. Its concern is with the "big questions" regarding the world, ourselves, and our place within reality's scheme of things. The salient task of the field is to elucidate the concepts and principles by whose means a clearer understanding of the ideas of existence and reality can be achieved. As such, metaphysics has been an established branch of philosophy since Aristotle's initial systematization of the subject in the fourth century B.C. And down to the present day it continues to be a lively area of investigation and deliberation.

In line with this tradition, the present book deals with a range of key metaphysical issues. Metaphysics, after all, has three prime areas of concern: (1) the world as such and the architecture of nature at large, (2) ourselves as nature's denizens and our potential for learning about it, and (3) the transcendent domain of possibility and value, which impels us to consider issues that reach above and beyond the resources of nature. The book makes a journey across this large and challenging domain, engaging issues ranging from world views to transcendental concerns. In the course of this journey it sets out an integrated view of the key philosophical problems, which is grounded in an idealistically value-oriented approach. It thus seeks to throw new light on philosophically central issues from a unified point of view.

Metaphysics is an "extra-ordinary" domain of inquiry; why, then, should at least some of us cultivate metaphysics and seek for a synoptic explanation of everything? After all, the explanatory process has to stop somewhere: we cannot go on giving explanations ad infinitum. So why not just call it a day and give up on the quest for a reason why things are as they are? In the end, the answer is simply, "Man by nature seeks to know," as Aristotle put it.

I am grateful to Estelle Burris for invaluable help in preparing this material for publication.

Nicholas Rescher
Pittsburgh, Pennsylvania
November 2016

INTRODUCTION

On The Mission of Philosophy

How should one conceive of philosophy as a human endeavor? What is the aim of the enterprise?

Many answers have been offered. But four of them are particularly prominent.

PHILOSOPHY AS LITERATURE. Philosophy is akin to *belles lettres*. It spreads out interesting ideas as possibilities for thoughtful deliberation in reading and conversation. Like the study of literature, its aim is intellectual stimulus, enlightenment, and cultural sophistication. Its work is an exploration of possibilities, and its study is a sort of tourism in the realm of ideas. Not this week Dordogne and next week Provence, but this week Plato and next week Nietzsche?

PHILOSOPHY AS MEGA-SCIENCE. Like science, philosophy is a venture in rational inquiry aimed at the determination of reality's facts. But where science seeks to understood the constituents and the processes that make up the natural and the social worlds, philosophy wants to explain how we humans fit into our place within the world as so characterized. It wants to explain the scope and the limits of our cognitive efforts and practical activities within the world as science describes it.

PHILOSOPHY AS NORMATIVE ASSESSOR. While most other cognitive inquiries depict the realm of what is, philosophizing is ultimately a venture in normativity and evaluative appreciation. Its prime concern is with questions of value, especially cognitive value (i.e., importance) and practical value (i.e., utility). And its prime task is axiological—to explore and expand the theory of rational appraisal.

1

PHILOSOPHY AS LIFE COACH. The definitive aim of philosophizing is a practical orientation. Its task is to provide reasonable guidance for the conduct of life. The motto of the collegiate φβκ Society gets it right: philosophy is the helmsman of life (*philosophia biou kybernētēs*). It seeks to instruct us about how to live "the good life."

Most philosophers adopt one or another of these approaches as authoritative. And as they see it, their favored version is solely correct and proper—people pursuing a rival path "are just not doing (real) philosophy."

But this exclusivist position is seriously flawed. For the best available option is a combination and amalgamation of all these alternatives. This should become clear when one considers the wide range of questions and objectives that need to be addressed:

(1) What are the subjects of philosophical concern? What issues are on the agenda? What sorts of questions arise? And what are the alternative possibilities for resolving them?

(2) Since philosophy is bound to address our place and position in the world, it cannot avoid attention to what science has to say about the world's composition and modus operandi and how we come to find out about these matters.

(3) Philosophy has both a theoretical and a practical dimension. Its task is not just to explain the world and our place in it, but to guide us in the management of our cognitive and practical affairs.

(4) To provide guidance, philosophy has to be concerned with what is important and what is unimportant, with what is of value for us and what is not. Concerned with the nature of the good, it cannot avoid addressing normative issues in its endeavor to provide guidance about thought and action.

And in dealing with the answers to the concerns just listed, all of the variant approaches described above—philosophy as literature, as megascience, as normative assessor, and as life coach—have a role. No single, limited line of approach can prove adequate to the entire project.

Philosophers have tended to focus on just one of these approaches and to see the others as incidental or irrelevant. But the inappropriateness of such a view should be clear. Statesmanship affords an illuminating model for philosophy here: a statesman cannot—or should not—wear blinders in looking at the problems and methods of the field. His proper task encompasses many dimensions of public affairs. Different approaches are required to handle the problems of public health, education, criminal justice, public information, and so on. The situation with philosophy is much the same. Philosophy is a complex, many-sided area of intellectual endeavor, and it thereby allows for many sorts of treatment. One must not labor under the delusion that any one part of it is the whole.

As traditionally conceived, the task of philosophy, specifically metaphysics, is to grapple with "the big questions" concerning man, nature, and man's role in reality's scheme of things. Science, to be sure, addresses these matters as well, but whereas science describes *how* things work in this world, metaphysics speculates about *why* they work in that sort of way. Science connects the constituents of reality to one another; metaphysics connects reality to possibility. And unlike the strictly descriptively informative concerns of science, the concerns of metaphysics are also normatively evaluative.

The issues that figure prominently in the agenda of philosophy and its various branches are inherent in the defining aim of the enterprise—to provide us with rationally cogent guidance for the management of our lives. This puts certain key questions at the heart of the discipline, namely:

- How do things work in the world? (Metaphysics)
- What is our own position in the world's scheme of things? (Philosophical Anthropology)
- How are we to find out things regarding both nature and ourselves? (Epistemology)
- How can we reason cogently about the facts at our disposal? (Logic)
- What is good for us: what goals and values are appropriate for beings situated as we are? (Axiology)
- What should we do: what ways of acting are appropriate for us? (Ethics)

And because the particular conditions and circumstances in which we find ourselves in the world differ almost endlessly in their particularity, it will be nearly impossible to find answers that gain universal acceptance and generalities that hold across the board. But nevertheless, the very rationality that defines our nature as beings in this world requires us to dedicate to these important issues our best efforts at resolution.

Accordingly, philosophy asks questions like these:

- Why is it that the world is constituted as is?
- Is nature's law structure necessary or contingent?

- What is it that gives people duties and obligations over and above those specified by law and by social convention?
- What is it that people ought to try to do with their lives?
- What does it take over and above the biology of being a *human* (a member of *Homo sapiens*) to be a *person* (a normatively engaged rational being)?
- What sorts of relations do and should exist among persons as such and how should we treat one another in view of this?

Moreover, philosophy is also a reflexive enterprise, a project a part of whose mandate is self-characterization. And this includes asking whether philosophical questions of the aforementioned sort are objectively legitimate at all, and what sort of measures are available for endeavoring to answer them. Or are these issues purely subjective matters of more or less arbitrary individual inclination?

Philosophy, so conceived, thus addresses issues of profound human concern. Granted, no one can manage to master or indeed even begin to answer all of its questions adequately. But one should never take the stance that issues outside one's particular sphere of interest don't really matter. And if the task is too large—if mastery of the whole is impracticable—then one can at least strive for a rudimentary understanding of the range of component issues and a clear understanding of at least one part of it. The philosopher cannot afford to be either a hedgehog, who knows a small terrain well but is ignorant of the larger setting, nor yet a fox, who knows superficially a wide area but no one part of it as thoroughly as the hedgehog. Instead, philosophers worthy of the name must try to the best of their ability to be a bit of both.

PHILOSOPHICAL ERROR

Insofar as we are benevolent and wish for people the best that life has to offer, we undoubtedly want them to have knowledge, virtue, and happiness; that is, we want them to be wise, good, and contented. And insofar as philosophy is "the guide to life," its function is to foster the understanding needed for the sensible pursuit of these goals.

In this light, the first and most profound error of philosophizing is to see its subject matter in misguided terms, with purposes apart from those that constitute its definitive aims.

In particular, it would be inaccurate to think that philosophy aims at presenting the truth, the whole truth, and nothing but the truth. That testimonial oath would be going too far. But what one can say is that philosophy aims in this general direction—that it tries to present the main aspects of the truth, insofar as this is needful and practicable, and in doing so that it seeks to avoid any outright falsification. In the circumstances, such a diminution of aspirations is only right and proper.

Even so, no one ever said that the work of a philosopher is easy. On the route to philosophical understanding, there are virtually endless ways of getting off the track. This alone would explain why it is difficult to make a systematic inventory of philosophical mistakes. Still, it is clear that there will be three major categories of defects in philosophical exposition:

— Errors of Commission
— Errors of Omission
— Errors of Transmission

Given that the aim is to secure rational conviction, philosophical deliberations cannot afford such errors, which are obstacles that stand in the way. After all, philosophizing is (inter alia) a venture in cognitive inquiry, and all of these types of errors involve violations of rational cogency.

To be sure, the avoidance of error is not a be-all and end-all. The way to philosophical understanding does not lie in the avoidance of errors alone. This desideratum may be a necessary condition for good philosophizing, but it is certainly not sufficient. All the same, it is a key point of a larger picture, and it is worthwhile to take a closer look at what it involves.

ERRORS OF COMMISSION

Of the innumerable flaws of commission that can blemish a philosophical exposition, some stand in the foreground:

— Inconsistency/Incoherence
— Implausibility/Stretching Credibility
— Probative Deficiency
— Oversimplification
— Overreaching
— Fallacy
— Trivial Pursuit: Misemphasis

Let us consider these more closely.

Inconsistency/Incoherence. Logical coherence is an indispensable requisite. One cannot appropriately say in one place that something affirms or entails *P* and in another place that it affirms or entails not-*P*. There would be no clearer sign of a failure to think seriously and sensibly about the issues.

Implausibility/Stretching Credibility. Philosophizing cannot stretch our credulity beyond reasonable limits. In particular, philosophical theories and speculations cannot or should not contradict our basic cognitive commitments. In particular, philosophy must not conflict with the basic facts that comprise our prephilosophical cognition, and accordingly it must not contravene logical fundamentals, scientific fact, everyday knowledge, and common sense.

Refutation by *reductio ad absurdum* holds good in philosophy as elsewhere. What is being contended must not entail absurd consequences—be it individually or in conjunction with well-established fact. A philosophy that denies craters on the moon or tea in China is not worth the paper it is printed on.

Philosophizing is (or should be) a serious business. A philosopher's views merit attention because of their constructive take on the issues, not because those views are bizarre, let alone outrageous. The motto *Credo quia absurdum* may have some merit for the theologian, but is improper for the philosopher.

Probative Deficiency. Inadequate substantiation is a crucial offense. The reason for philosophical discourse is to secure agreement. And one cannot expect to achieve this in the absence of substantiation for one's claims. One's contentions should be presented in an environment that renders them at least plausible and at best compelling. Often, of course, we must maintain conclusions that go beyond the securely known premises at our disposal. (We could not otherwise reason inductively.) But of course the extent to which such premise-transcending leaps of conjecture are appropriate is decidedly limited. The philosopher may not be able to demonstrate his contentions with mathematical cogency. But he should not forget them extensively and make claims that have no visible means of support. The philosopher should not overreach and presume too much from his audience in the sense of uncritically generous concessions.

Oversimplification. Basic principles of cognitive rationality must be honored in philosophy as elsewhere. One is the principle of rational economy: complications should pay their own way, as it were. They should not be introduced save when actually needed ("Occam's Razor").

Overreaching. An aspect of cognitive economy is that one should not take on more than one can afford—"to bite off more than one can chew," as the saying goes. One should extend the range of one's claims only insofar as one can provide adequate support for them. In philosophical as well as architectural construction, one should avoid erecting a structure that is greater in size and scope than its foundations can support.

Fallacy. Not only must substantive considerations used to support philosophical contentions be acceptable in themselves, but the line of reasoning that proceeds from them must not be fallacious. It must avoid such familiar pitfalls as circular reasoning, begging the question, infinite regression, and so on.

Trivial Pursuit: Misemphasis (allocation errors). Philosophizing must embody a sense of proportion: it should not devote elaborate attention to trivia and shortchange important issues. A failure to pay attention to significance leads to allocating one's deliberative efforts to matters out of proportion to their due. The legal precept *de minimis non curat lex* holds in spades with respect to philosophy. Becoming enmeshed in trivia is not a philosophical desideratum.

ERRORS OF OMISSION

Three principal forms of errors of omission can hinder the efficacy of philosophical exposition.

Under-substantiation. Substantive matters should never simply be taken for granted in philosophy; and the generosity of one's audience should never be presupposed. Substantial claims should always be substantiated.

Oversimplification. The full complexity of the issues must be acknowledged and taken in stride. As Socrates was wont to stress, matters are seldom as simple as they appear at first glance. Philosophical exposition must take account of the exceptions to the seeming rules.

Agenda Truncation. The big philosophical issues about man's place in nature's scheme of things are all closely linked and interconnected. One cannot be adequately addressed without dealing with its ramifications with respect to others. (For example, one cannot adequately deal with the moral aspects of freedom of the will without addressing the metaphysical issue of what is involved in an agent's being "in control" of his actions.) In such matters, adequacy requires following through with the trail of connectivity.

ERRORS OF TRANSMISSION

Philosophizing is a venture in communication. Ideas do not convey themselves; they must be explained and spelled out in ways that render them accessible to others both as regards their intelligibility and their acceptability. Specifically, this calls for avoiding the three principal forms of transmission errors:

Lack of clarity. Obviously one cannot expect people to accept what they do not understand. Mystery may be appropriate in matters of religion, but not in philosophy, where an inability or unwillingness to convey ideas in a meaningful and clear way is a grave failing.

Lack of organization. This is a failure to put first things first and to structure one's discussion so as to make it clear how the parts contribute to the whole.

Presumption. A philosopher has to reach his audience where it is. He cannot presume too much and cannot expect his audience to grant his position without due justification. Accordingly, he cannot maintain something that is uncertain on the basis of what is yet more so, or that which is obscure on the basis of something yet more so (*obscurum per obscurior*). In matters of persuasive exposition he must be a courteous client rather than a domineering dictator. Expository arrogance may gain him attention, but not conviction.

* * *

Philosophical exposition should transmit its message in an intelligible, accessible, and, where possible, persuasive form. And the various modes of philosophical error are to be avoided not because of communal disapproval or because a self-appointed "thought police" somehow penalizes them, but because they are counterproductive and self-defeating. Given that it is a key aim of the philosophical enterprise to secure the audience's rational conviction, philosophical ideas have to be presented in a way that can effectively achieve this objective. And the various philosophical flaws and errors described above are just that—flaws and errors—because they impede the achievement of this aim: securing conviction regarding the fundamentals of human existence on the basis of cogent reasons.

Chapter 1

ULTIMATE QUESTIONS

QUESTIONS

Among the fundamental questions of metaphysics is that of the nature of existence at the highest level of generality. This is traditionally characterized in Aristotle's phrase as the study of "being qua being"—of reality in general rather than specifically of this or that sort, whether animal or mineral or whatever. But another "ultimate question," posed by G. W. Leibniz, is: "Why is there anything at all?" Before that question can be addressed meaningfully, some clarification is essential.

To begin with, what sort of *thing* is to be at issue in this question? Are *numbers* to count as "things"? If so, then reasons of necessity—of abstract general principle—will do the job here. Or again, if *facts* (states of affairs) are to count as "things," then the answer is once more straightforward: there are such things because, although how they exist is controvertible, that they exist is not. And there is also—according to some thinkers—yet another necessary existent, namely, God. And so as long as such "things" as facts and numbers (not to mention deities) are allowed into the range of relevancy, the answer to the Leibnizian question is simply: "Because it has to be so and cannot possibly be otherwise."

However, this consideration is not really critical because the crucial question is not

Why is there something rather than nothing at all?

but rather

> Why is there something *contingent*—something whose existence is not necessary?

And so the "things" that will concern us here are real things and not mere thought-things, figments of the speculative imagination to which the characterization "real" does not apply. At bottom, that initial question is intended to be: "Why is there a realm of contingent existence—a real world with concrete objects in it? Why are there actually spatiotemporal entities when there might possibly be none?"

DISTRIBUTIVE EXPLANATION CANNOT DO THE JOB

Rational inquiry seeks to explain the phenomena—the condition of things with which experience confronts us. And any ultimate theory of explanation that can adequately account for contingent existence-at-large must be holistic: it must address the entirety of a collective whole, the world. To be sure, some theorists endorse what has come to be called the "Hume-Edwards thesis," namely: *If the existence of every member of a set is explained, then the existence of the set is thereby explained.*[1] And they then propose resolving the Leibnizian question seriatim, by explaining the existence of every existent through a causal explanation of its origin.

However, the fallacy here is not too difficult to detect. Consider the following two claims:

- If the existence of every sentence of a paragraph is explained, the existence of that paragraph is thereby explained.
- If the existence of each note of a symphony is explained, the existence of that symphony is thereby explained.

Both of these claims are clearly false as they stand. On the other hand, contrast these two with the following cognate revisions:

- If the existence of every sentence of a paragraph *as a sentence of that particular paragraph* is explained, then the existence of that paragraph is thereby explained.

- If the existence of every note of a symphony *as a part of that particular composition* is explained, then the existence of that symphony is thereby explained.

Both these theses are indeed true—but only subject to that added qualification. After all, to explain the existence of the spouses in a marriage is not automatically to achieve an explanation of the marital couple, seeing that this would call not just for explaining these participants distributively but also for explaining their collectively coordinated co-presence in the relationship in question. And the case is just the same with the Hume-Edwards thesis.

The explanatory invocation of the Hume-Edwards thesis fails to heed certain critical *conceptual* distinctions that are readily brought to light by means of a bit of symbolic machinery. So let us adopt the following abbreviations:

- $p @ q$ for "p [is true and] provides an adequate explanatory account for q," where the variables p and q range over factual claims.
- $E!x$ for "x exists," where the variable x ranges over existential possibilities. (In view of this we have it that $(\forall x)\Diamond E!x$.)

On this basis, it is clear that the idea that "Everything has an explanation" or "There is an explanation for everything" admits of two very different constructions:

Distributive explanation: "There is some case-specific explanation to account for each and any individual existent."
   (1) $(\forall x)(E!x \supset (\exists p)(p @ E!x)$
Collective explanation: "There is one single comprehensive explanation that accounts for all existents—the entire totality of them."[2]
   (2) $(\exists p)(\forall x)((E!x \supset p @ E!x))$

It is clear that very different questions are at issue and very different matters at stake with distributive and collective explanations. For distributive explanations explain the fact *that* every member of a certain set has the feature *F*; collective explanations account for *why* it is that this is so. And explaining how it is that all members of the club are male—which could be so by fortuitous circumstances—does not accomplish the job of explaining *why* this is so (e.g., because the bylaws require it). In posing different questions we must be prepared for the possibility of different answers.

So the Hume-Edwards thesis is of no real help in our explanatory quest. One has to look elsewhere.

ULTIMATE EXPLANATION

There is yet another "ultimate why question." It is not "*Why* does the universe exist" but rather "Why does the universe exist *as it is*: why is it that the nature of physical reality is as we find it to be?"

For better or for worse, this question cannot be answered on scientific principles. And there is a simple and decisive reason why this is so. Scientific explanations by their very constitution must make use of the laws of nature in their reasoning. But this strategy is simply unavailable in the present case. For those laws of nature required for scientific explanation are themselves a part—an essential and fundamental part—of the constitution of physical reality. And they are thereby a part of the problem and not instrumentalities available for its resolution.

The duly revised "ultimate why question" confronts us with a choice. Either we dismiss that question as being unavailable, inappropriate, and perhaps even "meaningless" (as logical positivists have always argued). Or we acknowledge that answering this question invites and indeed requires recourse to some sort of extraordinary explanation—one that transcends the cognitive resources of factual inquiry. And here the options become very limited. For here we enter into the region of teleology, where there are just two available alternatives.

On the one hand lies the *teleology of purpose*, which itself can in principle operate in two ways: either by the conscious purposiveness of an intelligent being (a creator deity) or by the unconscious finality of a natural impetus toward the creation of intelligent beings. On the other hand, a decidedly different approach envisions a *teleology of value*, which accounts for the nature of the world in axiological, value-involving terms as being for the best with respect to some (yet unspecified) mode of evaluative optimality.

Accordingly, five different approaches confront us with respect to that ultimate why question:

- dismissive positivism (à la the logical positivists of the 1930s)
- metaphysical inevitabilism (à la Spinoza)
- theological creationism (à la traditional scholasticism)
- anthropic evolutionism (à la anthropic theorists)
- evaluative optimalism (à la Leibniz)

Each option is available. And none is forced upon us by the inexorable necessity of reason itself. In the final analysis, "You pays your money, and you takes your choice," in line with your doctrinal views on the matter.

But is the outcome simply a matter of preference, personal taste, or inclination? By no means! Here, as elsewhere, *rational* choice must be based on the evidence—and thereby on the deliverances of experience.

So the question becomes: Given the sort of world that our body of available experience indicates this one to be, what sort of explanatory proceeding seems best? Here, however, the experience at issue will no longer be merely the observational experience of our (instrumentally augmented) human senses. Rather, in matters of the sort now at issue, it must be the cumulative evidence of the aggregate totality of one's life experience.

So where does this leave us?

THE NEED FOR ODDITY: ABANDONING CAUSALITY

The key point was made by Leibniz long ago:

> The reasons for the world [must] therefore lie in something extra-mundane, different from the chain of states or series of things whose aggregate constitutes the world. . . . So [to account for the world's being] there must exist something which is distinct from the plurality of beings, or from the world itself.[3]

In explaining the being and nature of concrete existence-as-a-whole, we cannot invoke some aspect of the being and nature of reality itself. To do so would be to beg the question—to make use of some part, feature, or aspect of the very thing that is to be explained. And of course this mode of explanation cannot function effectively in the present context. For any causal explanation carries us back to the starting point: the presupposition of this or that existent. But the question at issue puts this very circumstance into doubt. One cannot coherently invoke the existence of *something* in trying to explain the existence of *anything* whatever. In explaining the internality of the whole of real existence, one must go outside this realm.

It would accordingly be absurd to ask for some sort of *causal* account of reality-as-a-whole. Causality, after all, is a world-internal process: its functions show how some world-integral things and conditions arise out of others. It is the sort of account we use to explain how acorns yield trees and how lion parents produce baby lions. Causality is a matter of intra-world agency and requires world-internal inputs to do its work. It is not the sort of resource that could possibly be called upon to account for the world itself and to explain the origin of the totality of existents.

In the end, one cannot adequately explain contingent existence-at-large by an appeal to the nature of existence itself. The nature of contingent existence must be explained not on the basis of existing things or substances, but rather on the operation of principles that function with respect to the manifold of possibility.

Its formulation at this level of synoptic generality marks the "why-this-world?" question as a decidedly nonstandard question. For a standard existence-explanation will proceed in causally putative terms. The reason that X exists would be that there exist other items Y_1, Y_2, ... Y_n that interact causally so as to engender X. In standard existence explanations, what exists emerges through the causally productive machinations of other existents. But this sort of thing clearly will not do in the present context.

The question of existence-in-general cannot be dealt with as one of the standard generative sort, which asks for the existence of one thing to be explained causally in terms of the existence and functioning of another. We cannot say, "Well there's X in the world, and X explains the existence of things," because this simply shifts the issue to X, which after all is itself an existent. If we want *global* explanations of the existence of things in the world, we are going to have difficulty in getting them from existential premises pertaining to what the world is like. Does this mean we cannot get them at all?

And so, with ultimate questions, eccentricity is unavoidable. For such holistic questions are altogether extraordinary. Usually when we ask about things and their conditions we are after a developmental account—how they got to be so by a process of transformation from some earlier condition. This standard sort of issue-resolution is clearly impossible in the present case. The fact of it is that when we ask an extraordinary question, we must be prepared for an extraordinary answer.

A TWOFOLD TURNING

To secure our explanatory basis for contingent existence at large, one has to redirect one's thought in two directions: from actuality to possibility and from fact to value. Let us consider how these reorientations are to work.

The Turn to Metaphysical Possibility

To account for the being of contingent existence at large, one has to impose the burden of explanation on something that is itself entirely outside the realm of contingent existence and of existential fact. But where can one possibly look for explanatory resources if the realm of actuality, of "what there is," is not available? The answer is clear: we must look to the realm of possibility, of what *can possibly be*. For if reality is to have a basis, then *possibility* is the only available prospect. And to have any explanatory traction here, we must also invoke the concept of value—of what there ought to be. Thus, to resolve the problem of existence we must ultimately turn to a metaphysics of value.

To repeat the critical point, the domain of reality as a whole cannot be cogently explained by invoking some feature of its existential content. If there is to be an acceptable explanation, its probative basis must lie wholly outside this domain. It cannot be done within the realm of *things* or *substances* at all, but must step outside to proceed on the basis of some sort of *principle*.

To explain some actual condition of things without involving any other actual conditions of things is clearly a very tall order. And our room for maneuver is extremely limited. For if we cannot explain actualities at large in terms of actualities, we have little alternative but to explain them in terms of possibilities. What is thus called for here is a principle of explanation that can effect a transit from possibility to actuality, and thereby violates the medieval precept *de posse ad esse non valet consequentia.*

The Turn to Eliminative Value

But now comes a problem. If an adequate explanation of contingent existence is achievable only in terms of reference to something lying outside the realm of necessity and also outside the realm of concrete existence and contingent fact, then where can the explanation possibly go?

The only conceivable answer is this: it must go entirely outside the realm of fact to that of value.

To achieve a synoptically ultimate explanation of the domain of contingent existence/reality, we thus have to shift to another domain of deliberation altogether—and move outside of the evidential *realm of what is* to the normative *realm of what ought to be*, that is, from actuality to value.

And to realize this transition we must shift from the sphere of production to that of elimination. We must effect a revolutionary shift in the orientation of thought from productivity to reducibility, from fact to value, and from actuality to possibility.

In the realm of reality, creativity functions *productively* by engendering a yet-to-be-realized state. By contrast, in the realm of possibility, creativity is *reductive*; it functions by eliminating the prospect of some of the yet-to-be-realized conditions of things.

Ordinarily our concern with creativity is with the causal processes within nature. The second (metaphysical rather than physical) mode of productivity sounds rather strange to our ears. Nevertheless, at the level of ultimate explanation it emerges prominently into the foreground. In the realm of the real, creativity is innovative and brings new things to be. But on the side of possibility there can be nothing new and genuinely innovative: here, such novelty as there is proceeds by a selective elimination.

To be sure, the creative process in the realm of reality is temporal and subject to physical causality, whereas in the realm of possibility it is atemporal and subject to metaphysical selectivity on the ground of evaluative factors. Possibility-based explanation must implement the idea that contingent reality is what it is because that is somehow for the best. It must, that is to say, explain existence in terms of value and take what might be called the axiological turn. Again, the key point here was made by Leibniz:

Even if the world is not necessary [absolutely or] metaphysically, in the sense that its contrary would imply a contradiction or logical absurdity, it is nonetheless necessary physically [or evaluatively], determined in such a way that its contrary would imply imperfection or moral absurdity. And thus as possibility is the principle of essence, so perfection or degree of essence is the principle of existence.[4]

Granted, this sort of thing may sound strange. But in asking for an explanation of contingent existence as a whole, one is posing a decidedly extraordinary question, and when one insists upon doing this, one must be ready for a decidedly extraordinary answer. The bizarre nature of the answer is not an objection to it but the acknowledgment of a sine qua non condition of adequacy.

And so, one must reckon with the situation that an ultimate account of reality as a whole has to proceed not in terms of causal production but in terms of possibility elimination based on evaluative considerations. Let us examine how this approach would work.

THE CRUX: NOT CAUSAL PRODUCTION BUT POSSIBILITY ELIMINATION

The crux of the reasoning required here lies in the Sherlock Holmes principle: "When you have excluded the impossible, whatever remains, however improbable, must be the truth."[5] However, elimination in the realm of the possible cannot proceed *causally*: it has to proceed *normatively*. Those eliminated possibilities are ruled out because they are inherently unworthy—outranked and outflanked by other, superior alternatives. Inferior merit is existentially disqualifying. And this eliminative principle carries a crucial corollary: *Reality is optimific.* Accordingly, the answer to the question of what explains the elimination of the inferior alternatives lies in a metaphysical principle of optimality: *Given an exhaustive range of possible alternatives, it is the best of them that is actualized.*

But just why should it be that the best possibility is the actual one?

To begin with, this raises the preliminary question, "best" in what sense? What is to be the standard of merit here? Of course, "merit" here has to mean merit in terms of qualification for actual existence, and "best" has to mean best qualified in terms of the strength of the rationale for this status. In epistemology, the truth lies preeminently on the side of the strongest reasons; in metaphysics, authenticity lies on the side of the optimal option, the option on whose side lie the best and strongest reasons. And the basis for this principle of optimality lies in the nature of the principle itself: it is for the best that matters should stand so. Yet why is it that reality should merit the demands of reason? In the final analysis it is because reason itself demands our thinking it so. What it demands of us is a rational account, and an account that does not give rationality the lead in these matters cannot qualify as fully rational in itself. Kant maintained that for us, "ought" implies "can"; the tradition of Western metaphysics since Plato commits us to the conviction that for reality, "ought" implies "will." (The seemingly obvious objections to this idea are based on the world's manifold imperfections and will be addressed in chapter 10.)

THE STANDARD OF METAPHYSICAL VALUE: THE PIVOTAL ROLE OF INTELLIGENCE

The pivotal idea that the explanation of reality pivots on value—that the best available possibility is what will be actualized—spins like a useless gear that fails to engage the machinery of explanation until the operative standard of evaluation is identified. Only then will this "axiogenesis" approach acquire any explanatory traction. And so the question becomes: What sort of considerations can serve as the determinant of existential fitness here? What renders one world-arrangement superior and existentially more qualified than another?

It is clear that one cannot just optimize, any more than one can just maximize or minimize. For one has to optimize *something*, some feature or aspect of things. But if this merit-indicating factor is to be self-validating and self-sustaining, then the most promising candidate would seem to be intelligence itself—that is to say, the overall status and standing of intelligent beings at large. Any rational being is bound to see the loss of reason as a supreme tragedy. For an intelligent being—a rational creature—intelligence itself must have a prime place on the scale of values. Accordingly, intelligence and rationality best qualify as the self-sufficient standard of value at issue. The position taken here is thus oriented toward optimizing the conditions of existence for intelligent beings at large. It envisions a universe that provides for

- the randomness through which alone intelligent beings can emerge in the world through evolutionary processes based on chance-conditioned variation and selection.
- the chance-conditional novelty and innovation needed for an environment of sufficient complexity to engage the thought of intelligent beings.
- the order of regularity and lawfulness needed for a universe sufficiently orderly to allow complex creatures to develop and thrive.
- a lawful order in the modus operandi of nature that is sufficiently simple to be understood by imperfectly intelligent beings as a basis for grounding their decisions and actions in a complex world.

The arrangements of an intelligently contrived universe must, in short, manage things in a way that rational creatures would see as optimal from the vantage point of their own best interests. Such a world must realize a condition of optimalization under constraints—these constraints being a manifold of natural law favorable to the best interests of intelligent beings in the overall scheme of things.

But if reality is indeed optimal for the interests of intelligent beings, why is it not easier for them to understand the world's ways? Why should there be aspects of nature that perplex even an Einstein?

The answer is that it just is not in the best interest of intelligent beings that the world be very simple. Simplicity is not the only key aspect of merit. For one thing, the design of a world in which intelligent creatures arise by evolutionary processes requires a great deal of complexity. For another, an overly simple world would not provide the challenges needed for the interests and efforts of intelligent beings to evolve. The ultimate answer to the question of why an intelligence-congenial world will not be simple is that this would not be in the best interests of intelligent beings. Even as a good gardener must strike a proper balance between variegated complexity and harmonious order, so a world that is user-friendly for intelligent beings can be neither so simple as to be monotonous for them nor so complex and unharmonious as to baffle their appreciative apprehension. As Leibniz saw, the world has to be a duly harmonized mixture.

EXPLAINING THE OPTIMALITY PRINCIPLE:
SELF-EXPLANATION AS THE PIVOT

But what is it that accounts for that crucial principle of optimality? What sorts of considerations could possibly justify optimalism? Why should it be that what is for the best be actual? The answer here lies in the principle itself. It is literally self-explaining, given that realization of the optimality principle is itself the best alternative in accounting for the prevailing order of things.

Yet is this reasoning not rendered ineffective through circularity?

By no means! At this stage, circularity is not vicious but virtuous: it is not a flaw but an essential asset. For any *ultimate* explanation must be self-sustaining and rest on a principle that is self-validating. If the validity of the principle rested on something else—some deeper and different rationale of validation—then it would not be ultimate but would through this very circumstance be flawed.

And the optimality principle indeed has this feature of self-support, which is here not a vitiating circularity but an essential aspect of the problem—a decidedly virtuous circularity. After all, there is no decisive reason why that explanation has to be "deeper and different"—that is why the prospect of *self-explanation* has to be included at this fundamental level.[6] After all, we cannot go on putting the explanatory elephant on the back of the tortoise on the back of the alligator ad infinitum: as Aristotle already saw, the explanatory regress has to stop somewhere at the "final" theory—one that is literally "self-explanatory." In the end, we must expect that any ultimate principle must explain itself and cannot, in the very nature of things, admit of an external explanation in terms of something altogether different. The impetus to realization inherent in authentic value lies in the very nature of value itself. A rational person would not favor the inferior alternative; and a rational reality cannot do so either. And what better candidate could there be than the optimality principle itself, with the result that the divisions between real possibilities and merely theoretical possibilities are as they are (i.e., value-based) because that itself is for the best?[7]

So what has to be at work here is a proto-ontological law to the effect that under certain conditions, various theoretical possibilities become eliminated (i.e., are realization-ineligible) as real possibilities by virtue of their evaluative inferiority. And such a process will have to continue its operation in the possibilistic domain until at last only one privileged alternative remains. What we have here is a figurative struggle for the survival of the fittest, but now with matters being fought out not among competing actuals but among competing possibilities.

Such an axiogenetic approach enjoys the advantage of rational economy in that it proceeds uniformly. It provides a single rationale for both answers—namely, that "this is for the best." It accordingly also enjoys the significant merit of providing for the rational economy of explanatory principles at the level of metaphysical fundamentals.

In addressing the question of why the principle of optimality obtains, we have maintained it to be self-sustaining, obtaining because that is for the best. Granted, such an axiogenetic account of the principle goes against the grain of much metaphysical thinking, which is to explain matters by concrete causes—by the productive efficacy of existing objects—rather than by abstract laws and principles. And this line of thought naturally invites a theological implementation by invoking God as the instituting agent for the principle of optimality. This not implausible option will be addressed in greater detail in this book. For present purposes, however, it suffices to note that this theological treatment of the principle of optimality, while indeed available, is not mandated. A self-operated metaphysical axiology is in theory an alternative.

Chapter 2

WORLD VIEWS

CONCEPTUAL PERSPECTIVES ON UNDERSTANDING AND EVALUATION

As intelligent beings we make our way in the world by acting on the indications of thought. Our beliefs about what is and what might be going on are the bases on which we are prepared to act. Our views regarding the realities and possibilities of things are crucial resources here. The world as we see it sets the stage on which our actions are played out.

The German term *Weltanschauung* can mean either *view of the world* (i.e., conception of what the world is descriptively like) or *attitude toward the world* (i.e., evaluative stance toward the world in regard to its positivities or negativities). It is the former descriptive meaning rather that the latter evaluative and attitudinal one that will be at issue here.

World views provide us with a *conceptual framework*—a coordinated manifold of basic categories and concepts—for portraying the world and its ways. It comprises not only the basic conceptions that people use to explain nature's phenomena (be those explanations causal or coordinative or even occult), but also those they employ in evaluating features such as importance, significance, priority, and the like. By the use of such concept-schemes, both cognitive and evaluative, we render the world and our experiences intelligible and comprehensible to ourselves.

In some discussions the term "world view" or "world-picture" takes on a specifically cosmological sense, as when one speaks of the Aristotelian, Ptolemaic, Copernican, or Newtonian world view. But as the term generally figures in philosophical discussion, it encompasses much more than this; it goes beyond astronomy and cosmology to include not only matters of animate science (biology, anthropology) but also matters of sociocultural concern. The "world" at issue broadens beyond physical nature to encompass the biological, psychological, cultural, and even political domains, indeed, the entire stage-setting of human existence and concern.

Explicit focus on these issues goes back to the German neo-Kantian philosopher Wilhelm Dilthey (1833–1911), who was among the first to stress the differences among the world-conceptions of different philosophers and to take the resulting "strife of systems" as a central plank of his theoretical platform:

> The contest among rival world views cannot be brought to a decision at any significant point. The course of history effects a selection among them, but their main types stand forth alongside each other self-sufficiently, impassable yet indestructible. Owing their existence to no decisive demonstration, they can be destroyed by none. . . . Their rooting in human life persists and fortifies and continually produces ever new forms.[1]

This perspective points to a conception of philosophy in which the construction of a cogent world view is a definitive feature of the enterprise. Philosophical history is here taken to unfold as an ongoing refinement of preexisting doctrines, a development in the course of which ever more sophisticated and divergent doctrines emerge from the fundamental discords of older established programs. This development is marked by the persistence of conflict among different schools of thought—an ongoing rivalry of systems. The quarrel between idealists and realists, determinists and free-willers, skeptics and cognitivists, deontologists and consequentialists, and so on, all represent branchings in a river that flows on and on.

Among the key conceptual distinctions at issue in world views is that between phenomena that are typical or normal and those that are extraordinary, and correspondingly, the distinction between situations that are only natural and to be expected as against those that are regarded as problematic and bizarre. All this relates to one's basic framework of judgment about how things work in the world.

World views further relate both to matters of fact and to matters of value. And, evaluative matters apart, the issue-agenda of a world view will principally include the following areas of concern:

(1) *Existential issues*: What kinds of things are at issue with "existence-in-the-world" and how are they to be classified and described? What is the nature and structure of physical reality and of real possibility?

(2) *Explanatory issues*: What explains the existence of the world and its contents? What are their interactive processes and modus operandi? How are we to understand the interactive processes at work in the world?

(3) *Reflexive issues*: What is the special nature, place, role, and (perhaps) function or mission in the world's scheme of things of such intelligent beings as humans?

(4) *Transcendental issues*: What sorts of things have nonphysical being, that is, lie outside the realm of the world's material contents? What is to be said about the status of numbers, forces, gods, concepts, and other such immaterial objects? What is the basis of theoretical (rather than real or physical) possibility?

(5) *Methodological issues*: Are questions of the previously indicated sort meaningful and appropriate or not? If meaningful, what means are at our disposal for addressing them?

These areas of consideration constitute the realm in which the edifice of a world view comes to be constructed.

And here, *construction* is the operative term. For world views are not projected full-formed into our hands by some external potency but are ideational constraints of our own contriving. Like scientific theories, they are both inspired by experience and confirmed by it. But they are nevertheless human artifacts and not works of nature.

In Dilthey's wake, various other philosophers took to the idea, and among late-nineteenth-century thinkers the study of world views plays a significant role. Like Dilthey, some made it a centerpiece of their thinking, proposing to treat philosophy itself as a systemic study of world views focusing on such issues as:

- the nature and structure of world views
- the taxonomy of world views
- the historical development of thought about world views
- the rationale of world views
- the methodology of world-view formation and substantiation

One of the most fundamental issues in world-view formation is the role (if any) of the transcendental. The pivotal question here is this: Is the natural world entirely self-contained, or is there above and beyond the world a further super or supra-power or potency that functions independently of it and yet somehow affects or even controls its affairs and operations?

MODES OF EXPLANATORY ORDER

Among the most basic questions in forming a world view is this: Do events proceed in an orderly, intelligible, rationally cogent explanatory order—according to a manifold of regularities, laws, and principles that renders them rationally explainable and intelligible?

As regards this issue of the explanatory intelligibility of the world, there are three basic positions:

- *Nomic Anarchy*: the world is chaotic, random, anarchic—ultimately nothing is really altogether explicable.
- *Nomic Systematicity*: the world is all-pervasively lawful, orderly, and systematic—ultimately everything that occurs in it has a rational explanation. (The principle of sufficient reason is at issue here.)
- *Nomic Duality*: the world is an explanatory dualism—a mixture of order and disorder, with the upshot that various of its circumstances admit of rational explanation while others simply do not.

And with regard to the second and third positions, one can hold that the explanatory laws at work are any of the below:

- monolithically physical
- monolithically mental
- pluralistically diverse

Very different lines of thought can take such approaches, given that explanatory laws can be regarded as causal, teleologically magical, symbolic, or theistic. That is, very different sorts of explanatory models can be taken to be at work.

In the history of philosophy the idea that the world is a system of some sort has always stood at the forefront. But what kind of system?

REALITY MODELS AND WORLD HYPOTHESES

Just as nature abhors a vacuum, so the human mind shuns complications. It hews to the Ockhamite idea that complications, like entities, are not to be multiplied, with the caveat "beyond necessity" (*preater necessitatem*)— a caveat often conveniently forgotten. On this basis, world-view theoreticians have often been tempted by the reductive idea of a single-factor conception of the world, treating it as fundamentally monotone in nature. Along these lines, very different models for the universe have been projected, most prominently including:

- *Mechanism*: The world is one vast mechanical contrivance, a machine. (Democritus, de La Mettrie)
- *Organisms*: The world is one vast organism, a living being of some sort. (Plato?)
- *Pan-psychism*: The world is a vast complex of minds or mind-like entities. (Berkeley)
- *Pan-societism*: The world is a vast society of individual agents. (Leibniz, Whitehead)[2]

As indicated, different thinkers have thus adopted very different world models, ranging from the mechanism of J. O. de La Mettrie to the organicism of Plato's *Timaeus*. Some few have even adopted a more complex pluralism, most notably Leibniz, whose world view has aspects not only of the mechanist and organic types, but also of a political statism reflective of the hierarchical order of the ancien régime. (In the end, such a pluralistically diversified approach is likely the best philosophical policy—the safest policy in view of the complexity and multifaceted nature of our experience.)

VALUE PERSPECTIVE OR AXIOLOGICAL ORIENTATIONS

As already noted, above and beyond the descriptive dimension of world views there is also an evaluative dimension. Numerous components of this dimension can come into play here:

- the *aesthetic* (beautiful/ugly)
- the *ethical* (right/wrong)
- the *functional* (effective, ineffective)
- the *significant* (important/unimportant)
- the *affective* (pleasant/unpleasant)
- the *instrumental* (useful/useless)
- the *purposive* (productive/unproductive)
- the *rational* (sensible/absurd or correct/incorrect)

A theory of value will be a key component of any adequate world view. The questions of what we are to see as important, as desirable, or as meritorious are crucial in this regard. The dimension of value and evaluation—be these values substantial or nihilistic—is a key factor in the functions of a world view.

WORLD VIEWS AND NATURAL SCIENCE

Science provides us with extensive information about the natural world and its ways. No reasonable world view today can turn its back on science—the scientific picture of the world is something with which any such view will have to come to terms. But science has not of itself constituted a world view: its concerns address only part of the problem, not its comprehensive totality. For while science provides a descriptive text about the world, nevertheless, this text, like any other, calls for *interpretation*. Even if we accept natural science and take its declarations as fixed and given, many "big questions" yet remain.

After all, science does not instruct us about goals and values. It does not tell us what is good or important within the range of human effort or what is right in matters of human interaction. It may tell us what people earn, but not what they deserve. It may tell us what people think, but not what they are well advised to think. It may tell us the direction taken by people's actions, but not which direction is wise or sensible. And it does not address the issue of our orientation toward ourselves, our fellows, and indeed the world itself. Science describes the stage on which our actions transpire but has little to say about the dance we are to perform on that stage.

After all, the conception of our work in this world is yet another key aspect of a world view. We have only one life at our disposal, and it is brief in scope and limited in time. How then are we to dispose of it? What are we to make of ourselves? There are, of course, immediate limits on what we can achieve—the success of our efforts is "in the lap of the gods" and always beyond our control. But what we *try* to do—what it is that we aspire to and aim at—is up to us. And the direction in which sensible people should set their aims in this regard is a key formative factor of a person's world view.

WHICH WORLD VIEW IS ONE TO HOLD?

As rational beings, we are confronted with the challenge of forming an idea of what the world is like and what our place is within it. And the position that we take in these matters is—and cannot but be—a reflection of the course of our experience. For, as rational beings, all of the attitudes and judgments we form on such matters are going to be shaped by our own developmental history.

On this basis it is clearly in the best interests of rational beings—and in a way, obligatory for them—to develop their body of experience, vicarious experience included, in a sufficiently ample way to provide the background for the judicious resolution of the matter. A truly rational being would clearly expend effort in this direction.

Which of those varying world views deserves to be acknowledged? What sort of stance is the one to endorse and adopt in these matters? The answer is that it all depends. No particular world view is rationally enjoined on us by considerations of abstract reliability or general principle, given that there are genuine alternatives, all of which are, in theory, rationally viable. Some theorists take this very fact to negate the reliance on and the utility of a concern for world views. But the absence of a one-size-fits-all condition does not mean that there cannot be a one-size-fits-best condition with respect to the prevailing cognitive and cultural situation in which we find ourselves.

Most world-view theoreticians locate the impetus to adopt one position over against others in the psychology of the individual.[3] But this is very questionable. To all viable appearances, people's philosophical inclinations do not issue from their psychological makeup but rather from the course of their experience (personal, cultural, social, and so on). This is not the place to rehearse the nature-nurture dispute, but in reality, one's philosophical inclinations are formed less by natural endowment and disposition than by the manifold of conviction-influencing experiences that life brings one's way.

Here, as everywhere else, what one is rationally impelled to believe depends on the evidence at one's disposal, which in this case is not narrowly *observational* but rather broadly *experiential* in nature. And just as it is rational to harmonize and coordinate one's factual beliefs with the observational evidence, so it is rational to harmonize and coordinate one's philosophical beliefs with the experiential evidence. Thus an individual's proper choice is not free and unfettered. Instead, it is rationally directed (even if not actually restricted) by an individual course of experience. Given the individual's experience, the range of what are, for him or her, live options will be markedly reduced.

The experiential basis on which a world view will rest can be complex and many-sided. Some twentieth-century theorists took the line that it can and should consist of natural science alone, and accordingly they mandated a wholly science-based world view (*Wissenschaftliche Weltanschauung*). But this ignores the fact, first, that science does not speak with a single or uniform voice but instead exhibits considerable interest in conflict and variation; and second, that human experience has many important facets in matters of culture and social affairs that lie quite outside the scientific domain—issues that science, as we have it, simply does not address.

The fact that there is no unique mandate regarding world views stands in the way of there being any single, universally appropriate one. But this, of course, nowise precludes the prospect of a world view that is optimal for a particular individual for cogent and convincing reasons. After all, no one particular diet or physical regime is universally appropriate for everyone, and yet this does not preclude there being a physical regime that is best suited for a particular person. And the selection at issue is certainly not an arbitrary one, such that the outcome is arbitrary and a matter of utter indifference. So what we have here is not a matter of relativistic indifference but one of contextualistic appropriateness and situational cogency. Although the larger community doubtless confronts a pluralism of available alternatives, nevertheless a person's particular body of experience may well leave the rational individual with little choice. And there is no decisive obstacle to taking the view that this position is uniquely right and proper for people, given the manifold of their experience. After all, as rational beings they must base their conclusions on the available premises, and in these matters we have no premises at our disposal save those which experience—in its broadest possible conception—delivers into our hands.

But if I think that you are rational, would not the fact that your world view differs from mine undermine my confidence in it? Clearly it would and should do so only if either I believed that your body of relevant experience (i.e., your evidence for your position) was somehow ampler or superior to mine, or if I thought that your ability to exploit your information were markedly superior to mine. But human nature is such that neither of these conditions is likely to be met. As Descartes observed at the outset of his *Discourse on Method*, few among us deem ourselves deficient in basic matters of common sense. And even when we concede to others greater knowledge than our own, we are unlikely to concede greater wisdom to them.

Chapter 3

TERMINOLOGICAL CONTEXTUALITY

CONTEXTUALISM

Natural science has its own technical vocabulary, and even when this includes ordinary words taken from the language of everyday discourse, these words usually will no longer bear their ordinary sense. In numerous instances, scientific discourse employs such terms in an entirely different sense. The physicist's use of terms like *work*, *force*, and *energy* bears little resemblance to their role in ordinary language. The botanist's use of *male*, *female*, and *parent* departs markedly from their everyday employment. The medical use of terms such as *germ* or *tissue* differs from that of ordinary usage. Distinct enterprises and diverse linguistic realms have their own technical language with its own provisional usages. Be it in medicine, wine-connoisseurship, or natural science, different domains have different vocabularies and modes of discourse.

But which mode of discourse gets things correctly—science or common usage? When science uses terms differently from their use in ordinary discourse, who is in the right? Which is actually the correct use of the term? One is tempted to ask, "Will the proper meaning of the term please stand up and be recognized?"

While it may seem plausible and natural to ask this sort of thing, nevertheless, the question is inappropriate. For when one self-same term figures differently in two different linguistic settings, there is no right or wrong about its meaning. In English a "brief" can mean the documentation of a legal case, but in German it is a letter. In French, "chat" is a cat, in English it is a brief colloquy. Context apart, there is no such thing as right or wrong use.

To take a different line and try to impose the idea of conceptual correctness across diverse ranges of discourse is to commit a fundamental error—a fallacy of context blindness. For not only do words not have stable meanings outside the setting of a particular linguistic context, but their meaning within any such context is independent of what it might be elsewhere. What a word means in one linguistic context does not stand in conflict with its role elsewhere. The fact that the physicist's terms *work* or *force* have meanings different from those in ordinary English, and that very different things will have to be said about them in each context, does not conflict with—let alone invalidate—their communicative role in each context.

For the sake of an analogy, take the technical language of, say, wine lore. Here, *dryness* is not the opposite of *wetness* and has nothing to do with the fluidity of the wine but rather is a matter of lack of sweetness. And "full body" has nothing to do with shape and avoirdupois. Even when the same terms are used, the technical language of a domain can veer away from the conception of ordinary usage. And it would be absurd to ask, "What is the real meaning of 'sweetness'—that of the wine connoisseur or that of the ordinary man-in-the-street?"

When ordinary people take one line on whether or not a certain liquid (which happens to be wine) is or is not dry (which of course, qua liquid, it is not at all), whereas a wine connoisseur insists that it is very dry indeed, there is no fact about which they are disagreeing. They are talking about different issues, and their "disagreement" is simply a verbal illusion. And essentially the same is the case with regard to the "disagreement" between the "plain man" and the scientist regarding such matters as work or energy or space or time. Claims dealing with different substantive dimensions of things deal with different issues: to move from one to the other is "to change the subject."

The crucial point is that every linguistic domain is a law unto itself as far as matters of meaning are concerned. But when two realms of discourse disagree, is not the one going to be right and the other wrong? Not really!

For this would be so only if what the one said were inconsistent with the claims of the other. But in the absence of the requisite contact—of variant claims being made about the same thing—this cannot occur.

Every domain of discourse is *semantically autonomous*: Each is at liberty to lay down its own communicative ground rules. The fact that others proceed differently presents no obstacle. The classification of correct versus incorrect does not come into play.

EVERYDAY USAGE VS. SCIENTIFIC TERMINOLOGY

In the context of a cook's issues and concerns, the cook classifies tomatoes as vegetables, while in the context of a botanist's considerations, the botanist classifies it as a fruit. On his own limited home turf and within his own frame of reference, each proceeds appropriately. And in doing so, neither denies what the other is claiming. "Customary vegetables" is one sort of thing and "botanical vegetables" is yet another. One feature can be present in the absence of the other and vice versa. It is as though on my side of the fence there is green and on my neighbor's side there is brown. We are dealing with different sides (features, aspects) of the matter, and the discordant claims we make in regard to the color of the view from the fence actually do not disagree because he views the south side of the fence and I view the north side.

The same goes for space-time talk. We cannot ask, "What is the real time—that of the relativity theorist or that of the plain man?" It is not that one is real and the other fictive and illusionary. Both are perfectly proper in their own way and in their own domain. And insofar as they differ in their claims, there is simply no commonality of concept that reaches across these domains to preclude what is real in the one from being equally so in the other.

Accordingly, what is intended and what is communicated in ordinary language when it is said that the grass is green or the sky is blue is not—and cannot be—in conflict or disagreement with anything that is said about the mechanics of color perception in optics or the physiology of vision. Similarly, what is said about space or time in the theory of relativity does not clash with the space-time talk of everyday communication. The fact that Einsteinian relativity has things to say about space-time that differ from the space and time conceptions in ordinary talk in no way disagrees or conflicts with what is going on there—any more than the fact that Newtonian mechanics talks differently about *work*.

It simply cannot be said that the technical ranges of scientific consideration make different claims about *the same* objects of consideration. Rather, what they do is to make *different claims about different* (albeit in some ways analogous) *matters*.

Suppose you are looking over a science article in an old newspaper and you come across Einstein's classic equation with its equals sign. The paper is printed in the old style, with ink applied as a constellation of little dots. What you then see can be described and discussed in two radically different ways. It can be described in terms of small ink-dots of certain shapes, sizes, and placement relative to one another. It can also be described as the equals sign of a certain equation. Neither description is incorrect. But the descriptions have effectively nothing in common. They deal with entirely different issues: They address different matters of a different vocabulary. There is a complete lack of semantical connectivity between them.

And much the same is true when we compare the discourse of science and that of everyday life. The human language of ordinary discussion and that of contemporary micro- or macro-physics are essentially different things and talk about entirely different matters. And just the same situation holds for terms such as work or force or energy and for pretty well everything where a seeming commonality of language persists.

To be sure, someone could say, "I will grant that the scientist and the layman may deal with different properties of things and do so in different terms of reference and by means of different vocabularies. Yet surely that does not mean that they are talking about different things and are not dealing with the same objects." But this view of the matter is very questionable. For things are determined as the items they are in view of their processual, that is, functional, role. An ace of spades is not "the same card" in poker and in contract bridge. A given letter configuration (say, "ding") is not the same word in English and in German. A rain shower is not the same thing for the meteorologists and the landscape painter. An object becomes specified and determined as the object it is through the way in which we conceptualize it, and fundamentally different conceptualizations put different objects before us.

To say that in these matters science characterizes the same things better or more accurately than ordinary discourse is to make a claim that does not hold water, simply because science does not deal with "the same things" at all: it changes the subject. The physicist's work-talk is conceptually disconnected from that of ordinary usage, his time-determinations from those of the scheduler of transport services.

EDDINGTON'S TABLES

Two modes of conceptualization and deliberation are available to us with regard to the world's situations and occurrences: the pretheoretical descriptive perspective of everyday language and the fundamentally explanatory perspective of natural science.

Ever since classical antiquity, many philosophers have viewed humans as amphibians, living in two worlds. In the analogy of Plato's *Republic*, we live in the visible world of sunlight as well as the thought-world of Ideas. In Immanuel Kant's inaugural dissertation, we live both in the sensory *mundus sensibilis* and in the cognitive *mundus intelligibilis*. In German idealism, we live both in the world of science and in the world of human experience, and for the phenomenologist, we inhabit both the world of observational or scientific experience (*Erfahrung*) and the cultural world of everyday life—the life-world of everyday *Erlebnis*. And in his 1914 book *Our Knowledge of the External World*, Bertrand Russell contrasted "the world of physics" with that of "the world of sense." The former, as he saw it, is "a form of atomism [that] regards all matter as composed of two kinds of units, electrons and protons, both indestructible." The latter is a realm of sensory data, which present themselves in human perception as experienced qualities.[1] Perhaps the most widely diffused dual-realm theory of the twentieth century was launched by the English physicist and astronomer Arthur Eddington (1882–1944) in projecting the example of the "two tables" in his best-selling book, *The Nature of the Physical World*. Eddington here contrasted the table as the physicist sees it with the table of ordinary life experience. The latter is solid and filled with material. The former is largely empty space and is replete with electromagnetic phenomena. As he put it:

> I have settled down to the task of writing these lectures and have drawn up my chair to my two tables. Two tables! . . . One of them has been familiar to me from earliest years. It is a commonplace

object of that environment which I call the world. How shall I describe it? It has extension; it is comparatively permanent; it is coloured; above all it is *substantial*. After all if you are a plain commonsense man, not too much worried with scientific scruples, you will be confident that you understand the nature of an ordinary table. . . . Table No. 2 is my scientific table. It is a more recent acquaintance and I do not feel so familiar with it. . . . My scientific table is mostly emptiness. Sparsely scattered in that emptiness are numerous electric charges rushing about with great speed; but their combined bulk amounts to less than a billionth of the bulk of the table itself. Notwithstanding its strange construction it turns out to be an entirely efficient table. It supports my writing paper as satisfactorily as table No. 1. . . . But there is nothing substantial about my second table. It is nearly all empty space—space pervaded, it is true, by fields of force, but these are assigned to the category of "influences," not of "things". [And] even in the principal part which is not empty, we must not transfer the old notion of "substance" [since what is at issue is electromagnetic vibration and not "stuff"].[2]

Are the plain man and the scientist really talking about the same thing in the Eddington example? Seemingly, yes—by hypothesis they are both talking about the same table. But this is an optical illusion—or perhaps better, a *conceptual* illusion. The plain man is talking about the table all right. But in physics there just are no tables of the sort he has in view. There are indeed manifolds of process that lead people to hold that they see tables. There are, if you will, impression-of-table-creating processes. But they are just exactly that—process manifolds of a certain sort—and by no means tables. There is no such thing as a physicist's "version" or "picture" or "image" of a table. Technical physics simply has no truck with ordinary life's tables.

The fact is that scientific discourse and the discourse of everyday life have their own distinctive resources and their own distinctive aims. But they are neither in disagreement nor at cross purposes. They deal with entirely different aspects of reality. They are as dimensionally different as shape and color are different. Nothing on the one side can clash or conflict with the other. And so, there is not and cannot be any basis for saying that one is right and the other wrong.

CONTEXTUALISM IS NOT RELATIVISM

Consider a statement such as "There are no black swans hereabouts." The truth status of this claim obviously depends on the range of concern. If "hereabouts" refers to Pennsylvania, then that claim is true; but if it refers to the world, then it is false. And the same holds for "The table is hard and impenetrable." If the range of concern is everyday life, then this is clearly true, but if that range encompasses the physical sciences, the claim is then false. The context of consideration—the range of concern—makes all the difference. And the question "What is the correct range of concerns" makes no sense. There is not one correct deliberative setting any more than there is one correct spatial or temporal setting. The distinction between the two tables—labeling one real and the other apparent—is accordingly based on a seriously incorrect understanding of the situation.

Moreover, the situation is even more complicated. For science does not speak with a single voice. Its declarations vary over time. The science of the year 1500 and the science of today have different things to say, and the science of the year 3000 also will have different things to say. In scientific matters, we cannot just speak of the truth; we have to speak of the truth as X (the science of the year Z) has it. There is certainly no finality to "the science of today." The real truth is an idealization: the truth as "the perfect knower" sees it—or rather would see it if there were such a being. In practice we can never do more (but also should do no less) than to aim at giving our best estimate of the truth as far as the prevailing circumstances allow. And this too must be acknowledged before it makes sense to envision such a thing as "the table of the physicists."

And so in the end there is no quarrel and no disagreement between the assertions of the physical and those of the plain man. It is not that one is right and one wrong. You cannot be mistaken until you endorse something that just is not the case. And neither the physicist nor the plain man do this. Within their intended range of deliberations, each is perfectly correct.

Context determines meaning, and truth hinges on what is meant. And on this basis the discourse of physics and ordinary discourse are perfectly compatible.

When we examine an Eddingtonian contrast between "the table as ordinarily conceived" and "the table of the physicist," we come up against a problem. For the fact is, as already indicated above, that physics takes no notice of tables. They do not figure in the texts and treatises of the subject. The discursive machinery for talk about tables and such-like objects is simply not available in modern physics: tables as such are not on the agenda.

And for that very reason we cannot ask about "the physicist's (or scientist's) table" or debate about its color or its weight or style. Nothing but category confusion lies down this road. The essential presupposition of questions such as "Does 'the physicist's (or scientist's) table' or 'that table as the physicists conceive of it' have this or that feature?" is simply not available, because it presupposes something nonexistent. The physicist does not deal with that *table* at all.

And this conclusion holds not only for tables but also for work and force and space and time as well, as these items are ordinarily conceived. The physicist does not discuss these matters at all but rather abandons them (as ordinarily understood) and shifts the discussion to some technical issues of his own. The space-time talk of the physicist is about something quite different from what is at issue in the space-time talk of ordinary language. The language may be similar or even identical, but the physicist has in effect changed the subject.

In the final analysis, the question "Which is the real table—that of the plain man or that of the physicist?" does not make sense because there actually is no physicist's table at all. To be sure, one can shift the ground and ask at a different level of generality: "What is the proper and correct way to conceptualize the world's furnishings, that of scientific discourse or that of ordinary, everyday life?" But while this question seems to make better sense, the fact is that here too there is an erroneous presupposition, namely, that there is only one "proper and correct way" to conceptualize the world. The situation is complicated. Is it all a matter of scientific explanation or a matter of the management of the affairs of everyday life? In the laboratory there is one proper way of talking; in the furniture store, another. It is all a matter of appropriate context. We cannot say that one mode of discourse is more appropriate and correct than another without specifying the particular context of consideration, any more than we can say that our mode of perception is more correct and appropriate than our mode of physical description. There is no one-size-fits-all in matters of linguistic propriety. In these matters, too, terminological contextualization rules. The distinction between appearance and reality simply does not map into the distinction between scientific and everyday-life discourse.

The fact that different ranges of discourse can be semantically autonomous means that the claims formulated in the setting of one linguistic framework have to be appraised with respect to their meaning, logic, and truth by means of the ground rules and principles that are appropriate in that particular context. This sort of contextualism is totally apart from an indifferentist relativism. For the relativist, the choice among alternatives is rationally indifferent, a matter of arbitrary individual proceedings. The relativist's motto is, "Follow your inclinations. It makes no real difference which way you go: it is simply a matter of taste." But contextualism acknowledges and indeed insists on there being a right and wrong way to proceed: it holds that there are definite guidelines as to what is right and proper. And it goes on to hold that what is right or proper depends on the nature of the circumstances; that circumstances vary, and resolutions vary with them; that there are times when a hammer is the way to insert that metal pin and other times when a screwdriver is called for. Propriety is there, but its details vary with the conditions and circumstances. It is not indifferent whether you use a comma or a period in providing punctuation, but that which is called for as appropriate depends on the circumstances. It is, in the final analysis, a matter of functional efficacy—of what is for the best in the prevailing conditions. And this certainly does not depend on the whim or will of the agent.

Accordingly, relativism and contextualism are very different sorts of approaches and exhibit very different modes of procedure. Above all, they differ fundamentally on the issue of there being good reasons for issue-resolution. And in terminological matters, as elsewhere, this makes for a substantial difference.

Granted, human beings, the members of *Homo sapiens*, are not just sapient but are also fallible. And the views and contentions we maintain in everyday life—not to speak of matters of metaphysics and religion—may well involve various sorts of errors. But they are certainly not blocked or vitiated from the very outset by the fact that what is being maintained cannot be recast in the language of natural science. In the final analysis, natural science does not improve on the resources of ordinary discourse; as clearly shown above, it merely changes the subject.

And this situation has significant implications for metaphysics. For the very language in which our puzzlements arise and our questions are posed is in large measure remote from and discontinuous with the terms of reference in which science conducts its deliberations.

The problems of metaphysics may or may not admit of cogent solutions, but if they do, it will not be natural science that supplies them.

Chapter 4

ON CONTINGENCY AND NECESSITY

PROBLEMS OF TOTALITY

A prime task of metaphysics is to elucidate the conceptual instrumentalities through which our understanding of what is actual and possible becomes open to the deliberations of rational inquiry. Traditionally, metaphysics is characterized as the study of being in general, and in implementing this idea, three realms or modes of beings have been contemplated:

Realm 1: the things and processes of the physical universe as accessible through observational experience.

Realm 2: the conceptual instrumentalities (colors, shapes, types) needed for the description and explanation of Realm 1 items.

Realm 3: the conjectural, fictional, or hypothetical possibilities that can be concocted from the resources of Realm 2.

We may, of course, presume that there are hyperbolic possibilities that cannot be envisioned with the (still) reality-connected conceptual resources of Realm 2. But with these we can have no cognitive commerce whatsoever: like facts that no one will ever conceive of, such things unquestionably exist, but we can have no informative contact with them. They may be imagined to exist at the level of generality, but they can never be identified at the level of individualized specificity.

In its role as an inquiry into being qua being, a fundamental task for metaphysics is to ask whether there is one all-inclusive type or category—

one that encompasses everything whatsoever. But how are we to accomplish this? Where are we to obtain a term that affords the requisite universality of coverage?

The broadest term in philosophical usage is "thing" (Greek *chrêma*, Latin *res*, German *Ding*). But in fact none of these terms are sufficiently general in their normal usage, pertaining across the board to objects of consideration in an unrestricted way. (For example, it doesn't seem natural to apply them to numbers, colors, or Napoleon's defeat at Waterloo.) In standard usage, "thing" or "object" generally means *existing* thing or object—unless we are put on notice by the explicit addendum of "functional" or "suppositional" or "merely possible." What is needed is a term of truly unrestricted generality, and since neither ordinary discourse nor philosophical usage appears to provide one, we had best create one by terminological postulation.

Perhaps the closest one can come to this desideratum within the resources of ordinary English discourse is the word "item," and we shall here postulate that it does the job. Thus every possible object of discussion will qualify as an item: the Washington Monument, the number series, the Easter bunny, the preceding comma, and so on.

The boundaries of reality do not set any limits on membership in our category of "items." Nor do the boundaries of conceivability. Only the boundaries of logical possibility set limits. Round squares are out for sure, and so are magnetic numbers.

Items as here conceived thus constitute a domain that reaches beyond the traditional philosophical category of substance. Since any individual target of discussion or deliberation counts as an item, this domain will include the assassination of Julius Caesar, the London Earthquake of 1754, and the defeat of Napoleon at Waterloo. But these are processes rather than substances. Or again, consider the fact that Caesar was married to Calpurnia, or that Napoleon was for a time First Consul of France, or that Hitler hated Churchill. Such facts, too, are items, although facts are not substances. From the angle of traditional philosophical consideration, itemhood is a uniquely inclusive conception.

As these deliberations indicate, there is a conceptual and ontological gap between items and existents, that is, between the suppositional being of discussion objects and the authentic existence of the real world's furnishings. And just as natural science examines the descriptive nature and the actual modus operandi of spatiotemporal existents, metaphysics deliberates about the descriptive nature and functional modus operandi of those merely hypothetical particularities. Metaphysics seeks to broaden our perspective of deliberation through situating the real within the wider range of the possible, enabling us to come to terms with the question of how it is that reality is as it is when it might possibly be otherwise. Even at this level of generality, however, the principle *ex nihilo nihil* applies; necessity must admit of a rational grounding of some sort.

THE CONCEPT OF CONTINGENCY

From the very birth of logic in Aristotle's day it has been accepted that some propositions are true as a matter of fact, others as a matter of necessity. A fact is contingent when its obtaining is not necessary—that is, whenever the situation in its regard could be different from what it is. The conception of contingency looks to alternative possibilities and envisions that what is the case might be otherwise. A circumstance (state of affairs) is contingent when it is equally possible that it could or could not obtain, to the extent that this can be determined on the basis of one or the other of the following:

(1) general principles
(2) the condition of affairs prevailing before that time
(3) what is known or thought to be the condition of affairs prevailing before that time

Contingency accordingly has both temporal and atemporal senses— (2) and (3) as contrasted with (1)—and both ontological and epistemic senses— (1) and (2) as contrasted with (3). And so there will be categorical or absolute contingency as per (1), conditional contingency as per (2), and epistemic contingency as per (3).

A fact is necessary if it cannot possibly be different from what it is. That triangles have three sides is necessary because this being so is rooted in the very idea of what it is to be a triangle. But that right triangles are real is contingent: no contradiction ensues from supposing the situation otherwise.

Contingency is a conception that finds application in many different contexts and that functions somewhat differently from one case to the other. How contingency is to be construed is itself a contingent issue. And the concept of noncontingency is of course correspondingly diverse. Thus a state of affairs that is *not* contingent

— in sense (1) is either necessary or impossible
— in sense (2) is predetermined (and thus in principle predictable) one way or the other
— in sense (3) is predictable one way or the other as a foregone conclusion

It is thus clear that a complex set of issues revolve around the concept of contingency, which itself is a many-faceted and complex concept.

In matters of cognition, precisely those possibilities that, for all we know, would go one way or the other with respect to truth and falsity are the most urgent and obvious candidates for investigation, research, and inquiry.

And the situation is equally salient in matters of action. For here, whenever matters could, in the causal order of things, work themselves out either one way or the other with respect to something in which we have a stake or interest, two pressing questions arise. First, could we act so as to determine or at least influence the outcome? And second, should this prove to be beyond our powers, can we take measures to mitigate any possible unfavorable outcome?

Contingency is the theoretician's bane. For throughout all the pertinent contexts, contingency leaves a gap where fundamental general principles cannot settle matters. Further and less decisive means of determination have to come into play.

MODES OF NECESSITY

Why dwell on the concept of necessity? Because philosophers have generally been drawn to it given that the sphere of contingent truth—of non-necessary truth—belongs to the empirical sciences.

Here it is important to distinguish the two questions "What is necessity?" and "What is necessary?" Only after the first is satisfactorily resolved can the second be addressed profitably.

The conception of necessity has it that whatever is necessary must be as it is and cannot possibly be otherwise. The very idea that the case might be otherwise is unsustainable and incoherent. The root idea is that certain facts simply have to be as is, secure, and unquestionable—absolutely assured either by the impersonal arrangement of things or by the communication conceptions stipulated by intelligent agents.

In any case, the basic idea is that something is necessary (in one way or another) if its negation is incompatible with some body of definitively established and (at least pro-tem) incontestable truth.

Necessity is always something that is basis-relative, and contingency is so as well. With the matter approached from this angle, we arrive at the taxonomy of necessity set out in Display 4.1.

Display 4.1

THE MODES OF NECESSITY

That is necessary whose denial is logically incompatible with

- the laws and principles of logic (*logical necessity*)
- the fundamental rules and principles that govern meaningful discourse (*semantical* or *linguistic necessity*)
- the basic definitions and principles of mathematics (*mathematical necessity*)
- the decrees of God (*theoretical necessity*)
- The principles of metaphysics (*metaphysical necessity*)
- the laws of nature (*physical* or *natural necessity*)
- the established rules of social interactions (*social necessity*)
- the operative values of a certain domain of necessitation (*axiological necessity*)

Note: The first three of these are modes of *absolute* or *formal necessity*. The last three are modes of *conditional* or *material necessity*.

That cats are felines or that forks have tines are matters of semantical necessity. Given that the *concepts* of "cat," "feline," "fork," and "tine" are what they are, these claims are patently correct. However, that the English *word* "cat" means *cat*—namely, is used in relation to that particular concept—is only a matter of conditional necessity, whose truth depends on social conventions. The truths of logic, language, and mathematics are necessary because their rivals are ultimately incoherent. Perhaps the least familiar of the variant modes of necessity is that of axiological (or evaluative) necessitation. Consider the following situation. Suppose that four 0s and five 1s are allocated to a tic-tac-toe gridwork, subject to the condition that the more axial symmetry the better. Then our problem has but one solution, as shown in the graphic here.

1	0	1
0	1	0
1	0	1

Given the "physical" constraints at work, the "evaluative" consideration superadded to them allows for only one *optimal* solution. But given the axiological nature of the condition at issue, that solution, though necessary, is put in place by conditions of evaluative (axiological) necessity.

Necessity pivots on the idea that matters have to stand in a certain way because if they stood differently, that would create a significant rift in the fabric of fact. This line of thought pivots on the idea that

> p is and must be the case because things could only stand differently if, in saying that some fact is not necessary, we are prepared to claim that matters might have stood otherwise.

But how does that "if" function here—if what? We cannot simply say "if it were not the case." For that would be trivial and pointless. We have to be prepared to give meaningful sense to this idea of if-dependency—to offer some intelligible hypothesis to conceptualize the "if-supposition" at issue. And at this point the following spectrum of prospects comes to the fore, depending on whether

— matters of logic, mathematics, and formal science at large stood otherwise (which is absolutely impossible)
— God had willed it so (presumably a theological impossibility)
— the laws and principles of nature were different
— social customs and regulations were different
— a variant belief system has it so
— a given individual (X or Y or Z) has so decided
— pure chance would have had things turn out differently

Observe that each of these hypotheses creates fractures in the real—the manifold of actual fact—but that these fractures become less radical as we move down the list. At the top of the list we have to deal with wild, radical, and virtually absurd hypotheses, while as we proceed downward the hypotheses become increasingly viable, with fewer demands on our capacity for suspension of disbelief. The correlate assumptions involve the abandonment of increasingly weakened commitments, whose enmeshment with our view of reality is ever diminished. Ever weaker and less absolute modes of necessitation are at issue.

The fundamental mode of necessity that is relevant here is the *logical* necessity coordinate with being demonstrably true on logico-conceptual principles. This has two forms, the absolute and the conditional. We accordingly have it that:

- p is *categorically necessary*, symbolically $\Box p$, iff p is demonstrable on the basis of logico-conceptual considerations: $\vdash p$
- p is *conditionally necessary* relative to q, symbolically $\Box(p \mid q)$, iff p follows from q solely on the basis of logico-conceptual considerations: $q \vdash p$.

On this basis the four different modes of categorical necessity can be articulated, here symbolized as $\vdash X \dashv$ where X will be:

L   in the case of *logical* (or logico-conceptual) necessity
C   in the case of *cognitive* (or epistemic) necessity
P   in the case of *physical* (or natural) necessity
E   in the case of *ethical* (or moral) necessity

And there will also be four corresponding forms of conditional necessitation in line with the formula:

$$\vdash X \mid q \dashv p \text{ iff } \Box(p \mid X \& q) \text{ or equivalently } (X \& q) \vdash p$$

The resulting situation is summarized in Display 4.2, which clearly brings home the many-sided bearing of the idea of necessity.

CONTINGENCY AND NECESSITY

A proposition is contingent (in one or another of the relevant modes) when it expresses a contingent possibility, that is, a claim that is neither necessarily true not necessarily false:

$$\sim \vdash X \dashv p \ \& \ \sim \vdash X \dashv \sim p \text{ where X can be any of L, C, P, E}$$

And on this basis a proposition is a contingent *truth* when it is both contingent and true. And so there are going to be as many different modes of contingency (C) as there are of necessity ($\vdash X \dashv$). If something has to be as it is and could not possibly turn out otherwise, then any prospect of contingency is thereby removed. And, as noted above, there are distinct possibilities here.

The most basic and salient prospect here is the *logico-conceptual* (categorical or absolute) mode of necessity, which calls for being demonstrable on the basis of abstract general principles alone. With this mode of necessity symbolized by "$\Box$," we thus have:

$$\Box p \text{ iff } \vdash p$$

Absolutely necessary conclusions are thus those which can be seen to obtain solely on the basis of logico-conceptual considerations.

Moving beyond this, there is also the prospect of *conditional logico-conceptual necessity* with respect to some given condition C:

$$\Box(p \mid C) \text{ iff } C \vdash p$$

DIFFERENT MODES OF NECESSITY

- Logico-conceptual necessity: $\vdash_L$

  — p is logico-conceptually necessary, symbolically $\vdash_P$ or $\Box p$, iff p is demonstrable given logico-conceptual principles:

  $\vdash_L p$ or $\Box p$ iff $L \vdash p$

- Cognitive/epistemic necessity: $\vdash_C$

  — p is cognitively necessary, symbolically $\vdash_C p$, iff p is logico-conceptually necessary given the body of known information C:

  $\vdash_C p$ or $\Box(p \mid C)$ iff $C \vdash p$

- Physical/natural necessity: $\vdash_P$

  — p is physically necessary (in the unconditional mode) iff p is logico-conceptually necessary given the body of fundamental physical fact P:

  $\vdash_P p$ or $\Box(p \mid P)$ iff $P \vdash p$

  — p is physically necessary conditionally upon q iff p is logico-conceptually necessary given q together with the body of fundamental physical fact P:

  $\vdash_{P \mid q} p$ or $\Box(p \mid P \ \& \ q)$ iff $(P \ \& \ q) \vdash p$

- Ethico-moral necessity: $\vdash_E$

  — p is ethically necessary in the unconditional mode iff p is logico-conceptually necessary given the manifold of ethical principles and precepts E:

  $\vdash_E p$ or $\Box(p \mid E)$ iff $E \vdash p$

  — p is ethically necessary conditionally upon q iff p becomes logico-conceptually necessary when q is superimposed upon E:

  $\vdash_{E \mid q} p$ or $\Box(p \mid E \ \& \ q)$ iff $(E \ \& \ q) \vdash p$

Here p is not necessary absolutely but only a condition that C is satisfied. Thus, that today is Thursday is not necessary and is thereby contingent. (You might be reading this on Monday.) But that today is Thursday if yesterday was Wednesday is indeed necessary—a consequence of the very meaning of the terms of reference at issue and not the result of some potentially variable eventuation.

The conception of *ethical* necessity provides yet another gateway to contingency. It is grounded in the idea of conditional necessity relative to the requirements and structures of ethically appropriate comportment (E):

$$\vdash E \dashv p \text{ iff } \Box(p \mid E)$$

Ethical necessity is thus a matter of logico-conceptual necessity relative to the manifold of ethical principles (E). And on this basis, ethical contingency comes to

$$\sim \vdash E \dashv p \And \sim \vdash E \dashv \sim p$$

In cases of science, ethical contingency will be entirely indifferent whether or not p is to be realized. (Like stamp collecting, p's being realized is immaterial from an ethico-moral point of view.)

Physical necessity (symbolized as [P]) is another factor that is crucial for our present concerns. It is predicated on the idea of conditional necessitation relative to the body of true and fundamental facts prevailing in the natural sciences (S). We thus have

$$\vdash P \dashv p \text{ iff } \Box(p \mid S)$$

On this basis a physically contingent *truth* is a proposition p such that

$$p \And \sim \vdash P \dashv p \text{ or equivalently } p \And \sim \Box(p \mid S)$$

It will be a fact that obtains without being subordinated by the laws on the fundamentals of nature's modus operandi, as science reveals them to us.

The question of whether or not there are such truths—an issue much debated in traditional metaphysics—was settled in the affirmative in modern science by the discovery that some of nature's fundamental laws are merely stochastic, that is, they have a probabilistic rather than a definitely determinate bearing.

There is no single way to learn necessary truths, and their status as necessitation is not a function of their mode of acquisition. We can learn such truths in many ways: by "figuring them out," by mere instruction, by rational insight, and so on. Their status as necessary is a matter of the considerations that can establish their truth; how people *learn* that they are true is another matter altogether.

Only after we learn what the words "forks" and "tines" mean can the necessity of the contention "All (normal, unbroken) forks have tines" come into our awareness. Only after Newtonian mechanics has been developed can we secure a conviction of the necessity that every physical action must evoke an equal and contrary reaction. However, the necessity of necessary facts lies in what they affirm, and not in our affirmation of them. Like all other facts, necessary truths have to be learned: it is what they assert that is necessary, not our apprehension of them.

NECESSITY AND HUMAN FREEDOM

We see ourselves as to some extent in productive control of events—we assume that certain things that happen in this world would not in fact happen if we did not cause them to be so. Our statements would not be stated, our paintings painted, and our books written if we ourselves did not get in there and decide to state/paint/write them. The realization of those outcomes is not independent of our deliberate agency; those outcomes are especially dependent on our decisions and actions. Here we are in control— if our choices in point of decision and action were different, then some minuscule sector of reality would be different from what it is.

Human free agency is entirely a matter of temporal contingency. A human decision at time t is made freely if there is no time prior to t when that decision is necessitated by the then-existing condition of things. This means that there is no time t that constitutes a point of no return, one that exempts the decision from possible recall. The decision becomes a fait accompli at no point prior to the decision itself.

TECHNICAL APPENDIX

It must be stressed that there is a significant difference between what the medieval schoolmen characterized as consequential necessity (*necessitas consequantiae*) with respect to a body of fact F, namely, $\Box(F \rightarrow p)$, and what they called consequent necessity (*necessitas consequentis*), namely, $F \rightarrow \Box p$. Observe that when F is p itself, the former will be true by logic alone, but the latter certainly need not be, given that not every truth is necessarily so.

Since F is, by hypothesis, a body of fact, we have it that [F] p—that is F $\vdash p$—and accordingly

$$[F]\, p \rightarrow p$$

Several points regarding the resultant formal logic of necessity deserve note. Observe moreover that now

$$[F][F]\, p \text{ iff } F \rightarrow (F \rightarrow p)$$

In standard logic the right-hand side comes to $F \rightarrow p$, or, equivalently, [F] p. Thus [F] p iff [F][F] p, so that our logic of necessity will have the structure of a Lewis S5 system.

Chapter 5

RANDOMNESS AND REASON

RANDOMNESS ENVISIONED

The role that chance, randomness, and purely fortuitous occurrence play in reality's scheme of things constitutes one of the most fundamental and persistent issues in the history of metaphysics.

Since the days of the ancient Stoics the idea of the lawful orderliness of the world has been prominent in Western philosophy. And chance, randomness, and chaos have usually been deemed anathema in an orderly and rationally functioning world, with mere chance seen as the hallmark of rationally unacceptable disorder. As Albert Einstein famously put it, "God does not play dice with his universe."[1]

All the same, such randomness-aversion is decidedly questionable. For in diverse settings, both in regard to nature and to human affairs, the interests of rationality and order are in fact best served via a recourse to arbitrary chance.

RANDOMNESS IN PHYSICS

Let us begin with physics. The role of probabilities in nature has been a controversial issue. In his metaphysical moments, Einstein was convinced that there was no proper place for randomness in nature. And so he held there was no place for probabilities in physics—or at least not at the level of fundamentals. As he wrote to David Bohm in 1954, "I do not believe in micro- or macro-laws, but only in structure laws that lay claim to a universally binding validity."[2] All the same, it seems to be an ironic fact that sometimes universally binding laws can open the door to mere chance. For if those binding laws are to serve the interests of simplicity across an entire ensemble of possible state-conditions, then recourse to probabilities can become necessary. Once the economic factors of the effectiveness and efficiency of operation are on the agenda, probabilities can enter in, given that some optimization problems are best addressed by probabilistic machinery.

Accordingly, even a chance-averse Einstein could in principle come to terms with this idea. For what he would want is for quantum probabilities to be obtained by derivation under the aegis of rationally cogent basic principles. Specifically, he would ask for a higher-level perspective on physical principles that would engender the probabilistic detail of quantum theory as the demonstrably adequate resolution of a problem of optimization under constraints—a projection of the classic standpoint of rational mechanics onto the latter-day realm of quantum mechanics.[3] And there really seems to be no ultimately compelling reason based on fundamental principles why he cannot have his way here.

Einstein rejected randomness because he wanted a rational universe. But it is in fact sensible to think that even a thoroughly rational cosmos can make room for random processes and chance occurrences.

To convey a general idea of such a pathway to probability, consider a simple analogy: an illustration of a type familiar from classic rational mechanics, which endeavored to show how various laws of nature are as they are because conformity to them provides for maximal efficiency, effectiveness, and economy of operation.

Let us assume that a physical system calls for a limitation of its constituents from one state to another. And now assume that this can be accomplished by one of two revolving-door turnstile passageways between the two states, each of which can allow the passage of one constituent per unit of time. Consider two possible and plausible lawful rules for unit transit:

(1) Effect transit via a determinate passageway (say, the nearest).
(2) Effect transit via a passageway selected 50:50 at random.

In these conditions, the second rule would clearly make the transfer of units more efficient (i.e., faster) than the first rule. For with the first rule of a fixed determination, a condition of crowding could easily transpire, via something akin to a traffic jam. In order to achieve efficiency throughout the entire ensemble of possible initial conditions, then, the behavior of individual constituents may well have to be governed by laws geared to probabilities.

Further, consider the prospect that the two connective turnstiles rotate at different speeds, say, one at twice the rate of the other. Then the optimizing rule for individual units would not be to effect a transit with one-to-one-randomness between the two turnstiles but rather to head for the faster turnstile at a two-to-one ratio of probability. For maximum efficiency, the operative probability would then have to be adjusted to the mechanical mode of turnstile operation. Probability would thus become derivative from nonprobabilistic features of the modus operandi of the physical set-up at issue via considerations of efficiency and economy.

What we have here is the realization of a mode of operation which, in allowing the individual subunits of a system "to throw the dice," as it were, in line with probabilistic variation, enables the system as a whole a way that is optimally effective, efficient, and economical. As such illustrations indicate, the advantage of a system's functioning in point of economy, stability, or viability may lie in the fact that its components behave randomly in certain respects. For rigid regularity involves overload, and randomness helps to keep things on an even keel. Take two more analogies, from human affairs. Not every passenger on a boat should be on the same side of the boat; and in evacuating an unevenly occupied building, the instruction "Go to the nearest exit" may not be as effective as "Just leave" (by whatever exit you wish or can find).

The salient point is that if certain global conditions are to be realized with maximal efficiency in a physical system, then its constituent elements may have to conform to probabilistic laws of behavior. On such an approach, probabilities need not enter by unexplained fiat; they can prove to have an explanatory rationale in terms of fundamental principles. And it was apparently just this sort of thing that Einstein had in view.

Einstein's basic desideratum was the exclusion of probabilities that lack a rationale grounded in considerations of general principle: "That there should be statistical laws that require God to throw dice in each individual case, I find highly disagreeable."[4] But of course the situation becomes rather different when probabilities do not just spring into operation ex nihilo but instead emerge as part of a solution to a problem of optimization under plausible constraints.[5] For in the end, there is good reason to think that even in physics the ideology of rational order can allow a role for randomness and pure chance. Einstein did not hesitate to declare, "When I am judging a theory I ask myself whether, if I were God, I would have arranged the world in such a way."[6] But such a view need not necessarily merit the rejection of probabilities altogether from a divinely instituted, rational scheme of things.

But let us now return to the human perspective.

RANDOMNESS IN MORAL PHILOSOPHY

In the human sphere, randomness even has a constructive role to play in matters of moral propriety. One dilemma of fairness lies in the consideration that there are many circumstances in which a realization of the desideratum of aligning results with claims becomes impossible to achieve because of the inherent incompatibility of the claims at issue. A classic illustration of this situation arises in connection with equal claims to an indivisible good. And an analogous situation arises with any *insufficiency of resources for meeting equivalent claims*. Thus suppose that someone owes $100 to each of two otherwise equivalent creditors but only has $120. If each creditor requires payment in full in order to buy some essential medical treatment, one might as well proceed by random selection. Given that we cannot achieve an equality of outcome, an equality of opportunity is the best we can realize. The result, which leaves one claimant empty-handed, is certainly not optimal—one can hardly say that justice is satisfied. But in the circumstances, one must concede that the result is fair—in the sense that equally qualified situations are issuing from the same decision method—random selection. (One lesson here is that justice and fairness cannot be equated.)[7]

Again, let the following situation be assumed:

A mad scientist has rigged up an electrocution apparatus and is forcing *A*, *B*, and *C* to participate in his evil scheme. The setup is such that their innocent friend *X* will be fatally electrocuted unless *just exactly two* of the trio throw a disconnect switch. However, they have to proceed independently, without any knowledge of what their mates are doing. Should they throw that switch?

Display 5.1

A SURVEY OF POSSIBILITIES

	A	B	C	The fate of X
1.	T	T	T	–
2.	T	T	N	+
3.	T	N	T	+
4.	T	N	N	–
5.	N	T	T	+
6.	N	T	N	–
7.	N	N	T	–
8.	N	N	N	–

As Display 5.1 shows, there are overall eight theoretically available possibilities for these individuals with respect to the choice: throw (T) or not-throw (N). And each of our three subjects has the prospect of reasoning along any of the following five seemingly plausible lines. (We shall look at this situation from A's point of view, so that A = I myself, noting that B and C face an identical situation):

Case 1. B and C and I are all rational agents facing exactly the problem and are thus bound to arrive at the same resolution. It does not matter what I choose to do, seeing that B and C, being similarly situated, are also bound to choose likewise. So choices 1 and 8 are the only real options. Accordingly, poor X is doomed irrespective of what I choose to do.

Case 2. Overall those eight alternatives seem equally available. But if I choose T, then X will be saved in two cases, while if I choose N, he will be saved in only one. So I had best throw that switch, which appears to double X's prospects of survival.

Case 3. B and C are smart fellows. They are going to reason as per case 2 that they ought to throw the switch. And therefore I must opt out and choose N. (But, alas, here again if they reason likewise, poor X is doomed.)

Case 4. I might as well simply toss a coin, counting on the others to do likewise. With three of the eight cases now in his favor, that will give X at least a 3/8 (i.e., 38%) chance of survival.

Case 5. I should resort to a probabilistically mixed strategy—as in case 4, but not case 4 itself. Rather, suppose that I select T with probability x and N with probability $1 - x$. Then calculation reveals that the value of x that maximizes the chances of saving X (namely, 4/9 or 44%) is $x = 2/3$.

Accordingly, these five lines of reasoning lead to the different conclusions:

(1) Choice Indifference between T and N
(2) Choice of T
(3) Choice of N
(4) Probabilistic Indifference between T and N
(5) Favor T over N probabilistically at a ratio of 2-to-1

All things considered, alternative 5 clearly does the best job of ensuring X's survival.

When a selection among alternatives is delegated to a random process, it may be that the only reason for adopting that *particular* resolution is this very circumstance itself. Moreover, the delegation of a choice or decision to a random process does not relieve the delegator of responsibility for the outcome. Random selection does not abrogate responsibility. (The commander who orders five arbitrarily selected citizens to be shot as retribution for some offense is still responsible for the murder of these innocents.)

When an outcome is selected at random, there simply is no case-specific reason for its determination. In this regard, randomness is the very *antithesis* of rationality. However, this is not the end of the story. For there may well be good reason for having the outcome be selected randomly. So the seeming conflict is resolved through the distinction between processes and product. There may be a sound rational basis for making a determination randomly.

In the final analysis, the operation of chance does not mean a conflict with the principle of sufficient reason. For the very fact that something is the outcome of a random process will in certain circumstances constitute the sufficient reasons for its actualization.

But back to the main point, which is this. In human affairs it is sometimes best to proceed randomly. This is especially so in matters of what might be called "strategic interaction." In the children's game of "scissors-stone-paper," the best plan is to make one's selection randomly to ensure an even chance of winning. Any other policy will result in a detectable bias of which the opponent can take advantage in the long run. Again, in war planning of the classical sort, a commander does well to vary his attacks randomly, for example between the left and the right wings of his army, to keep his opponent off balance. And the conflict between encoders and their cryptographic opponents is similar. The effective use of ciphers is critically dependent on concealing meaningful messages in a fog of apparent randomness—and the more randomness, the higher the level of secrecy.

CONCLUSION

The acceptance of randomness in matters of decision through the mediation of probabilistic indeterminacy can prove to be rationally appropriate with respect to a wide variety of contexts. With respect to nature, it can make for greater efficiency in processes of state transition. And in human affairs, too, it can serve many useful purposes. Specifically, it can serve to

— ensure fairness in distributing positivities or negativities
— avert predictability in situations of conflict or competition
— enhance secrecy in communication
— maximize efficiency in certain goal-directed processes
— make rational optimality possible in certain decision contexts

The fact of it is that both with persons and in nature overall, rationally optimal arrangements are often most efficiently and effectively met by resolutions effected through randomness. And so there is no inherent conflict or contradiction between randomness and reason.

Chapter 6

ISSUES OF SELF-REFERENCE AND PARADOX

SELF-REFERENCE AND SELF-REFERENTIAL STATEMENTS

Ever since Descartes put the self at the center of metaphysical reflection, the issue of self-reference and reflexivity has been at the forefront of philosophical deliberation. But where Descartes sought for certainty via the focus on one's self, later thinkers found not only uncertainty but paradox. For the Cartesian idea that "short of divine aid I can be certain of nothing except what relates to myself" has a paradoxical air about it. So let us begin with the basics of the matter.

The discursive reflexivity of self-reference is a widely diffused phenomenon. It can occur with respect to:

— assertions/statements/propositions/claims
— specifications, identifications
— definitions
— predictions/prophecies
— questions
— instructions/requests

Statements can involve two modes of self-reference: the *direct* and the *indirect* (or *oblique*), and either sort can be true or false. Model instances of directly self-referential statements are:

- This statement is short. (True)
- This statement is framed in a French sentence. (False)

Such directly self-referential statements explicitly attribute some feature to themselves. By contrast, obliquely self-referential statements are not about themselves as such, but about an entire class of statements to which they themselves belong. Two instances of these are:

- All statements make an assertion.
- All statements on this page are framed in Greek sentences.

In many cases, obliquely self-referential statements (including the two above) require factual information for their specific identification. The message conveyed by such self-referential statements hinges not just in their own content but on facts over and above those provided in the statements. Thus, for example, construing the last two sample statements requires knowing that they are written on this page. Their falsity is accordingly not a matter of abstract necessity but hinges on certain contingent facts affecting the determination of their reference.

However, self-referential statements can also prove to be true or false necessarily, as a matter of general principle. Thus consider:

- This statement has a beginning. (True)
- This statement concerns statements. (True)
- This statement makes a statement. (True)
- This statement conveys significant information. (False)
- All statements are true. (False)
- This statement is presented in words of one syllable. (False)

All of these statements have their truth-status determined through a necessity rooted in general principles with respect to the concepts at issue.

However, it should be stressed that self-reference and self-instantiation are wholly different issues. Thus consider the statement:

- Some statements are true.

Although this statement is in no sense self-referential, it is nevertheless self-substantiating in that it ensures the truth of the claim that it makes.

Concern for problems of self-reference originated with the liar paradox (*pseudomenos*) of Eubulides: "Does the man who says 'I am lying' lie?" (Also, "Does the witness who declares 'I am perjuring myself' perjure himself?")[1] The problem that arises here was posed via the following dilemma:

> The declaration that I lie will be either true or false. But if this declaration is true, then I lie, and my declaration will be false. But if that declaration is false, then what it says—namely that I lie—is not the case and I must be speaking the truth. Thus either way the truth status being assigned is inappropriate.

Eubulides' riddle was immensely popular in classical antiquity.[2] And it gave rise to the problem encapsulated in the ancient story of Epimenides the Cretan, who is supposed to have said "All Cretans are liars"—with "liar" being understood in the sense of a "*congenital* liar," someone incapable of telling the truth.[3]

SELF-FALSIFYING STATEMENTS: PARADOXES

Self-referential statements can be unproblematic and meaningful. But they need not be. It all depends.

Medieval logicians devoted much attention to *insolubilia*—reflexive propositions that deny about themselves some feature they actually have—for example, "This proposition is meaningless." And this sort of issue has continued to worry logicians of the present. They are reluctant to admit the radical solution of dismissing self-reference altogether, lest they throw out the baby along with the bath water—eliminating seemingly harmless and innocuous claims such as "This statement is about statements."

The mediaevals, however, proposed addressing the problem by means of a distinction. They proposed distinguishing between meaningful propositions proper (*propositiones*) and mere verbalisms (*proportiones vacatis*). The latter may fail to convey authentic propositions and thereby be meaningless rather than true or false. The *insolubilia*, so they held, fall into this latter category and are *improprie dicta*.[4]

Thus John Buridan maintained that statements which cannot in the nature of things be classified as true or false are thereby inherently untenable.[5] And Paul of Venice was even more explicit. He held that a statement such as "What I now say is false" is not a proper statement at all.[6] It is neither true not false but stands in an indifferently untenable vacillation between the two (*non est verum nec falsum, sel medium indifferens ad utrumque*).[7] It is, strictly speaking, no proposition at all. (*Nullum insolubile est verum et falsum, quia nullum tale es propositio.*)[8]

Self-referentially paradoxical statements are characterized as such through the feature of truth-statement instability. In virtue of their telling, if they are classified as true, then they will have to be reclassified as false and the other way around. They are inferentially vacuous; no useful information can be extracted from them. Thus consider:

- All statements are false.
- The statement expressed by the sentence written on this line is false.
- No statement I make today is true.
- No universal generalization is true.
- Every claim made in this book is false.

All such paradoxical statements are self-inconsistent.

In general we have it that:

This statement is X = The statement whose truth is being affirmed herewith is X = This very statement is itself X.

But if X were to be something like "senseless" or "meaningless" or "false," we would straightway have a self-contradiction. Exactly this feature also renders statements like "This statement is false" paradoxical and thereby informatively vacuous.

SELF-REFERENTIAL SPECIFICATION

Let us now turn from *statements* to *item-specifications* at large. Instances of paradoxical specifications are:

- the smallest integer that has never been mentioned
- the oldest centurion of Julius Caesar's army whom no one has mentioned since the death of Trajan

Self-referential specifications are problematic when they fail to bear upon what is identified and available, for instance:

- The Executive Committee is to consist of all persons appointed to it by the mayor.

Here there is no problem. The "it" refers anaphorically to a well-defined, preexisting group previously constituted through appointment by the mayor.

But contrast this with

- The Executive Committee is to be self-constituted and is to consist of all persons elected by itself.

Here, "itself" refers to what is being constituted by this formula and pre-supposes its own constituting. For that committee to exist, it has to come into being via an act that can only be performed by an already existing committee. The specification presupposes the prior availability of some-thing supposedly being constituted via the formula. It presupposes the realization of what is supposedly being defined. This sort of illicitly self-referring presupposition is paradoxical and self-defeating. It calls at one and the same time for affirming and for denying the existence of something.

Specificatory paradoxes include:

- the woman in yon corner who doesn't exist
- the tallest man in London who never set foot in England
- the first math problem I solved that defeated all my efforts
- the first-ever proof of an unprovable theorem

One clearly cannot identify something as the X that has the property F while at the same time maintaining that nothing ever has that property.

PREDICTIVE SELF-REFERENCE

There certainly are such things as self-referring predictions, for instance:

- Someday this present prediction will have originated in the past. (True)
- Someday someone will realize that no predictions were made this month. (False)
- Tomorrow it will transpire that this prediction was made (on that day's) yesterday. (True)

All of these predictions, be they true or false, necessary or contingent, are unproblematic and readily intelligible.

However, with predictions, just as with questions, there can be paradoxes. Thus consider:

- None of my predictions will ever come true.

Note that if what is claimed is true, then the prediction is false. But if it is false, then nothing anomalous results—unless this is the only prediction I ever make, in which case its coming true would again be anomalous.

Of course predictions can also be self-defeating rather than self-refuting. Thus if influential and knowledgeable economists predict a market boom or bust for some commodity next year, they may well accelerate the contrary development, thereby making the prediction bring about its own falsification. However, this sort of self-defeat is rather a causal than a conceptual phenomenon.

And the same sort of thing holds good with respect to the statement:

- All of the predictions I make today will be falsified.

Such predictions are paradoxical. The claim that they have been verified is self-contradictory.

SELF-REFERENTIAL QUESTIONS AND INSTRUCTIONS

Self-referential questions ask about themselves, as with the following:

- Is this a yes/no question?
- Does this question have an answer?

Some questions, while not strictly self-referential, are nevertheless self-resolving in that they themselves provide the material for answering the very question they pose. Thus, for example, consider:

- Are there questions?
- Can questions be posed?
- Are any questions being posed on this page?
- Can questions ask about questions?
- Is this question among those being considered by you today?
- Is it possible to frame this question in French?

All of these questions can be answered in the affirmative and in themselves provide the material for a correct answer. In effect, these questions answer themselves—and in this case do so affirmatively. In each case a correct answer can take the form: "Yes, as is shown by that question itself."

Not only can questions be self-referential, they can also be self-exemplifying, for instance:

- What is an example of a question that mentions rabbits?

By contrast, paradoxical questions are questions which by their very nature admit no possible answer. An instance is provided by the following question:

- Is *No* the correct answer to this yes/no question?

It is clear that neither *Yes* nor *No* can be the proper answer here. We are driven into inconsistency no matter where we turn:

— *Yes* is the correct answer to the question of whether all duly relevant questions, this one included, are correctly answered by *No*.
— *No* is the correct answer to the question of whether the question at issue has a correct answer.

The question rests on a false presupposition, namely, that it has a correct answer. It is by nature not a proper but a paradoxical question.

Consider the following obliquely self-referential question:

> Do all of the yes/no
> questions posed in this
> box have a negative answer?

Note that a *Yes* answer would be straightforwardly self-contradictory. And a *No* answer would also be self-contradictory, barring the existence of other "invisible" questions in that box. The question at issue is effectively paradoxical.

Instructions and questions are in pretty much the same boat. Thus consider the question:

- What is an example of an *F* (say elephant)?

To all intents and purposes this is tantamount to the instruction:

- Provide an example of an *F*!

All of the issues that can arise regarding questions can also arise with regard to instructions.

An example of an instruction that is self-referential is:

- Be herewith instructed to obey all valid instructions.

Some such instructions are clearly paradoxical, as for example:

- Count from one to ten without including six.
- Name all of the American presidents without mentioning Benjamin Harrison.
- Bake an apple pie without apples.
- Walk from the Tuileries to the Eiffel Tower without crossing a street.

That such instructions are paradoxical is attested by the fact that the claim that they have been carried out presents an impossibility. Thus, for example, consider:

- Jones counted from one to ten without including six.

Considering what "counting from one to ten" requires, the claim that it has been done is clearly incompatible with the omission of six.

CONCLUSION

Self-reference can function in many different communicative contexts, ranging from assertions to questions. But the prospect of paradox looms throughout this entire range. For in every self-referential situation there is the possibility of a conflict between what an expression claims to do and what it actually does, between promise and performance.

And an entire domain of metaphysical deliberation regarding the nature of truth, meaning, and understanding is opened up through the implications and ramifications of self-reference.

Chapter 7

EXPLANATION AND THE PRINCIPLE OF SUFFICIENT REASON

ONTOLOGICAL VS. EPISTEMIC EXPLANATION

To explain something is to account for it in such a way as to make it understandable. This process has both a factual and a hypothetical mode: in the factual mode, one explains how it is that something is indeed the case; in the hypothetical mode, one explains how even when something is not or may not be so, it might nevertheless have become so. The present discussion will focus on the former, factual mode. And here, to explain a fact F one must provide an account of F's relation to relevantly obtaining conditions and circumstances $R(F)$ in such a way that shows how F's obtaining is at least likely and, ideally, necessary.

Only acknowledged facts, be they real or hypothetically postulated, require epistemic explanation. For explanatory issues become moot when the purported facts to be explained are themselves questionable—for instance, UFO visitations and Loch Ness monster sightings. Moreover, the explanatory venture will also become problematic when we simply lack the information to deal with the issues adequately in the prevailing state of our knowledge. Acupuncture and hypnosis would seem to afford instances of this situation. For the present, however, we shall concern ourselves with the explanation of acknowledged facts.

Explanation so conceived accordingly has two components: the fact F at issue and the explanatory rationale $R(F)$ that is provided to account for F. In general, $R(F)$ will consist of further facts (actual or presumptive) $F_1, F_2, \ldots F_n$, which are compiled to provide the requisite explanatory basis.

It is instructive to contrast the questions:

(1) Why F?
(2) Why F rather than G? (where G is a condition alternative to and incompatible with F).

With (1) we are called on to show how it is that reality encompasses F, while with (2) we confront the further issue of why reality did not (as it conceivably might have) come to encompass not-F.

To be sure, it seems at first sight that (2) is simply redundant with (1). After all, when we have explained that p, then, when q is (by hypothesis) incompatible with p, have we not automatically ruled out q and thus provided an answer for (2)?

However, this plausible line of reasoning does not really work out. Consider an illustration. Columbus made landfall in the New World on October 12, 1492. How are we to explain this event on this date? One good explanation is that on October 10, he was seventy nautical miles to the east and had mild easterly winds before him that necessitated tacking. But why did he not make landfall on the 11th? Because to do this would have required wind conditions different from those that prevailed. Yet there is nothing in the former (1)-style explanation that provides an answer to the indicated (2)-style explanatory question.

Or again, let it be the case that the average age of active American dentists is currently 36.5 years. Explaining *that* this is the case is laborious but in principle unproblematic: just inventory all active American dentists and then calculate the average of their ages. But explaining *why* this is the case—let alone explaining why just this average and not, say, 36.7, is another matter. A great deal else is now required. One would, for example, have to consider why various elderly dentists choose to retire rather than continuing in harness. That second question asks for a great deal more than the first. What the medieval schoolmen called a *demonstratio quia*—a that-demonstration—is available. But explaining *why* this fact obtains, namely, providing a demonstration *propter quid*, is more difficult. The situation would appear to be simply one of how things just happened to work out, without a specifiable reason—there is no basis of available fact to provide the basis for a rational account.

As regards factual explanation, there are basically two distinct, albeit interrelated, questions: (1) the ontological issue of *what brings it about* that a certain fact obtains and thereby answers the question of what it is that makes this to be the case, and (2) the epistemological question of *what entitles us to claim* the truth of this contention. The difference at issue is reflected in the questions "What conditions must be met for it to be true that the cat is on the mat?" and "What conditions must be met for us to be entitled to claim that the cat is on the mat?" The former is a matter of *truth-conditions*, the latter is one of *acceptability-conditions*. The one relates to the situation regarding the fact at issue in the objective scheme of things; the other relates also to the issue of the information and evidence that is at one's disposal with regard to such a fact.

This difference here is that between truth-making and claim-authorizing, which is reflected in the medieval distinction between ontological *rationes essendi* and cognitive *rationes cognoscendi*. Thus, suppose I accept a certain claim. And let it be that I do so simply and solely because you affirm that *p* and I trust you completely in such matters. This, then, is my *ratio cognoscendi*: a trust in the correctness of your claims. The acceptability conditions are thus in place. But of course, this is completely distinct from that claim's *ratio essendi*. The considerations that make a certain claim true may be quite disconnected from those that provide for our knowledge of that claim. Two decidedly different sorts of explanation are at issue here.

The theory of explanation faces many problems.

Problem 1. What is the relation between $R(F)$ and F itself? What sort of relation would obtain between a fact F and its explanatory rationale $R(F)$ for this explanation to be adequate? Clearly, some sort of consequential grounding is called for. But just what is at issue here?

Problem 2. Can $R(F)$ include F itself? Or is such "explanatory circularity" vicious and self-defeating?

Problem 3. Often a given fact F will admit of alternative possible explanations $R_1(F)$ and $R_2(F)$. What sorts of considerations will render one of these superior to the others?

Problem 4. Does an adequate explanation need to be pervasive in that the facts F_i at issue in the explanatory rationale $R(F)$ must themselves be explained? And if such explanatory totality were required, would the explanatory regress not automatically defeat the whole enterprise?

Problem 5. But if the explanatory regress were terminated at some point, resulting in unexplained explainers, how would this square with the aims of the enterprise? What sort of axiomatic ultimates would viably constitute the end-of-the-line in explanatory regression?

Clearly, any adequate account of the process of explanation will have to come to terms with these problems, and the present discussion will address the issues that arise in this connection.

THE PRINCIPLE OF SUFFICIENT REASON (PSR)

There is good reason for concerning ourselves with explanations. As beings who make their way in the world through the use of information, we *Homo sapiens* want to know and understand what is going on about us. We seek everywhere for the explanation of facts. And to reassure us that this quest is not in vain, philosophers have projected a "principle of sufficient reason" (PSR), according to which every true fact admits of an (onto-logical) explanation of why it is so rather than otherwise. What is in contemplation here is, in effect, a principle of ontological pan-explicability. From one point of view, the principle asserts the rationality of the real: when something is so, there is a reason for it. Accordingly, the PSR has it that *all* facts have explanations for being as they are, even though we may not be able to provide these explanations. However, the principle claims only that there *is* an explanation of the facts; it affords no assurance that we can actually *find or identify* it.[1]

For the PSR to be properly understood, various qualifications and caveats are necessary. In particular, the principle itself says nothing about the *sort* of explanation at issue. It is entirely open-ended in this regard, and a vast number of options are clearly available here. Consider just a few examples:

- *causal productivity* (Why did the car's engine stop?)
- *agent motivation* (Why did Smith enter the room?)
- *conceptual/mathematical demonstration* (Why is $\sqrt{4}$ less than 3?)

- *functional purposiveness* (Why do bicycles have pedals? Why do people require sleep?)

While all such explanations proceed under the aegis of lawful generality, many different sorts of lawful process can provide for the ontological explanation of facts.

TWO BASIC TYPES OF ONTOLOGICAL EXPLANATION: SUBSUMPTIVE AND COORDINATIVE (OR SYSTEMIC)

An explanation of the facts of reality standardly proceeds with regard to underlying generalities—that is, laws. And in general, laws of nature account for facts by incorporating them into the context of a larger generality. This can happen in two ways, namely, the evidentially subsumptive and the systemically coordinative. These correspond to two modes of explanatory procedure. On the one side is the model of mathematics, of exfoliative development from first principles—axioms and definitions that are (or should be) self-evident and are fundamental in the order of justification. But there is also another mode of procedure, which is not axiomatically reductive but probatively productive, namely, with reference to those generalities and principles that best coordinate, systematize, and harmoniously orchestrate the claims we deem it necessary and desirable to endorse, and thereupon to endorse on this very basis contentions that optimally satisfy this information-harmonizing desideratum. (It is just this sort of consideration that explains why those axiomatic generalities and principles were selected for their role.)

Subsumptive reasons explain facts "from above" with reference to overarching generalities. Systemic reasons, by contrast, explain facts "from around" with reference to a wider context of surrounding facts.

In this way, coordinative explanation accounts for the fact to be explained by enbedding it in a web of other facts. Here, law subordination is not required, but rather merely a fit within a wider framework of lawfulness. Facts thus become explained by fitting harmoniously into a larger manifold of relevant order.

In matters of theoretical science, this type of contextual explanation may be relatively rare. But in applied science it is commonplace, and it is familiar from and pervasive in the sciences of human affairs. In the explanation of economic phenomena (e.g., bank runs, bubbles, or market crashes) or in the management of technology (e.g., traffic jams or airplane disasters), let alone political affairs (e.g., elections, revolutions, migrations), this mode of occurrence-explanation is standard.

VARIETIES OF LAWFULNESS AND MODES OF GENERALITY

Ontological explanation places the fact to be explained into a framework of environing generality afforded by the laws of nature. The generality at issue can be

— universal
— general but not strictly universal
— substantially predominant
— merely occasional

With ontological explanation the probative link between the rationale $R(F)$ and the fact F can so vary as to render that fact

— inevitable
— (highly) probable
— likely
— nontrivially probable
— possible

With explanations at large there are thus different levels of explanatory stringency, extending from the conclusively categorical to the merely possibilistic.

Of course, even the weakest of these linkages can still do explanatory work. And the different modes of explanation involve different, albeit interrelated, tasks. At the level of inevitability we come to understand why the explanation must be the case. With probabilistic explanation we understand how it is that the explanation is very likely the case. With possibilistic explanation we understand how it is that the explanation becomes possible. Inevitabilistic explanation carries necessity in its wake: it shows how it is that the explanation must obtain in the prevailing circumstances.

But do we really get actual explanations at those lower levels of explanatory potency? An affirmative answer is indicated by such situations as the following. Suppose that you ask me for the name of the man we met in the street last Sunday. I tell you that at the time I knew it but now I have forgotten it. And that's the fact of it. How is that fact to be explained? The very best and most that can be drawn along these lines is simply this: "People sometimes forget names, at least temporarily, especially when they reach my age. And that's what has happened here." What more of an explanation could there possibly be? What more could one reasonably ask for? What we have here is an explanation alright, albeit a paradigmatically problematic one.

Overall, such systemic explanation is coordinative rather than subsumptive. Such explanation is a matter of establishing that the fact being explained affords a natural way for rounding off the larger context of pre-established facts in the interest of providing an understandable and informative whole.

Take, for example, the explanation of a bank run or of the market collapse of a particular stock. We have no "covering laws" to account for such an occurrence. But various well-known phenomena are relevant to those sorts of developments, for example:

• information diffusion (rumor)
• personal panicking
• social contagion

So what we have here is a coordinative explanation, where various tendencies and processes come into a systemic, web-like interplay to provide a unified account. Circumstances and processes join to create a predictive web or complex (Gestalt), where the unfolding of a certain result is "only natural and to be expected." We have a categorical explanation not as a result of law subsumption but rather as one of process-coordination.

REGRESSION ISSUES

It is often said that the presence of unexplained premises in an explanatory account prevents that account from being completely adequate and cogent. But the matter is not all that clear. For consider the following situation:

Smith has to travel from point X to point Y and has two equally satisfactory routes for doing so, routes A and B. To settle the matter he tosses a coin: heads for A and tails for B. The coin comes up A, and Smith proceeds accordingly.

Can we now explain why Smith traveled from X to Y via route A? Of course! For consider the following explanatory account, already spelled out in the situation above:

(1) Two equally plausible routes were available to Smith, routes A and B.
(2) Smith decided to resolve the matter by a coin toss.
(3) In coming up heads, the coin toss settled the issue in favor of alternative A.
(4) Smith accordingly conducted his journey by this route in line with his plan.

Clearly, premises (1)–(3) afford a complete and adequate explanation of why Smith traveled from X to Y via route A. But nevertheless, premise (3) is an "unexplained explainer." For assuming that the coin-toss outcome is a matter of pure randomness and chance, (3) represents a fact for which there is no decisive explanation. But nevertheless, this circumstance does not preclude its role in providing a complete and cogent explanation.

The only thing that matters in the context of explaining Smith's travel is the fact *that* the coin toss favored alternative A; *why* it did so is irrelevant to the explanatory issue at hand. In providing explanations, we need not go beyond the requirements of the case. The given explanation is perfectly *sufficient unto the specific explanatory problem at hand*. And this situation prevails pervasively.

To be sure, there is no reason to think that when we have completed a particular explanation, we have reached rock bottom in regard to the overall project of explanatory understanding. In practice we can carry matters only so far, and even in theory we need only do so. No doubt those explanatory facts will themselves admit of explanation. But that does not need to be practiced to settle the explanatory question at hand. Smith refers to Jones's dog by using the word "dog." Why does he do so? Because he is an English speaker, and in English dogs are called dogs. But we do not need to explain those latter facts as well: their mere authenticity suffices for our explanatory needs.

LIMITS TO SUBSUMPTIVE EXPLANATION

Explanations are coordinated to our knowledge of the prevailing circumstances. A die is thrown. It comes up 6. Can we explain this? It is all a matter of time. Let it be true that the die settles at 6 at the time *t*. Then the information about what was going on at $t - \epsilon$ (for a trivially small ϵ) would certainly explain why 6 resulted. Of course, if our information were limited to what was available 3 seconds earlier (let alone 3 days earlier), this would in no way suffice for explanation.

Subsumptive explanation has its problems. For it deals with the facts to be explained on the basis of underlying lawful generalities. Thus, for example, the fact that yon tree is shedding its leaves is explained by noting that (1) it is an elm tree, (2) elm trees are deciduous—that is, they annually shed their leaves in the autumn, and (3) it is now autumn in this region.

It is clear that such an explanatory proceeding can encounter two sorts of limits: *anarchy* and *ultimacy* with respect to explanatory generalization.

With *anarchy* there simply are no such laws. Some examples of anarchy-inherent problems include:

- Why [assuming this to be so] is there
  — no American novel of exactly 24,048 words?
  — no ö sound in the American English pronunciation?
  — no mammal indigenous to Antarctica?
- Why [assuming this to be so] is it that
  — the average age of American dentists is 36.5 years?
  — I have forgotten the name of my first Latin teacher?
  — there is an even (rather than odd) number of elephants alive in Africa?

Here the facts at issue encounter problems with regard to their embedding in a framework of general principles. In each case we can provide a minimalistic explanation for how it is that the result in question can come to be—that is, an explanation for its possibility. But explaining the actual details of the matter is something else again.

Subsumptive expandability also becomes problematic with regard to such "ultimate" facts as:

- Why is the speed of light what it is?
- Why is there conservation of energy?

Ultimate unexplainability presents difficult issues. Facts of this sort are subsumptively "ultimate" because, within the factual domain at issue, there simply is no other, more fundamental fact that would be invoked for its explanation. With such facts we reach "the end of the line" in the regressive process of subsumptive generalization. No more fundamental explanatory generalization is to be had.

Inexplainability results when the role of chance and fortuitous haphazard is very large. Thus, consider the challenge of explaining why a hurricane flattened exactly 338 homes in a certain coastal city.

REASON'S SELF-RELIANCE IS NOT VICIOUS BUT VIRTUOUS

The only satisfactory explanation for anything—even for the existence of intelligence and its requirements—will have to be an intelligent explanation. In taking intelligence to provide its own ultimate explanatory basis, we proceed in a way that is cyclical and indeed even "circular." But this simply reflects the structural coherence of rational systematization. And there is nothing viciously self-defeating about such self-reliance. For while vicious circularity stultifies by "begging the question," virtuous circularity merely coordinates related elements in their mutual interlinkage. The former presupposes what is to be proved, the latter simply shows how things are connected together in a well-coordinated and mutually supportive interrelationship.

And this is crucial in the present range of deliberations. It is clear that to be able to adequately resolve our ultimate questions, the principle at work cannot rest on further extraneous considerations. For the question of why the truth of things is what it actually is will arise with respect to the principle itself, and if it is to resolve such matters, it must do so with respect to itself as well. It must, in short, be self-sustaining and self-grounding. Otherwise the requisite ultimacy will not be achieved.

The only validation of rational intelligence that can reasonably be asked for—and the only one worth having—must lie in considerations of the systemic self-sufficiency of reason. The self-endorsement of an intelligence-based explanation is not problematic but altogether appropriate.

After all, even to ask the question "Why should it be that reality is intelligible?" is to manifest one's commitment to the principle at issue, since asking a question is to expect an answer—and a sensible one at that.

There is simply no satisfactory alternative to using intelligence in its own explanation. For when a self-validating principle of explanation is needed, then intelligence and reason appear on the scene as ready volunteers, providing a natural pivot for the presently envisioned optimalism.

Accustomed as we are to living and thinking within the sphere of actuality, the conceptual change of perspectival context in the move to mere possibility is bound to seem extraordinary. It is bound to seem strange by ordinary standards, because those ordinary standards simply do not and cannot apply at this level of deliberation. We here face a question whose inherent nature is far removed from the usual range of questions needing explanation. Only an answer that lies entirely outside the box of accustomed thinking can be adequate.

CONCLUSION

In assessing the tenability-credentials of the PSR, we have to come to terms with the circumstance that there are salient distinct ranges of possible variation: the domain of factuality, the modes of explanation, and the stringency of the result. This situation is briefly summarized in Display 7.1.

Are all facts actually explainable? It is clear that the extent to which the PSR obtains will expand accordingly as

- the domain at issue is diminished
- the modes of explanation are increased
- the stringency of acceptable explanation is diminished

And clearly, if we are increasingly undemanding with respect to what we ask of an explanatory project, the prospect of its potential success will increase substantially.

Display 7.1

ISSUES OF EXPLANATION

I. DOMAIN OF EXPLANATORY FACTUALITY

- *Facts regarding nature*

    — occurrences
    — processes
    — laws
    — principles

- *Facts regarding abstract concepts*

    — logic
    — mathematics
    — information/language/semantics

II. MODES OF (Ontological) EXPLANATION

- *Subsumptive* (under lawful generalities)
- *Coordinative* (within informational contexts)

III. DEGREES OF EXPLANATORY STRINGENCY

This will vary over the following range, according as $R(F)$ renders F:

    — inevitable
    — highly likely (probable)
    — expectable
    — possible

In particular, if we limit the range of explanatory issues to the domain of natural occurrences, if we are prepared to accept both subsumptive and coordinative explanations, and if we are content to have our explanation of events function at the level of the lawfully possible, there can be little question as to pan-explicability within this restricted procedural sphere. But in the end, the issue becomes one of the scope and scale of the demands we are prepared to make upon the explanatory project. When we pose the question "Does the principle of sufficient reason hold good?" the answer is: "It all depends."

Finally, there is the question of the standing of the principle itself. The PSR certainly is not a conceptual truism: "facts are explainable" is not like "dogs are canines," and explicability is certainly not inherent in the conception of factuality as such. Nor is the PSR an inductive generalization from the circumstance that we are able to explain the facts we have heretofore investigated. Induction, after all, is based on the material of available experience, and the reach and range of the PSR is too vast for it to be based on so small a foundation. To be realistic, one has to look on the principle as an idealization. For the PSR is not merely a cognitive principle regarding the epistemology of understanding: it is rooted in a deeply metaphysical commitment regarding the "rationality of the real." In endorsing it, one is taking on board a substantial manifold of metaphysical presuppositions and commitments.

Chapter 8

INTELLIGENT DESIGN
REVISITED IN THE LIGHT OF
EVOLUTIONARY NEOPLATONISM

LEVELS OF BEING: THE THREE PRIME HYPOSTASES

Neoplatonism, with its emphasis on the ultimate rationality of the real, has a distinguished past, and it may well also have a promising future. But this is likely to remain at a considerable remove because its doctrines are distant from the sympathies and orthodoxies of the present age. It is not easy to make plausible to contemporaries even what it is that the Neoplatonists wanted. The present discussion will try to offer a perspective on Neoplatonist metaphysics that makes its key doctrines less strange and more plausible to the contemporary mind.

Neoplatonism implements the idea that there are basically three levels of being: reals, observables, and thinkables.

The *reals* are things that are physically encountered in space and time in the course of our ordinary experience—the physical objects of our environing world. Like trees, rocks, and cats, they occupy sectors of space-time.

The *observables* are the discernable features, properties, modes of comportment, and processes that pertain to the reals. They do not occupy space-time as much as exhibit themselves within it. Unlike concrete reals, which stolidly continue in place and cannot be repeated, the self-same observable properties and processes can recur on different occasions.

The *thinkables* are abstractions that do not, as such, admit of spatio-temporal manifestations at all. They are instruments of thought-artifice and have the status of what philosophers have called "creatures of reason" (*entia rationis*). The three-ness of that trio of books on the table is observable, but threeness as such is not. The greenness of that blade of grass is observable, but greenness as such is not. We can experientially encounter exemplifying instances of an abstraction but not the abstraction itself—even as we can meet up with an inscription of the letter *A* but not that letter itself. The inscription has a location in space-time, the letter as such does not.

From this perspective we arrive at the conception, going back to Plotinus, of a tripartite order of hypostases—of levels or modes of being—namely, the realms of

- *Experiential Reality* as-a-whole: the domain of the reals—the all-comprehensive universe (*to ôn*) of existence-at-large. It encompasses all actual being and constitutes the realm in which we live and within which all of our experience transpires.
- *Intelligible Order*: the order of thought or soul (*psychê*), encompassing the intelligible structure of things, the taxonomic manifold partitioning reality into orderly natural kinds in line with the lawful modus operandi of the items at issue. It encompasses what is understandable, describable, and explicable, amenable to the grasp of intelligence. It is the realm of orderly structure and operation where mind exercises its explanatory grasp.
- *Rational Normativity*: the order of reason (*nous*) concerned with the realm of value and the intellectual appreciation of merit (*to agathos*). It is the sphere of teleology and final causality—of the intellectual apprehension of positivity in appreciating the constructive role of things.[1]

In sum, what we have here are three modes of intellectual encounter with reality: experiential apprehension, lawful comprehension, and rational appreciation.

From a variant yet related perspective, these three orders deal, respectively, with *what is, what is possible,* and *what is meritorious.* And as a rough approximation, one might consider these as correlative with three levels of

sophistication in our understanding of the world: the levels of ordinary experience, natural science ("physics"), and metaphysics, respectively. And in
the end we have an *epistrophê*, a transit that ultimately returns to its starting
point from the vantage point of a higher level of rational intelligibility,
enabling us to see the rational structure of existence from a teleological
perspective with all of its ramifications—thus enabling us to see how it is
that the cosmos is arranged for the best in maximizing the harmonious
coordination of the whole.

EVOLUTIONARY NEOPLATONISM

From the aspect of reason (*nous*), the Neoplatonists put forward a scheme
of assessment determined by relation to time, that is, by the concepts
of temporality, omnitemporality, and extra-temporality. This trichotomy
underwrites a value-scheme geared ultimately toward ensuring security
against the ravages of time.

It is constructive to look at the situation in the light of cosmic evolution as presented by modern science, with the sequential development of
different modes of process, each subject to its own ways of operation. First,
after the big bang came various sorts of quantum phenomena, then functional stabilities led to chemical processes, then organisms merged and biology came upon the scene, then increasingly elaborate societies emerged,
and with them a complex phenomenology of social, political, and economic comportment that provided scope for a new range of social sciences
for which the earlier stages of the cosmos had no place. Cosmic evolution
thus unfolded a vast range of increasing complexity and sophistication in
the nature of reality, culminating in the emergence of intelligent beings
able to some extent to comprehend the cosmic drama in which they themselves play their part.

The approach we shall take here is based on the idea of an orderly
and directionally definite cosmic evolution—a developed course of reality through successive changes of lawful complexity and sophistication,
evolving along the following lines:

- Protoexistence (raw being)
- Structure and Order: the realm of mathematics

- Nature and Physics: the order of material being
- Life: the order of organic being
- Intelligence: the order of intelligent being
- Artifice: the creators of intelligent life; technology

In the Neoplatonic perspective, this situation can be seen as an ongoing exfoliation of differentiated complexity, moving through successive stages of elaboration:

- The proto-existential starting point of undifferentiated potential is "The One" (*to hen*).
- The process of ongoing exfoliation of increasingly complex and elaborately differentiated orders of being can be characterized as "progression" (*prohodos*).
- The energizing force (*dynamis*) that drives this process of increasing complexity can be called "*nous*" (Intellect or Reason) in its nisus toward intelligible order and its realization by intelligent beings.
- A key object of reason (*nous*) is to bring evaluative intelligence to an appreciation of "the Good" of the intelligence-appreciated value in existence.

As the Neoplatonists saw it, we inhabit a universe that is designed rationally in a manner congenial to the everlasting aspirations of reason. Analogously, we ourselves envision a universe designed for the emergent development of intelligent beings in the cosmos who are able to use their intelligence to realize the benefit of inhabiting an intelligible universe. On this basis, the fact remains that, despite our diminished dedication to teleology, the metaphysical stance of Neoplatonism should not—or need not—be viewed as totally far-fetched and outlandish.

INTELLIGENT DESIGN REVISITED

The widely controverted issue of the world's intelligent design—a prime Neoplatonic conception—has in recent decades evoked a good deal more heat than light.[2] And this is due in no small part to a failure to heed some critical distinctions.

In speaking of intelligent design, a crucial conceptual distinction must be borne in mind, namely, that between the *operational* conception of being designed intelligently and the *originative* conception of coming to be through the productive activity of an intelligent being. The former relates adjectivally to the way in which something functions—its mode of operating—and the latter relates adjectivally to the source of its origination. The former involves the hypothetical issue of how an intelligent agent *would* perform, the latter a historical issue of how an intelligent agent did perform creatively. But entirely different matters are at issue here. Thus, when one says that something functions intelligently, this can be construed in parallel with saying that it functions reliably, erratically, or clumsily. One is here describing the manner of its operation and not ascribing its origination to an agent or agency that is reliable, erratic, or clumsy.

The issue of intelligent design involves three very different questions, namely, whether the world is designed:

- *with* intelligence, that is, in an intelligent manner
- *for* intelligence, that is, in a manner favorable to the existence and operation of intelligent beings
- *by* intelligence, that is, by the productive operation of an intelligent agent or potency

These different issues will have to be addressed in very different terms of reference. Let us consider them in turn.

BEING INTELLIGENTLY DESIGNED:
THE META-SCIENTIFIC ASPECT

As one acute commentator tellingly puts it, "The alpha and omega of Neo-platonism is the assumption of the wholly transcendent One understood as the [coordinative] highest principle of all things."[3] And the Neoplatonic enterprise of structure, order, taxonomy, and intelligent organization has its developmental aspect as well. In its depiction of existence there is ongoing differentiation, for over time there is an ongoing differentiation and an increasing complexity of types and kinds. To be sure, at the level of explanatory understanding there is also increasing order, unification, and synthesis—Mind's power of explanatory synthesis is everywhere at work. In a world that is increasingly complex at the descriptive level, according to the Neoplatonists, there is an ever more extensive and profound orchestrating of rational connectivity by a comprehensive and comprehensible principle, the Neoplatonic One.

Is the world intelligently designed? Is it constructed as an intelligent designer would have it?

Well, what would an intelligently designed world have to be like? It would, for sure, have to be a manifold of phenomena operating under the aegis of a coherent body of laws. And clear signs of this are given by the rational order of nature as a manifold governed by principles of lawful order: conservation, continuity, economy, explicability, symmetry, harmony, efficacy, and the like. As the reader of D'Arcy Wentworth Thompsons's classic work *On Growth and Form* soon comes to realize, nature is by all available indications an effective problem solver. It works out its resolution of issues in a simple, efficient, and economical way. As the myriad examples provided by Thompson indicate, when asked to place four *X*s in a tic-tac-toe square, biological nature would consider only two solutions (see diagram). These solutions alone are the most symmetric—and the most easily graspable in both visual and conceptual terms.

Once we resolve the theoretical question of what it is for a system to be intelligently designed (simple but pervasive laws, ontological economy, efficient processes, harmoniously symmetric structures, and what have you), the issue of whether the physical universe constitutes an intelligently designed system becomes a straightforwardly scientific question. In the final analysis, this is going to have to be a question of the sort of world-picture that scientific inquiry manages to put into our hands. Are the ways of the world intelligible or explained by rational principles? Can they be rationally systematized on what one would nowadays call efficient computational principles?

Clearly, a failure to achieve intelligent design occurs in such cases as

- *Inconsistency*: failure to treat like cases alike. If the solution to a problem is optimally efficient and effective, it should clearly be used in every instance of the problem.
- *Inefficiency*: the realization of results that could equally well be achieved by less demanding means.
- *Needless complexity*: functioning in ways whose operations can be realized by fewer and simpler principles.
- *Fecklessness*: systemic failures to reapply successful procedures and to abandon unsuccessful ones.

In this respect, a good case can be made for holding that nature avoids processes that function unintelligently. However, maintaining this view is not just an exercise in speculative metaphysics: in principle, it can and should be investigated by large-scale exercises in computer simulation of cosmic evolution under the aegis of natural laws. Attesting to it are all of those numerous factors of aesthetic elegance, rational economy, and complex harmonization that we encounter in the study of the world's modus operandi. And clear signs of it are given by the rational order of nature as a manifold governed by principles of lawful order: conservation, continuity, economy, explicability, symmetry, harmony, efficacy, and the like.

And here one could proceed by postulating cosmic systems with laws of operation on whose basis rational operations would efficiently lead to circumstances favorable to the emergence and thriving of intelligent beings. This would call for producing:

- A cosmos, not a chaos. It functions under the aegis of a harmonious, coherent, and intelligible system of laws.
- A self-supportive and self-sufficiently effective manifold of existence.

- An existential manifold functioning as a system that permits and facilitates the emergence of intelligent beings.
- A system that is user-friendly for its intelligences, in the sense of operating on principles simple and straightforward enough to be cognitively available to them to a substantial degree.
- A system in which those emergent intelligences are afforded the prospect of realizing conditions of life as physical and also as cogent to them as the previous conditions allow.

The sort of computational modeling required here is evidentially difficult but surely not beyond the reach of realizability. There is, after all, reason to think that nature has already carried out the exercise.

In this context, some key features of intelligent design would be:

- Economy of means in the use of resources
- Regularity of process in the development of structure (as with linear or experimental growth)
- Symmetry of structure in the products of production
- Connectivity of process in the mode of operation of things

All of these are features that render nature's ways more readily accessible to intelligent beings. And all of them are patently aspects of the workings of nature that in principle can be achieved in natural ways.

In particular, it must be emphasized that evolution by natural selection is a totally natural process accounting for the state of things on the basis of nature's laws. There is no appeal here to the purposes of an intelligent agent, and being intelligently designed is merely descriptive of the way in which something functions. In saying that the world is designed *with* intelligence, nothing is necessarily claimed about its being designed *by* intelligence. The whole idea of purposive production by an intelligent agent is absent from the evolutionary picture. It is much like saying "Water seeks its own level" or "Magnets attract iron filings." It describes how these things act and interact productively. And it does not anthropomorphize the matter by holding that this is something that water consciously *tries* to do or that those iron filings somehow *feel* an attraction.

In summary, holding that the universe is designed intelligently does not require claiming that an intelligence *did* contrive it, but only that its nature is harmoniously structured *as though* an intelligence contrived it. And it should be clear that this aspect of intelligent design pivots on natural science, although it emerges not so much *in* natural science but rather *from* natural science. For it pivots on the question whether the lawful modus operandi of nature, as science depicts it, provides for an elegant, effective, and efficient systematization of natural phenomena. Does the scientific picture of nature's rules and regulations provide the means for harmonious accounts that explain and predict nature's phenomena? Can the rational enterprise of understanding the mind via science achieve this objective in a successful and effective way? Scientific inquiry into the nature of "nature" can and should be our guide here.

DESIGN BY INTELLIGENCE: THE THEOLOGICAL ASPECT

Even with an intelligently designed world, the question remains whether it is designed *by* intelligence—that is, through the operation of intelligent agency or potency. The issues at stake here are quite different ones. They are matters of theology. They reach beyond the world itself into the realm of the transcendental, or, put differently, beyond the nature of nature into a supra-natural sphere. Nature here is seen as the artifact of a supernatural potency, something that resides not just above and beyond nature but rather in a totally transcendental region.

What is required at this point is a reply to the questions: Is the circumstance that the universe, as it stands, makes possible and promotes the emergence and development of intelligent beings due to the productive operations of an intelligent being or power? Is the cosmos rationally intelligible due to its origination through the productive operation of a rational intelligence of some sort?

The deliberations needed to resolve this question are neither merely scientific nor even merely metaphysical. The transcendental issues they raise go beyond the limits of scientific naturalism and even metaphysical supra-naturalism into the region of theology. Neither the factual inquiry of science nor yet the coordinative speculation of metaphysics can carry us this far. An admixture of transcendental faith is required to reach this destination—a conjectural dedication to the analogy of artifice. And on this basis, it can be argued that value ("the good") becomes a key factor for understanding and explaining the nature of things.

Critical here are two points: the first is purely negative and lies in the consideration that there is nothing in the realms of factual inquiry or metaphysical conjecture to block or impede such a transcendental leap of faith. Inquiring reason, in its widest sense, yields nothing that prevents this leap and affords no insuperable obstacle. But of course, such an argument for an intelligence-friendly theism is not a demonstration but merely a plausible consideration. The conclusion to which it leads us is not really *required* but rather merely *invited*—an invitation that thinkers of a strongly scientistic and/or naturalistic inclination are likely to refuse, but that many of us nevertheless accept.

Granted, further difficulties and various objections face us. One type of objection runs as follows: Is evolution by variation and survivalistic selection not an enormously wasteful mode of operation? And is it not cumbersome and much too slow? Does this sort of moving not rule intelligence out of it?

Not really. For where the objector complains of *wastage*, a more generous spirit might see a Leibnizian principle of fertility at work, which gives a wide variety of life forms their chance for a moment in the limelight. (Perhaps the objector wouldn't think much of being a dinosaur, but then, numerous small children wouldn't agree.) Anyway, perhaps it is better to be a microbe than to be a Wasn't that just Isn't—to invoke Dr. Seuss. Or again, one person's wastage is another's energizer—to invoke Leibniz.

But what of all that suffering that falls to the lot of organic existence? Perhaps it is just collateral damage in the cosmic struggle toward intelligent life. But this is not the place nor time for producing a theodicy and addressing the theological problem of the existence of evil. The salient point is simply that the wastage objection is not automatically telling and that various lines of reply are available to deflect its impact.

Now on to slowness. Surely the proper response to the lethargy objection is to ask: What's the rush? In relation to a virtually infinite vastness of time, any finite initial timespan is but an instant.

Of course, there must be time enough for evolutionary processes to work out. There must be *sufficiency*. But nothing patent is achieved by *minimality* unless there is some mysterious reason why economy of time should be prioritized over other desiderata, such as variety, fertility, or the like.

CONCLUSION: THE KEY LESSON

It has been the aim of these deliberations to inject some much-needed clarity into the discussion of intelligent design. In particular, we have insisted upon taking into account three relevant questions, as discussed above:

(1) Is our natural world intelligently designed—that is, designed *with* intelligence?
(2) Is our natural world designed *for* intelligence—that is, designed teleologically to be a congenial home for intelligent beings?
(3) Is our natural world designed *by* intelligence—brought about through the agency of an intelligent being or potency?

The present deliberations have maintained that these are very different and distinct questions—and, in fact, are questions belonging to altogether different areas of inquiry and deliberation. This emerges from the following considerations about the question of intelligent design:

(1) It is in essence a *meta-scientific* or, if you will, metaphysical question: Insofar as it can be answered, this will have to be done on the basis of what science teaches us about nature's lawful order and mode of operation. This is essentially a matter of determining what an intelligently designed world would be like, an issue that can be constructively addressed once science has done its work.[4]
(2) It is in essence a *philosophical* (metaphysical) question: Insofar as it can be answered, this will have to be done on the basis of a conjecturally projected, metaphysical view of the interpretation of the limits of teleology in nature.
(3) It is in essence a *theological* question, whose answer reaches out into the realm of the transcendentally supernatural in posing issues that are, in the final analysis, not matters of factual or theoretical inquiry but of religious faith.

These considerations, of course, are related. There is little point in raising the philosophical question unless the scientific question is answered conformably; and little point in raising the theoretical question unless the philosophical picture is duly favorable. But this is a one-way street that does not automatically run in the opposite direction. Being intelligently designed does not mean being congenially designed *for* intelligence, and it would certainly not necessarily imply being designed *by* intelligence.

Accordingly, there is good reason for disentangling and separating the scientific, philosophical, and theological aspects of the matter, thus recognizing that distinctive problems are involved, different questions are at issue, and different modes of deliberation are required to deal with each of them. And when this separation of powers is clearly effected and the questions at issue disentangled, we come up against what might be called the fundamental principle of epistemology: *Different questions call for different answers.* Specifically, in the present case:

(1) That our universe is designed *with* intelligence is a thesis that requires—and apparently receives—considerable evidential substantiation from scientific inquiry.

(2) That our universe is designed *for* intelligence is a not implausibly arguable thesis of metaphysical speculation.

(3) That our universe is designed *by* intelligence is a theological doctrine that transcends empirical and speculative inquiry alike and remains to be addressed through the mediation of people's religious faith and their convictions regarding matters of a transcendentally theological cast.

POSTSCRIPT

Intelligent design theory encounters other difficulties as well. The following four are of particular weight:

(1) If the world is indeed intelligently designed, why is its design not simpler and more readily intelligible? Why are the world's ways not simpler to understand?

(2) Why has the evolution of intelligent beings not been more direct? Why should there have been so much collateral damage and wastage along the evolutionary route?

(3) If the world is indeed "intelligence-friendly" and its arrangements made with a view to the interests of intelligent beings, why is the life of such beings such a vale of tears? Why so much suffering? Why are the world's ways not kinder and more congenial to the interests of intelligent beings?

(4) If the development of intelligent beings is the telos of cosmic evolution, why are there not more of us on innumerable planets? And why are those presently here not a great deal more intelligent?

These issues certainly need to be addressed, but this will demand further deliberations, to which we now turn.

Chapter 9

WHAT IF THINGS
WERE DIFFERENT?

BELIEF-CONTRAVENING HYPOTHESES

Our knowledge of reality encompasses not only what is but also what might have been. After all, things might have been very different. Caesar might not have crossed the Rubicon. Napoleon might never have left Elba. Surely we can reason sensibly from such contrary-to-fact assumptions so as to obtain instructive knowledge about unrealized possibilities.

But is this really so? There are, in fact, good grounds for thinking that reasoning from fact-contravening suppositions is far more problematic than appears at first sight.

A "counterfactual conditional" along the lines of "If Napoleon had stayed on Elba, then the battle of Waterloo would not have been fought" is, in effect, *a conditional that elicits a consequence from an antecedent that represents a belief-contravening hypothesis.*[1] And the reality is that, in the context of other prevailing beliefs, *counterfactual hypotheses are always paradoxical.*[2]

Facts conjoin to constitute a *dense* structure, as the mathematicians use this term in relation (say) to real numbers. Every determinable fact is so drastically hemmed in by others that even when we erase it, it can always be restored on the basis of what remains. The fabric of fact is woven tight. Suppose that we make only a very small alteration in the descriptive composition of the real, say, by adding one pebble to the river bank. But which pebble? Where are we to get it, and what are we to put in its place? And where are we to put the air or the water that this new pebble displaces? And when we put that material in a new spot, just how are we to make room for it? And how are we to make room for the so-displaced material? Moreover, the region within six inches of the new pebble used to hold N pebbles. It now holds presumably $N + 1$. But whence that extra pebble? Of which region are we to say that it now holds $N - 1$ pebbles? And if it is that region yonder, then how did the pebble get here from there? By a miraculous instantaneous transport? By a little boy picking it up and throwing it? But then which little boy? And how did he get there? And if he threw it, then what happened to the air that his throw displaced, which would otherwise have gone undisturbed?

And what about the structure of the environing electromagnetic, thermal, and gravitational fields? Just how are these to be preserved as they were, given the removal and/or shift of the pebble? How is matter to be readjusted to preserve consistency here? Or are we to do so by changing the fundamental laws of physics? Hypothetical perturbations of reality confront us with problems without end. Every hypothetical change in the physical makeup of the real sets in motion a vast cascade of physical changes, either in the physical makeup of the real or in the laws of nature— or both. We cannot make hypothetical redistributions in the real world without thereby raising difficult questions. Counterfactual suppositions always create problems.

After all, when p is the case, then both $p \vee q$ and $p \vee \sim q$ are also the case. And so when we "revise" the register of accepted truths by putting $\sim p$ in place of p, we will at once obtain the contradictory result that both q and not-q. If consistency is to be preserved in the face of that hypothetical truth revision, we must (inter alia) immediately make one of the two theses $p \vee q$ and $p \vee \sim q$ yield way to the other or else abandon *both* of these theses. But once a suitable (albeit clearly extra-logical) mechanism of precedence and priority determination is at hand, then we will be able to determine coherently what sorts of "consequences" will follow from a fact-contravening hypothesis.

COUNTERFACTUALITY AND PLAUSIBILITY

Counterfactual suppositions are those that are at odds with the accepted facts. For present purposes, however, we shall also include as counterfactual those that merely go against our beliefs regarding the facts, or are belief-contravening. The present concern, then, is with conditional statements that address supposition-based questions of the form "If *P* were the case (which is it not), then what?" Its focus is the evaluation of conditionals on the model of:

If *A* were the case (which is it not), then *C*. (Here *A* stands for the antecedent and *C* for the consequent.)

In general, such conditionals do not present veridical claims, strictly speaking, but rather *conjectures*. And as such they do not fall into the evaluative-range of true/false, but rather into that of greater or lesser plausibility. Overall, one can classify the plausibility of counterfactuals into five categories:

— incontestable
— plausible
— problematic
— implausible
— absurd

But just how does this work?

Any counterfactual conditional of the form "If *A* were the case (which it is not), then *C*" is set in a cognitive context—here to be designated <*A*, *C*>—where certain background facts are taken to be known. Thus consider the conditional:

If Tom had let go of the ball, it would have dropped to the ground.

Here <*A*, *C*>, the body of relevant fact, contains the following:

(1) Tom sustained the rock.
(2) There was nothing else to sustain it.
(3) The rock did not drop to the ground.
(4) Heavy, unsustained objects always drop to the ground.

But now suppose

Not-(1): Tom ceased to sustain the rock.

There are three ways to restore consistency here so as to arrive at consistent revisions of <*A*, *C*>. They lead to the following conditionals:

- If Tom had let go of the rock, it would have dropped to the ground (because unsupported objects drop to the ground). [Here (3) is abandoned.]
- If Tom had let go of the rock, unsupported objects would not always drop to the ground (because the ball did not drop). [Here fact (4) is abandoned.]
- If Tom had let go of the rock, something else would have sustained it (because it did not drop). [Here (2) is abandoned.]

All of these counterfactuals are in theory available in the circumstances. The plausibility of the first lies in the fact that in such matters it is rationally preferable to abandon specific occurrences (the ball's not dropping) rather than to abandon general relationships (the dropping of unsupported objects) or wide-ranging conditions (the absence of a rock-sustainer).

On this basis, the plausibility status of the counterfactual conditionals hinges on the status of what is required for consistency-resolution. Maximum plausibility (i.e., unquestionable acceptability) obtains when virtually no readjustment at all is required. This would be the case with such counterfactuals as

If Gustave Eiffel had erected two of his towers (*A*), there would have been more than one of them (*C*).

On the other hand, consider

If Gustave Eiffel had erected two of his towers (*A*), then one of them would not be in Paris (*Q*).

Validating this counterfactual would call for a substantial body of rather elaborate revisions in our background information.

COUNTERFACTUAL CONDITIONALS

As the preceding considerations indicate, the critical fact about counterfactual deliberation is that even highly plausible counterfactuals will lead to inconsistent results.

Consider, for example, a version of the Lottery Paradox. Let it be that X is asked to choose an integer between 1 and 1,000,000 and that X chooses 972. And now consider the counterfactual:

If X had not chosen 972, he would not have chosen 973 either.

To all appearances this is highly plausible. But if we repeat the exercise for all of the other (equally highly plausible) possibilities, we end up in a contradiction. And as we reach into the background of accepted fact to establish the cognitive context for a counterfactual supposition, we find that this can always be accomplished in several equally plausible ways. The only thing we can securely infer is the disjunction of all these alternatives.

To exhibit this point yet more vividly, consider the following facts:

(1) Bizet was French.
(2) Verdi was Italian.
(3) Compatriots are people who share the same nationality.

And let us ask the counterfactual question

What if Bizet and Verdi had been compatriots?

We could now reason:

If Bizet and Verdi had been compatriots, then Bizet would have been Italian (since Verdi was Italian). [In point of retention/rejection we have (2), (3) / (1).]

But by parity of reasoning we also have:

If Bizet and Verdi had been compatriots, then Verdi would have been French (since Bizet was French). [In point of retention/rejection, we have (1), (3) / (2).]

These counterfactuals mutually cancel one another. The only safe course is to adopt:

If Bizet and Verdi had been compatriots, then either Bizet would have been Italian or Verdi would have been French (since Bizet was French and Verdi was Italian). [In point of retention/rejection, we have (1)-or-(2), (3) / (1)-and-(2).]

As this example shows, conflicting counterfactuals only become unproblematic at the level of disjunctive possibility.

In the end, only three sorts of counterfactuals are absolutely secure:

(1) Counterfactuals inherent in logico-conceptual facts—"If Hitler had had a son, then Hitler would have been a father." Here the consequent follows logically from the antecedent.

(2) Disjunctively exhaustive counterfactuals as per the Bizet-Verdi example above.

(3) Possibilistic counterfactuals regarding what *might* rather then what *would* be—"If Bizet and Verdi had been compatriots, then Bizet might have been Italian." Here the consequent stakes a merely possibilistic claim.

In such cases the conditionals are categorically assured and qualify as unproblematic truths. But elsewhere, more convoluted considerations come into play, and counterfactuals have to be classed as conjectural: they are not true/false but are to some degree speculative.

To be sure, speculative counterfactuals are not created equal. Some are plausible and qualify as rationally acceptable, while others lack the necessary credentials. To secure clearer insight into the conditions at work here, consider the counterfactual "If this rubber band were made of copper, it would conduct electricity." The situation is as follows:

(1) This stick is made of wood.
(2) This stick is not made of copper.
(3) Wood does not conduct electricity.
(4) Copper does conduct electricity.
(5) This stick does not conduct electricity.

And now let us introduce the (1)-modifying assumption:

(6) This stick is made of copper.

How is consistency to be restored?

Note that our initial givens fall into two groups: general laws (3), (4), and particular facts (1), (2), (5). Now when (6) is introduced as an issue-definitive hypothesis, we of course have to abandon (1) and (2) in the wake of this assumption. But that still does not restore consistency since (6) and (4) yield not-(5). There is, however, a way out. It is provided by the standard epistemic policy of *prioritizing more general principles such as laws over particular facts in counterfactual contexts*. In the situation before us this means that it is (5) rather than (4) that should now be abandoned. We thus arrive at the natural (5)-rejecting counterfactual conditional:

(A) If this stick were made of copper, then it would conduct electricity (since copper conducts electricity).

in place of the "unnatural," (4)-rejecting counterfactual conditional:

(B) If this stick were made of copper, then copper would not conduct electricity (since this stick does not conduct electricity).

Suppose, however, that for the sake of contrast we take the radical step of altering the fabric of natural law by contemplating the assumption:

(7) Wood conducts electricity.

We would now of course have to abandon (3) in the wake of this issue-definitive hypothesis. But again, this is not enough, given that (7) and

(1) will yield not-(5). At this point, however, we must resort to the principle: *In counterfactual contexts, particular mode-of-composition statements take priority over particular mode-of-behavior-statements.*[3] And this means that it is once more (5) that should be abandoned. We thus arrive at the "natural" counterfactual:

> If wood conducted electricity, then this stick would conduct electricity (since it is made of wood).

in place of the "unnatural" counterfactual:

> If wood conducted electricity, then this stick would not be made of wood (since it does not conduct electricity).

Since *alternative* outcomes are always possible in such cases, a logical analysis of the situation will not of itself be sufficient to eliminate the basic indeterminacy inherent in counterfactual situations. We once again require a principle of precedence and priority to indicate what has to give way in case of a conflict.

TENACITY

As used here, the *tenacity* of accepted contentions is a distinctive and characteristic conception. What it determines is survivability in the case of supposition conflicts. It is not a matter of evidentiation, of familiarity, or of generality. The only familiar conception that comes close to it is that of cognitive enmeshment, as in the question "If circumstances forced the abandonment of this contention, how radical and extensive would be the revisions you would have to make in the overall body of your beliefs?" For in prioritizing the role of tenacity in belief-revision we are, in effect, opting for the smallest *overall* revision in our belief-commitments, the aim being one of minimizing disruption and saving as much as possible. Tenacity, then, is a function of the extent of overall enmeshment of beliefs in the failure of our knowledge.

The determinative considerations for the comparative tenacity (inertia) and staying power of contentions in the face of belief-contravening suppositions is the extent of their enmeshment within the overall manifold of accepted fact. Their invariability depends on their epistemic entrenchment—their connectivity in the context of environing acceptances. In line with this principle, comparative tenacity is ruled by the hierarchy of factors set out in Display 9.1.

Display 9.1

HIERARCHY OF TENACITY

(A) logico-conceptual necessities
(B) laws of nature
(C) established generalities
(D) contingent facts of larger scope
(E) contingent facts of lesser scope
(F) chance occurrences
(G) suppositions and conjectures

Note: The earlier the alphabetic order of a claim, the greater its comparative tenacity.

On this basis, the staying power (epistemic tenacity) of a contention that is under threat of destabilization in the wake of a counterfactual assumption depends on the extent of its enmeshment in the manifold of relevant cognition. And this, in turn, pivots on the extent to which its abandonment would engender revision within that manifold—the extent to which its abandonment would constrain changes in the overall system of preestablished knowledge. In sum, epistemic triage in the nature of counterfactual suppositions is governed by the principle of least communal harm. We save those whose dismissal must create the greatest overall damage (destabilization) within the overall group of related commitments. The pivotal question becomes, What would the destabilization at issue affect within the range of alternatives listed in Display 9.1?

It is exactly this factor of tenacity that validates the distinction between counterfactuals that are rational and plausible and those that are counter-inductive. Thus, consider a cognitive situation in which the following body of facts is taken as given:

(1) John threw the switch.
(2) No one else even located the switch.
(3) The light went on.
(4) The switch controls the flow of electrical current.
(5) The flow of current operated the light.

Let us now make the supposition

Not-(1): John did not throw the switch.

With this now superadded to (1)–(5), we have an inconsistency on our hands. In the interests of consistency and coherence, something has to go.

Of course (1) is an obvious candidate here. But even then, an inconsistency remains, and one of the remaining theses will also have to be abandoned.

In effect, we now have the following four possible counterfactual conditionals before us. If John has not thrown the switch, then

(2)-rejection: Someone else must have done so.
(3)-rejection: The light would not have gone on.
(4)-rejection: The switch does not control the flow of current.
(5)-rejection: The flow of current does not operate the light.

Some of our commitments can be saved; others must be abandoned. Triage becomes unavoidable. Four different ways of breaking the chain of inconsistency are available. So what is the proper way of proceeding?

But now consider the status of those claims:

(2) is a matter of the overall course of events, and so (D) per Display 9.1.
(3) is a matter of specific occurrence, and so (E) per Display 9.1.
(4) is a matter of generality of occurrence, and so (C) per Display 9.1.
(5) is a matter of lawful processuality, and so (B) per Display 9.1.

In breaking the chain of inconsistency at its weakest link in point of tenacity with belief (3), we in effect validate the conditional:

If John had not thrown the switch, the light would not have gone on.

This counterfactual is thus the appropriate claim in the circumstances rather than its various rivals.

And this is a general course of procedure. When restoring consistency in the wake of belief-contravening suppositions, we seek to break the chain of inconsistency at its weakest link—by abandoning just those contentions whose tenacity is weakest. Accordingly, suppositional triage based on tenacity-governed weakest-link considerations affords the key to counter-factual reasoning. For "counterfactuals" call for determining the epistemically optimal consequences of belief-contravening suppositions. And just this accounts for the fact that, in general, the appropriate appraisal category of counterfactuals is not true/false but rather plausible/implausible. For in the end, those counterfactual conditions are not inferences based on local considerations alone but require recourse to their epistemically conceptualized generalities of cognitive tenacity, by which counterfactuals are validated along a sliding scale of plausibility. (This is why counterfactuals must in general be graded by comparative plausibility rather than classed as true/false.)

To deal effectively with counterfactual conditionals, we have to be in a position to distinguish, within the group of logically eligible alternatives, between more and less "natural" ways of reconciling a belief-contravening hypothesis with the entire set of residual beliefs that continue to be collectively inconsistent with it. Thus, observe that the choice between (A) and (B) above offers us an option between abandoning a law of nature (as in "Copper conducts electricity") and readjusting the features of a particular object, that rubber band. Following the policy of minimizing the scope of environmental changes in the wake of hypotheses, we will obviously opt for the second alternative.

And in general, such a mechanism is provided by general epistemic principles of the sort considered above. (Nonexistent possibilities—let alone possible worlds—are irrelevant here.)

FURTHER ILLUSTRATIONS

Making sense of counterfactuals is a matter of establishing precedence and priority among the relevant beliefs that are at work in the setting of particular questions. And what is needed is a localized micro-process and not a globalized macro-process. For when we make belief-contravening suppositions in ordinary workday situations, we are not shifting the frame of reference to the world at large—let alone having recourse to other possible worlds—but are merely testing the comparative tenacity and staying power of our actual claims within their contextual neighborhood. As with an Agatha Christie detective story, a closer scrutiny of the proximate suspects immediately involved in the context at issue is happily always sufficient to resolve the mystery. Let us illustrate this general circumstance by a concrete example.

The distinction between "natural" and "unnatural" counterfactuals is crucial. Consider the following example, due to David Lewis. By hypothesis we know the following:

(1) J. F. Kennedy was assassinated.
(2) L. H. Oswald assassinated Kennedy.
(3) No one other than Oswald assassinated Kennedy.

Imagine now that we are instructed to suppose not-(2), Kennedy was not killed by Oswald. Then we clearly cannot retain both (1) and (3), since in the presence of not-(2), (3) entails that no one assassinated Kennedy, which contradicts (1). Either (1) or (3) must go—one must be subordinated to the other. And now the very way in which a counterfactual is formulated instructs us as to the appropriate resolutions:

(A) If Oswald did not assassinate Kennedy, then someone else did. [This subordinates (3) to (1).]
(B) If Oswald had not assassinated Kennedy, then Kennedy would not have been assassinated at all. [This subordinates (1) to (3).]

However, if we were to supplement our beliefs (1)–(3) with a conspiracy theory by way of adopting

(4) Kennedy was the assassination victim of a successful conspiracy.

then we would also arrive at

(C) If Oswald had not assassinated Kennedy, then someone else would have. [This subordinates (3) to (4).]

The very way in which these conditionals are formulated informs us about (and corresponds to) the sorts of subordination relationships that are at work among those "factual" items that we take ourselves to know within the information-context of the counterfactual at issue.

In the analysis of counterfactuals, there is simply no need to look beyond the cluster of propositions immediately relevant to the particular ones at issue. To carry out cogent hypothetical reasoning, one does not need to have recourse to anything as complex and problematic as alternative worlds: a very moderate sector of reality suffices for all our needs. All that is required is some way of settling issues of precedence and priority among the conflicting suppositions that are immediately involved.

THE UNMANAGEABILITY OF WORLDS

With definite counterfactuals, evaluating the plausibility of specific conditionals of the form

If P were so, then Q would be so.

will usually be possible because the presence of Q will generally limit the range of relevant considerations to within a manageable scope. However, definitely open-ended questions of the form

If P were so, then what?

are deeply problematic. For this sort of question looks to consequences as a whole and pushes us beyond the P/Q locality. And at any given level of plausibility (short of certainty), the range of consequences is going to contain inconsistencies. And so anything that would require the total range to be taken into consideration will become unmanageable. Thus, for example, consider a question of world improvement such as:

If P were so, would this be a good thing?

Exactly because its range is open-ended, this sort of question becomes unmanageable. For we now have to deal not with manageable scenarios but with an intractable open-endedness.

And the globalization of conjecture is rendered particularly problematic by the fact that plausibilities (like probabilities) cannot simply be conjoined. For both "If P then Q_1" and "If P then Q_2" can be individually plausible without "If P then Q_1-and-Q_2" being so. Plausibilities have to be dealt with collectively because distributively individualized plausibilities cannot be conjoined.

The decisive drawback and deficit of the possible-worlds approach to counterfactuals that is so popular among contemporary semanticists lie in its inherent intractability. This becomes apparent through such examples as "If four were greater than five, then arithmetic would be involved in a contradiction." We clearly cannot handle this by contemplating the situation in those possible worlds where four is greater than five, since obviously there are none. Nevertheless, no one would have any difficulty making sense of that counterfactual, and in fact the present aporetic analysis validates it straightforwardly.[4] But there is no (sensible) question here of a recourse to "nonexistent worlds": nothing as far-reaching, metaphysical, and demanding as an ontology of possible worlds is required.

As contemporary possible-world theorists generally see it, we can and should be prepared to contemplate altogether different worlds, worlds removed from and indeed incompatible with our own in their makeup and their modus operandi.[5] But what do such worlds involve?

For one thing, they must be *worlds*. As such, they will have to be manifolds of concrete reality. To qualify as such, the constituent individuals of a possible world must also be *concrete* as regards the definiteness of its makeup. Specifically, a *world* must be descriptively definite and complete—that is, any descriptively specifiable feature either must hold of the world or fail to hold of it; there is no other alternative, no prospect of being indecisive with regard to its makeup.[6] A world must be decisive about what to be like. In consequence, the law of excluded middle must apply: the world and its constituents must exhibit a definiteness of composition through which any particular sort of situation either definitely does or definitely does not obtain. The individuals in a possible world cannot be "around six feet tall"—they have to commit to a definite size.[7]

After all, a world is not just some sketchily described state of affairs. It will have to be a "saturated" or "maximal" state of affairs at large—a state that affairs-in-toto can assume, a synoptic totality that suffices to resolve, if not everything, then at least everything that is in theory resolvable.[8]

(Unlike the state of affairs described by "A pen is writing this sentence," a world cannot leave unresolved whether that pen is writing with black ink or blue.) If an authentic world is to be at issue (be it existent or not), this entity must "make up its mind," so to speak, about what features it does or does not have.[9] Any assertion that purports to be about it must thus be either definitively true or definitively false—however difficult (or even impossible) a determination one way or the other may prove to be for particular inquirers, epistemologically speaking. Authentic worlds do and must accordingly have a wholly definite character.[10]

And just here lies the problem. For we can never manage to *identify* such a totality. Consider a state of affairs indicated by a claim such as "The pen on the table is red." An item cannot just be red: it has to be a definite shade of red—generic redness will not do. Nor is it a state of affairs that "There are two or three people in the room"—an actual state of affairs has to make up its mind. Nor again is it a state of affairs that "The butler did not do it." The actual situation here is left too indefinite to provide for the sort of thing that a state of affairs requires. No matter how much we say about some "state of affairs," the totality of concrete fact will go beyond it. As regards those merely possible worlds, we simply have no way to get there from here.

The point is not that we could not obtain different universes if we altered the initial conditions of the world or even the laws of nature. Rather, the point is that the situation of "what would happen if" would become ultimately intractable with any universe sufficiently complex to be of interest in the present context.

And this consideration is probatively crucial. For to provide a cogent refutation of optimalism, its opponent has to make good on that putative improvability by presenting a cogent case for contending that some definitely identified possibility would be superior. But world design is too big a job for us. Actually identifying alternative worlds is impracticable for us as a matter of basic principle.

The shortcoming of the currently fashionable possible-worlds approach consists in its being predicated on distinctly problematic presumptions. Possible-world semanticists proceed as though possible worlds were somehow given, as available instrumentalities that we have at hand to work with. But where these worlds come from—how we can actually get there from here—is a question they simply ignore. They never tell us how we are to arrive at possible worlds given our de facto starting point in this one. They proceed as though one could obtain by mere fiat that which would have to be the work of honest toil.

A critic might reply: "But surely it's not all that difficult. A variant world could, for example, be just like this one except for Caesar's deciding not to cross the Rubicon on that fateful occasion." Very well. But now just exactly what does happen in such a world? Does Caesar change his mind a nanosecond later and proceed as before, with just a minor delay? Is he carried across by *force majeure* and then decides to carry on as he was doing? And if he doesn't cross, then exactly what does he do? And what will all those who interacted with him afterwards be doing instead? The resulting list of questions is endless. The idea of identifying a possible world in some descriptive way or other is simply infeasible.

What of an alternative possible world that is just like this one, except for springing into existence on January 1, 1900? Surely it is descriptively unproblematic, since what exists in it and what is to happen to these items is determinately fixed. But the matter is not so straightforward. For while the *things* and *events* of that "world" are now determined, its *laws* are not. Clearly they cannot be the same as those of our world, where chickens come from eggs and do not spring into existence ex nihilo. But just what are the laws operative in this johnny-come-lately world? The answer is far from determinate. Once we leave the secure footing of the actual, we are inevitably "all at sea" as regards the prevailing situation.

As W. V. Quine forcefully emphasized long ago,[11] nonexistent possible worlds become something of a philosophical enormity when taken sufficiently seriously to be seen as somehow existing in their own right. To be sure, there is nothing particularly problematic about the idea of *scenarios*, viewed merely as oversimplified conceptual thought-artifacts answering to thoroughly incomplete world descriptions.[12] But alternative possible worlds are something else again. Semantical theorists who talk about other possible worlds have the audacity to lay claims to entities of a sort of which they are unable to provide even a single identifiable example.[13]

MAKING THE ACTUAL WORLD DO

Fortunately, to validate counterfactuals as informatively productive and appropriate assertions we need not go so far as to undertake conjectural global forays into other-worldly domains. It suffices to take note of the relevant local ground rules for prioritizing claims and judging their tenacity. Counterfactual reasoning is a cognitively crucial device that does not stand in need of a metaphysics of nonexistent possible worlds.

The management of counterfactuals is in many ways complex and problematic. But within the limits where established criteria of claim tenacity are available, they are a viable and meaningful resource. Thus we know perfectly well that, for example, "If Hitlerite Germany had developed an atomic bomb by 1943, the war would have taken a very different course." But what renders this conditional acceptable is simply an understanding of conditions in *this* world, and not a hypothetical transit into some alternative reality. Possible worlds are not only intractable in themselves but, with regard to counterfactual reasoning, unnecessary as well.

Chapter 10

ON THE IMPROVABILITY
OF THE WORLD

THE IMPROVABILITY THESIS AND
THE ISSUE OF "NATURAL EVIL"

Can this world of ours conceivably qualify as the best possible world? Until quite recently, no philosopher since Leibniz's day grappled seriously with the question of whether it is feasible to regard the actual order of nature as the optimal resolution of the problem of world-realization under *plausible* constraints—constraints, that is, that could reasonably be seen as appropriate requirements for realizing a coherent universe.[1] After all, the Leibnizian claim that this is the best possible world may seem to be absurd because so much appears to be amiss with the world. Yet the idea that the world is indeed improvable is not without its problems.

Since classical antiquity, theorists of an atheistic inclination have deployed the argument that if this world indeed were the product of the productive agency of an intelligent creator, then it would be far better than it is. As they see it, the world's imperfection in encompassing such "natural evils" as cataclysmic disasters, epidemic diseases, accidental injuries, and the like, mark it as improvable and thereby counts against the prospect of an intelligent creator. (The world's *moral* imperfection, rooted in the wicked misdeeds of its intelligent agents—that is, the "problem of moral evil"—poses separate and distinct issues.)[2] The imperfection of the natural world—its potential for improvement—is adduced as a decisive obstacle to divine creation. After all, if even we mere humans can envision ways of improving the world, how can it possibly be the product of divine creation? And so the problem of how an omnipotent and benevolent God can create an imperfect world looks to be a faith-defying paradox.

The idea that the actual world as we have it is the best possible goes back to Plato's *Timaeus*. Here we are told that the cosmos is "the best thing that has come into being" because

> The divine being [*theos*] wished that everything should be good and nothing imperfect *as far as possible* [*kata dunamin*] . . . since he judged that order [*taxis*] was better than disorder. For him who is the supremely good, it neither was nor is permissible to do anything other than what is the best [among the possibilities].[3]

Plato envisioned a world that, imperfections notwithstanding, is nevertheless "for the best" in being just as perfect as the conditions of a physically realized world will permit. And Leibniz agreed with this position.

Alfonso X, king of Castile (1221–84), known as "the learned" (*el-Sabio*) and as "the Astronomer" (*el Astrólogo*), who wrote prolifically on astronomical matters, deserves the eternal gratitude of scholars for his efforts to ensure the transmission of Greco-Arabic scholarship to Latinate Europe. But he is nowadays known mainly for his audacious declaration—issued in the wake of the Ptolemaic system of astronomy with its profusion of cycles and epicycles—that "If the Lord Almighty had consulted me before embarking on his creation, I would have recommended something simpler." And many has been the theorist who, walking in Alfonzo's footsteps, has thought that improvements could be made upon the Creator's handiwork.

Voltaire insisted that a benign Creator would certainly have averted the Lisbon earthquake of 1755, which killed many of his most dedicated devotees, among others. And, predicating his reasoning on the doctrine of evolution, Bertrand Russell wrote: "If I were granted omnipotence, and millions of years to experiment in, I should not think Man much to boast of as the final result of my efforts."[4] And in another place he writes, "If God really thinks well of the human . . . . why not proceed as in *Genesis* to create man at once?"[5]

Voltaire was certainly not alone in thinking it absurd of Leibniz to deem this vale of tears to be the best of possible worlds. And in just this vein, David Hume insisted that, if the world were indeed the product of a benevolent and omnipotent Creator, its arrangements would be far better than they are:

> A being, therefore, who knows the secret principles of the universe, might easily, by particular volitions, turn these accidents to the good of mankind, and render the whole world happy, . . . Some small touches, given to Caligula's brain in his infancy, might have converted him into a Trajan. One wave, a little higher than the rest, by burying Caesar and his fortune in the bottom of the ocean, might have restored liberty to a considerable part of mankind.[6]

And Hume went on to offer some helpful suggestions:

> The author of nature is inconceivably powerful: His force is supposed great, if not altogether inexhaustible. Nor is there any reason, as far as we can judge, to make him observe this strict frugality in his dealings with his creatures. It would have been better, were his power extremely limited, to have created fewer animals, and to have endowed these with more faculties for their happiness and preservation.[7]

And more recently, in his discussion of the problem of evil, Alvin Plantinga has suggested that God could have improved upon this world by arranging for Hitler to die in his sleep prior to inaugurating the Holocaust genocide of European Jewry.[8] The idea that a divinely created world would have to be a good deal better than this one has long intrigued philosophers. Again and again, optimalism has faced the charge of emulating a Dr. Pangloss, who will acknowledge no evil in the world—much like that familiar trio of monkeys who "see no evil, hear no evil, speak no evil." One theorist after another has maintained that, given the chance, he or she could readily improve on the natural world's arrangements by this, that, or the other modification.

And from there it is only one short and easy step to the conclusion that a benevolent creative deity does not exist.[9] Thus Bertrand Russell bolsters his anti-theistic argument with the acid comment that "an omnipotent Being who created a world containing evil not due to sin must Himself be at least partially evil."[10] After all, it seems only plausible to suppose that if there indeed is a deity acting as the intelligent contriver of the universe, he/she/it would have prevented all sorts of misfortunes and disasters.[11]

The present deliberations will try to cast doubt upon this idea of the world's improvability. They endeavor to rebut the seemingly plausible "improvability thesis," namely, that a better world might be obtained by fixing some of the many things that are wrong with the world as it stands. However, the key point here is that while it is easy to conceive of a world that is better than ours in this or that respect, a difference in any respect (even one that is small) would engender an unending cascade of differences in other respects (some potentially enormous). And so there is in prospect— and optimalists would argue, in reality—an overall destabilization of the world order that would yield a greatly inferior result. We can have no warranted confidence that any "inspired" reality would not issue in something far worse. To think we can improve on God's world is inappropriate hubris.

One important preliminary must be noted. Both the "improvementists" and their optimalist opponents must be in agreement on one fundamental point, namely, that there is a cogent and objective standard for world assessment. Claiming that the world is improvable and claiming that it is optimal both require a standard for merit assessment. Now for present purposes we will take this standard to be *the best condition for the real interests of the world's intelligent beings*. However, best conditions can here be construed in two decidedly different ways. The one is the *actualities* relating to their welfare and well-being. The other is the *possibilities* at their disposal—with the open prospect that they may well mess them up. On the surface, this second alternative doubtless appears more plausible.

It is, to be sure, theoretically possible to contemplate a different standard of world-merit, one that looks, for example, to the proliferation of different varieties of organic life. But this is not the sort of thing that those who complain about the world's imperfection have in mind. They tend to be much more parochial and see our human condition as pivotal. The shift from humans to intelligent creatures at large is doubtless as far as they would be prepared to go, and for dialectical purposes this is the view adopted here.[12]

ON THE INFEASIBILITY OF LOCAL TINKERING: BURLEY'S PRINCIPLE AS A LOGICAL OBSTACLE

For starters, one key obstacle that stands in the way of the improvability thesis is the pervasive interconnectedness of things. Man is, as the ancients have it, by nature an intelligent animal, and this automatically carries with it the inherent limitation of the frailties of the flesh. If you want animals, you must provide them with organic food. And a food chain brings with it a nature rough in tooth and claw. All worldly arrangements have a downside that involves imperfection. Imperfections of various sorts accompany any class of items, so that a world cannot be devoid of imperfections—if imperfection indeed is, as it must be, an involvement with limitations of some sort. But consider a somewhat more drastic alternative. What if we lived in a Berkeleyan world whose "nature" is not material and whose intelligences are disembodied spirits? Such a world would of course dispense with physical evils and injuries (and with physical pleasures as well). All the same, affective anguish and psychic distress would certainly remain. Alienation of affection can cause greater anguish than physical injury. And who is to say that in a psychical world, spiritual injuries are not felt even more acutely, and that disembodiment would do finite beings a disfavor?

There just is no real prospect of local tinkering with the world without wider ramifications. In this world—and indeed in any possible world—states of affairs are interconnected, and local changes always have pervasive consequences. Any local "fix" always has involvements throughout, and in consequence, no tweaking or tinkering may be able to effect an improvement. This very important fact can be seen from two points of view—the logico-theoretical and the empirico-substantive. Let us begin with the former.

As Walter Burley already observed in the fourteenth century, any and every change of one truth can potentially destabilize any other.[13] Thus let T be the set of all truths, and now consider the situation of Display 10.1, which sets out the idea of Burley's Principle. The logic of the situation is such that the introduction of any falsehood whatever into the set of all truths destabilizes everything: any other truth must then be abandoned. The systematic integrity of fact means that the idea of changing one item while leaving all the rest alone is simply impracticable.

Display 10.1

THE GIST OF BURLEY'S PRINCIPLE

(1) Let p and q two be arbitrary truths, with $p \in T$ and $q \in T$.
     And let us now suppose p to be false.
(2) $(p \lor \sim q) \in T$ by (1)
(3) $\sim p$ by supposition
(4) $\sim q$ from (2), (3)

Note: T is the manifold of all truths.

The structure of fact is an intricately woven fabric. One cannot sever one part of it without unraveling other parts of the real. As discussed in chapter 9, facts engender a *dense* structure, as the mathematicians use this term. Every determinable fact is so drastically hemmed in by others that even when we erase it, it can always be restored on the basis of what remains. The logical fabric of fact is woven tight. Facts are so closely intermeshed with each other as to form a connected network.

As far as the logic of the situation goes, any change anywhere in the manifold of truth has reverberations everywhere.[14] Once we embark on a reality-modifying assumption, then as far as pure logic is concerned, all bets are off. At the level of abstract logic, the introduction of belief-contravening hypotheses puts everything at risk: nothing is quite safe any more. To maintain consistency, we must revamp the entire fabric of fact, which is to say that we confront a task of Sisyphian proportions. (This is something that those who make glib use of the idea of other possible worlds all too easily forget.) The world is too complex to be remade in our thought. Reality's reach has a grip that it will never entirely relax: the cutting of any thread in the fabric of fact leads to an unraveling of the whole.

Yet there are, of course, aspects of improvability that lie beyond the logic of the situation. And they too require attention.

THE BUTTERFLY EFFECT AS A SUBSTANTIVE OBSTACLE TO TINKERING

Consider the following objection: "How can one possibly claim the world to be all that meritorious and benignly contrived? Surely, envisioning a better world would not be all that hard. After all, it wouldn't have taken much to arrange some small accident that would have removed a Hitler or a Stalin from the scene. To figure out how this sort of thing could be arranged—to the world's vast improvement!—is not rocket science!"

Alas, even rocket science is not good enough. For what stands in the way here is the massive obstacle of what is known as the "butterfly effect." This phenomenon roots in the *sensitive dependence of outcomes on initial conditions* in chaos theory, where a tiny variation in the initial conditions of a dynamical system can issue in immense variations in the long-term behavior of the system. E. N. Lorenz first analyzed the effect in a pioneering 1963 paper, leading to the comment of one meteorologist that "if the theory were correct, one flap of a butterfly's wings would be enough to alter the course of the weather forever."[15] With this process, changing even one tiny aspect of nature—one single butterfly flutter—could have the most massive repercussions: tsunamis, droughts, ice ages, there is no limit. With this phenomenology in play, rewriting the course of the cosmos in the wake of even the smallest hypothetical change is an utter impracticability.[16]

A *chaotic condition*, as natural scientists nowadays use this term, obtains when we have a situation that is tenable or viable in certain circumstances but where a change in these circumstances—even one that is extremely minute—will unravel and destabilize the overall situation with imponderable consequences, producing results that cannot be foreseen in informative detail. Every hypothetical change in the physical makeup of such a world, however small, sets in motion a cascade of further changes either in regard to the world's furnishings or in the laws of nature. And for all that we can tell, reality is just like that, as the pebble example discussed in chapter 9 illustrates.

Limits of necessity can be rooted not only in the fundamental principles of logic (logical impossibility) but also in the laws of nature (physical impossibility). For every scientific law is in effect a specification of impossibility. If it indeed is a law that iron conducts electricity, then a piece of nonconducting iron thereby becomes unrealizable. Accordingly, limits of necessity are instantiated by such aspirations as squaring the circle or accelerating spaceships into hyperdrive at translight speed. Many things that we might like to do—to avoid ageing, to erase the errors of the past, to transmute lead into gold—are just not practicable. Nature's modus operandi precludes the realization of such aspirations. We finite creatures had best abandon them because the iron necessity of natural law stands in the way of their realization.

But is the butterfly effect not an artifact of the laws of nature—the rules by which nature plays the game in the production of phenomena? And would not an omnipotent God alter those rules so that the world's occurrences are no longer inextricably intertwined? These are tricky questions that require some conceptual unraveling. An omnipotent creator could ex hypothesi create a chaos. But he could not create a cosmos that affords a friendly home for intelligent beings without thereby creating the sort of coordinated fabric of intelligible lawfulness that carries a butterfly effect in its wake. For how else could those intelligent agents make their way in the world? An existential manifold could possibly dispense with the lawful coordination that underpins the butterfly effect, but an intelligence-supportive ("noophelic") nature could not possibly do so.

We then have to reckon with the prospect that the lawful order inherent in the butterfly effect could not be abandoned without massive collateral damage to the intelligible order of things.

MONKEY'S PAW ISSUES

But could not the amount of human suffering that there is in the world be reduced in some different order of things? Certainly it could. But the next questions are, At what cost? At the price of there being no world at all? At the price of there being no humans in the world? At the price of having all humans be ignorant, dull, and unintelligent? At the price of having only humans without empathy, sympathy, or care for one another? The proper response to all of these questions is simply: Who knows? No one can say with any assurance that the cost of such an "improvement" would be acceptable.

The idea of collateral damage has important ramifications here. It is, unfortunately, entirely possible for the removal of even a Hitler or Stalin from the world stage to be achievable only at the price of visiting upon mankind an even greater disaster. To render this idea graphic, one should consider W. W. Jacobs's chilling story "The Monkey's Paw," whose protagonist is miraculously granted wishes that actually come true—but always at a fearsome price.[17]

The salient point here is straightforward. Granted, the world's *particular* existing negativities are in theory remediable. But to arrange for remedying them might well require accepting an even larger array of negativities overall (the monkey's paw dilemma). The cost of avoiding those manifest evils of this world would then be the realization of an even larger volume of misfortune.

What the monkey's paw dilemma means is that we can no longer be glibly facile about our ability to tinker with reality to effect improvements in the world by somehow removing this or that among its patent imperfections through well-intentioned readjustments. For what would need to be shown is that such a repair would not yield unintended and indeed altogether unforeseen consequences, resulting in an overall inferior result. The prospect of collateral damage would have to be sidelined. And this would be no easy task—and indeed could prove to be one far beyond our feeble powers.

To "fix" some negative aspect of the world would involve a change of how things happen within it, namely, altering the laws of nature under whose aegis things happen as they do. And the effects of this will prove imponderable. For as one recent writer has cogently argued:

> If water is to have the various properties in virtue of which it plays its beneficial part in the economy of the physical world and the life of mankind, it cannot at the same time lack its obnoxious capacity to drown us. The specific gravity of water is as much a necessary outcome of its ultimate constitution as its freezing point, or its thirst-quenching and cleansing functions. There cannot be assigned to any substance an arbitrarily selected group of qualities, from which all that ever may prove unfortunate to any sentient organism can be eliminated especially if . . . the world . . . is to be a calculable cosmos.[18]

What is crucial in this regard is the operation of natural laws. Our universe is an orderly cosmos instead of an anarchic jumble. And only this kind of cosmos can provide a home for beings whose actions are grounded by thought. Only through some degree of understanding of the orderly modus operandi of a world can an intelligent being whose actions are guided by beliefs operate. And in a realm in which what happens proceeds in accord with natural laws, a finite embodied being is inevitably at risk of mishap. Bruce Reichenbach has it right: "Natural evils are a consequence of natural objects acting according to natural laws upon sentient, natural creatures."[19] And those natural laws make the world a package deal.

But someone will now object as follows: "This reliance on the butterfly effect is problematic. For this effect is the result of the fact that, in certain respects, the laws of nature have yielded a system of the sort that mathematicians characterize as chaotic. Surely one could change the laws of nature to avoid this result." It is no doubt so. But now we have leapt from the frying pan into the fire. For in taking this line, we propose to fiddle not merely with this or that specific occurrence in world history, but with the very laws of nature themselves. And this embarks us on the uncharted waters of a monumental second-order butterfly effect—one whose implications and ramifications are incalculable for finite intelligences. The point is simple: Yes, the world's particular existing negativities are indeed remediable in theory. But to avert them in practice might well require accepting an even larger array of negativities overall. The cost of avoiding those manifest evils of this world would then be the realization of an even larger mass of misfortune. And the very possibility of this prospect shows that the improvability argument does not suffice to accomplish its aim.

THE PACKAGE-DEAL PREDICAMENT: THE TEETER-TOTTER EFFECT

Someone might object: "But surely if one effected this-or-that modification in the world *without changing anything else*, one would improve matters thereby." The difficulty here lies in that pivotal phrase "without changing anything else." In anything worthy of the name "world," the constituent components are interrelated and interconnected. We cannot change one without changing innumerable others. The situation is not unlike that of language. Change the letter "u" in "gust" to an "i," and everything changes—shape, meaning, pronunciation.

Granted, most of us would have little difficulty in imagining a few of our fellow humans without whom the world would be better off—or so we think. But the problem is that in a lawful world, getting rid of them would have to be achieved in a way that effects broader changes—more virulent diseases, more enterprising murderers, stronger impetus to suicide—all of which have wider and potentially deleterious consequences. A world is an infinitely complex arrangement of interrelated features and factors. And it is bound to have these coordinated in a complex interrelated harmony. Modify this and you disturb that.

After all, changes to the existing order of things do not come cost-free. Could *Homo sapiens* be improved by yet another pair of eyes, located at the back of the head? Presumably not. The redesign of this biosystem could not be effected without incurring additional vulnerabilities. And the mechanisms for processing the additional information provided would involve added complications that would doubtless not be cost-effective in added benefit. Nature has doubtless seen to it that we are as well adjusted to our bio-niche as the world's fabric of natural law permits. And there is no reason to refrain from seeing this sort of situation replicated on a cosmic scale.

The upshot of these considerations is thus clear. The idea that the world's defects can be fixed by tinkering is decidedly implausible. And given the fact that re-engineering the world-as-a-whole lies beyond our feeble powers, we have to face up to the consideration that—for all we can tell—this is indeed the best of possible worlds, and that changing the existing condition of the universe in any way whatsoever will diminish the sum-total of its positivities. We have to face the prospect that there is no "quick fix" for the negativities of this world.

The world we actually have—and indeed any possible alternative to it—is a coordinated whole. Once we start to tinker with it, it disappears on us. For in seeking to change it, we create conditions where there is no longer any anaphoric "it" to deal with. To tinker with a world is to annihilate it.

PROBLEMS OF CONJURING WITH POSSIBLE WORLDS

At this point it is needful to address the objection advanced by various "world-improvement counterfactualists" who propose that "if only this or that had been arranged for instead of the situation as is, the world would be a far better place." This inviting line of thought confronts inseparable difficulties.

To recognize them, one must look again at the nature of counterfactual reasoning. The only practicable way to address the large-scale question

If P were so (which it is not), then what?

is via a manifold of particularized, small-scale conditionals of the form

If P were so (which it is not), then Q would in consequence be so.

Note that when this schema is concretized via due particularization, we will obtain multiple conditionals along the lines of the following illustration.

If Napoleon had won the battle of Waterloo, then
(1)   Wellington would have lost this battle.
(2)   Napoleon would not have been shipped off to St. Helena.
(3)   France would have regained Canada.
(4)   French would have replaced English in Britain.

It is evident that these counterfactuals must be classed as, respectively, (1) trivial, (2) plausible, (3) implausible, and (4) absurd.

Now it would be eminently convenient if our initial question

If P were so, then what?

could be answered by having the consequent incorporate the totality of Q-consequents of the form

If P were so, then Q

that qualify as trivially true or plausible.

This, however, is simply not practicable. Some of them are bound to conflict with others, as noted in the preceding chapter. And the infeasibility of counting plausible counterfactuals can also be seen from another point of view, namely, that of a sorites-style reasoning such as the following:

— If Pickett's charge had succeeded, Lee would have won at Gettysburg.
— If Lee had won at Gettysburg, Sherman would not have been able to take Atlanta in the summer of 1864.
— If Atlanta had not fallen before the 1864 election, Lincoln would have lost to McClellan.
— If McClellan had won the U.S. presidency in 1864, the Civil War would have ended in a negotiated peace settlement.
— If the Civil War had ended in a negotiated peace, the Confederate States of America would have become an independent nation.
— If the Confederate States of America had become an independent nation, the United States of America would not have undertaken a war with Spain in 1898.
— If there had been no Spanish-American War, there would have been no Theodore Roosevelt presidency.
— If there had been no Theodore Roosevelt presidency, there would have been no Wilson presidency.
— If there had been no Wilson presidency, there would have been no League of Nations.
— If there had been no League of Nations, there would have been no United Nations.

The lesson is clear. Specifically, targeted counterfactuals of the form

If P were so (which it is not), then Q would be so.

are rationally tractable. One can appropriately access their tenability status and view them as definitely or at least plausibly acceptable.

But open-ended questions of the form

If *p* were so (which it is not), then what would ensue overall?

are simply imponderable. Particular considerations preclude such open-ended aggregations. There is no rationally viable way to provide a cogent answer to this sort of open-ended global question.

And this situation has important consequences in the present context of deliberation. For it means that those counterfactual questions that transcend local particularities and can be assessed only on a global, synoptically holistic, basis must be dismissed as rationally intractable.

This has significant implications for improvability questions. Granted, hypotheticals of the form

> If this or that change in world history had occurred, would the condition of the Russian peasant have improved?

may well be tractable. But nevertheless, globally holistic questions of the type "Would this have been better for world history as a whole?" will remain imponderable and intractable.

"But surely it is possible for there to be a world without earthquakes!" Indeed it is. But the move from a descriptive possibility (no earthquakes) to an authentic *world* requires a lot of fleshing out. (For example, if no earth, then no earthquakes.) The problem here lies in the move from possible *states* (no earthquakes) to possible *worlds*. To meet the dialectical needs of the situation, it will not do to invoke the mere possibility of a superior world. The objector will have to make good his challenge by specifying one in detail. And herein lies the insuperable difficulty.

At this juncture, an important point comes into play with respect to actual versus possible. With actuals there is a crucial difference between generic and specific knowledge—between knowing *that* something has a feature and knowing *which* item has that feature. Here, $K(\exists x \in S)Fx$—that is, knowing that some x in S has the property F—is possible without knowing of some specific x that it has F: $(\exists x \in S)KFx$. But with mere possibilities, the preceding distinction does not apply. The only way of knowing *that* some mere (nonexistent) possibility has a certain feature is by specifying the possibility that possesses this feature. Real objects have an identity apart from their specification. But mere possibilities do not. And this renders the task of specifying a superior world unachievable for us.

"But surely *some* alternative world would be superior to ours—though I concede an inability to provide an illustrative example." This sounds plausible enough. Surely some military officer is in the Pentagon right now—though I don't have a clue as to who that individual might be. But this sort of response will not work, being based on a seriously flawed analogy. For we know a great deal about the Pentagon and its general modus operandi. But there is nothing comparable going on with respect to merely possible worlds—no general principles of functioning that would lead to a comparable result.

Granted, it is in a broad sense *conceivable* that optimalism fails and that some alternative world might be superior to this one. But this does not bear on the dialectical situation at issue. For the argument at issue here is that of the atheist who insists that this world cannot be a divine creation on the grounds of its imperfection. "Even I," he says, "with my imperfect intellect can come up with ways of improving upon this world." And in *this* dialectical context, the mere possibility invoked above will not do the job.

WITH WORLDS, PERFECTION IS NOT A PROSPECT

A further salient consideration is that with worlds, perfection is not an intelligible prospect. Whenever the overall merit of a complex whole requires a harmonization among different and systematically *competitive* aspects of merit, it makes no sense to require *perfection* (i.e., maximization with respect to every aspect of merit). We will have to settle for *optimization*—the optimal harmonization of those different aspects, represented by their holistically best-achievable overall combination.

Now as the medieval schoolmen already emphasized, God's omnipotence consists in an ability to do anything that is possible; doing the impossible is not at issue. Neither can God make the self-same proposition *both* true and false, nor can he make 2 plus 2 come out to be 5, nor can he forget facts. Nor can God make a lesser number exceed a larger one, or turn virtue into vice, or make an inferior state of things a superior state. The truths of logic and mathematics and the conceptual truths about the nature of things are not alterable, and this holds for God as much as anyone. But—and this is crucial—the impossibility of God's doing the impossible is not an obstacle to his omnipotence. God can certainly create a good world and indeed an optimal one. But even He cannot make a manifold of finite being that is flawless and perfect.

Given the inherent tension between various modes of merit, a natural world cannot be both *perfect* and exhibit all possibilities to a maximal degree. As Plato already insisted, the imperfectability of the natural universe is an inevitable aspect of its physical materiality, its embodiment (*somatoeides*).[20] And Plato was followed in this view by the entire Neoplatonic tradition.[21]

All this harks back to the discussion of the ontological argument for the existence of God, with its familiar point that such a thing as "a perfect mountain" is simply not in the range of possibility. For world-imperfection is built into the very nature of things. Limitedness is unavoidable with finite beings. Humans cannot be superhuman—if they are to exist at all, they must exist as the type of things they inherently are. In an organically complex world, the interests of some species may have to be subordinated to those of others (e.g., as providers of food). Moreover, the interests of particular individuals may have to be subordinated to those of the entire species, just as a fire that destroys some trees may nourish the soil for the ampler development of others later on.

Perfection is unattainable with respect to created worlds. One salient reason for this is the phenomenon of what might be called *desideratum conflicts*, where in advancing with one positivity, we automatically diminish another. What we have here is vividly manifested in the phenomenon of *positivity complementarity* that obtains when two parameters of merit are so closely interconnected that more of the one automatically means less of the other.

One might characterize as a teeter-totter condition any arrangement where an improvement in regard to one aspect can be achieved only at the cost of worsening matters in another respect. And whenever two inherently positive factors (such as familiarity and novelty) are locked into such a teeter-totter relationship, we cannot have it both ways. Whenever this situation is in play, it stands decisively in the way of absolute perfection.

Consider a simple example, the case of a domestic garden. On the one hand, we may want the garden of a house to be extensive—to provide privacy, attractive vistas, scope for diverse planting, and so on. But on the other hand, we may also want the garden to be small—affordable to install, convenient to manage, affordable to maintain. But of course, we can't have it both ways: the garden cannot be *both* large *and* small. The desiderata at issue are locked into a teeter-totter type of conflict.

Again, any criminal justice system realizable in this imperfect world is going to have inappropriate negatives through letting some of the guilty go free, while also admitting false positives by condemning some innocents. And the more we rearrange things to diminish one flaw, the greater scope we give to the other. And so it goes in other situations without number. The two types of errors are locked together in a teeter-totter balance of complementarity that keeps perfection at bay. Throughout such situations, realizing more of one desideratum entails a correlative decrease in the other. We cannot have it both ways; the ideal of an *absolute perfection* that maximizes every parameter of merit at one and the same time is out of reach. Thus in the interest of viability, some sort of compromise must be negotiated, seeing that the concurrent maximization of desiderata is now unrealizable.

World optimization is always maximization under various existential constraints imposed by the taxonomic nature of the things whose realization is being contemplated. And such constraints mean that while the world may well be as good as it can be *as a whole*—that is, aggregatively merit-maximizing—nevertheless, it is not correspondingly merit-maximizing in its parts taken distributively. The condition of many of these parts is far from optimal and can certainly be improved. But the merit of the parts is so interconnected and intertwined that improvement in one area is bound to carry with it diminution in another.

The medieval schoolmen already had the correct take on the issue. They were inclined to look at perfection as a matter of completeness. For them, "perfect" and "whole" were virtually identical concepts.[22] However, they went on to insist that an optimal whole need not be perfect in each of its constituent aspects, and that increasing the perfection of some part or aspect will throw the whole out of balance. As St. Thomas put it, "God permitted imperfections in creation when they are necessary for the greater good of the whole."[23]

And so, imperfection does not preclude optimality. All that is required here is that—notwithstanding whatever imperfections there are and whatever positivities there might be—no other possible world arrangement ranks higher overall. An imperfect world is not thereby automatically improvable. For in reality, the project of improvement faces major obstacles.

As Leibniz insisted, optimality is one thing and perfection another. And our world can abandon any claims to the latter without compromising its claims to the former. For things to be "as good as they get" does not require perfection.

THE SPECTRE OF SPINOZISM

At this point it might seem that the specter of Spinozism looms ominously before us. For the point of contending that this is the *best* of possible worlds—that, for better or worse, this is as good as it gets—is clearly preempted by the Spinozistic idea that this is the *only* possible world. If so, then there are simply no alternatives to our world, and thus this world of ours is necessary. The question of its optimality thereby falls somewhere between trivial and immaterial.[24]

However, at this point it is essential to draw a distinction that was already stressed by Leibniz. For such necessity is certainly not tenable if we look to *logical* possibility and necessity. Alternative world-manifolds are always *logically* possible, given that logic confines itself to generalities—all of its theses and structure being abstract and universal in nature. Logic cannot mandate the existence of something unique and concrete. However, a specific existent world that contains concreta lies beyond the reach of logical necessity on anything like the standard conception of logic.[25] Particularity is always contingent, and any coherent manifold of particular truths is bound to have logically coherent alternatives.[26]

And thus, if necessity is to be realized in matters of existence, it will have to be not of the strictly logico-conceptual mode but rather of the *metaphysical* and, indeed as presently contemplated, *axiological* mode. However, necessity will then have lost its sting. For what we now have is, in effect, a Leibnizian theory of the *metaphysical* necessity of world optimization. For Spinoza, the world as it is is the one and only possibility. For Leibniz, it is the one and only *optimal* possibility. The difference turns on a single word. But this word is one that is obviously far-reaching in import.[27]

OPTIMALISM DOES NOT DEMAND OPTIMISM

The traditional approaches to *natural* or *physical* evils look to several alternative ways of addressing the problem, preeminently including the following:

- An *illusionism* that dismisses natural evil as merely apparent and not real. This is the approach of Oriental mysticism and of the Panglossian unrealism that Voltaire mistakenly attributed to Leibniz.
- A *facilitationism* that sees natural evil as part of the indispensable causal means to a greater good. (The melodrama must have its villain so that the persecuted heroine can fully appreciate the delights of a heroic rescue.)
- A *compensationism* that sees natural evil as compensated for in the larger scheme of things—either in this world or in the next. (This, according to Kant, is the key rationale for belief in an afterlife.)
- A *holism* that sees natural evil as the collateral damage that is unavoidable in even the best of possible arrangements contrived with a view to the realization of salient positivities. (This is in essence the Leibnizian view of the universe as a package deal that inextricably links the positive and the negative.)

The optimalistic approach of the present discussion best approximates the last of these options. It takes the line that physical evil represents the price of an entry ticket into the best arrangement possible within the limits of inevitable constraints. The world's physical evils are the inescapable consequences of the fact that intelligent beings of limited capacity are placed within a world-order whose lawfulness is sufficiently complex for their rational development but also sufficiently simple to afford them the cognitive access needed for the management of their affairs.

However, the idea that this is the best of possible worlds emphatically does not commit one to an overly rosy view of it. For what optimalism maintains is merely that this world, however imperfect, is such that any other possible world (and thus an actively fleshed-out *world* and not just some incomplete *scenario*) will involve a still greater balance of negativity over positivity. Accordingly, none of the traditional complaints about this world's evils and deficiencies refute the prospect of its being the best of possible worlds. For its being the very best of the possibilities need not and will not require being *perfect*. Even the best of possible worlds can admit all manner of imperfections: it is just a matter of there being fewer of them, on balance, than is the case with any of the other alternatives. Saying that this is the best of possible worlds is not necessarily to give it unqualified praise.

In short, as an argument against the Leibnizian view, the lucubrations of Voltaire's *Candide* are a nonstarter. There, Dr. Pangloss's skeptical pupil pressed him with the question: "Si c'est ici le meilleur des mondes possibles, que sont donc les autres?" (If this be the best of possible worlds, then what in heaven's name will the others be like?).[28] But a perfectly good answer was available to the good doctor, which, despite its cogency, he was reluctant to give, namely: "Even worse!" The facile optimism of Dr. Pangloss, the butt of Voltaire's parody *Candide*, misses the mark if Leibniz (and not some naive and simple-minded Leibnizian proponent) is intended as its target.

A seemingly telling objection to optimalism is the challenge of *fairness,* which effectively runs as follows: Even if one grants that the world as is represents the optimally achievable resolution to the problem of world creation, is it not deeply unfair that some of its members should, for no failing of their own making and responsibility, occupy a position inferior to that of others? The proper handling of this objection is not simple but requires recourse to some rather subtle distinctions. For fairness is a matter of proportioning outcomes to claims. And just as people come into the world without clothes, so they enter it without claims. It is incontestably *lamentable* that some of the denizens of even the best of possible worlds should fare badly. Their condition is unhappy and unfortunate. They deserve our sympathy in full measure. But victims of unfairness they are not. For unfairness only arises with preexisting claims. And in the context of realizing world-possibilities there simply are none. Those whose lot comes up short in possible worlds may be unfortunate, but they are not victims of unfairness. They have no preexisting claims upon reality—or upon God.

Yet is it not *unjust* that some should thrive and others suffer? Here it would seem that one can do no better than to revert to the previous consideration that perfect worlds—and in particular, worlds in which all individuals are treated with perfect justice—just are not on offer. There simply are no perfect *worlds* any more than there are perfect humans. And we cannot ask it of anyone—not even of God—that they should do better than the best that is possible.

CONCLUSION

The upshot of these neo-Leibnizian deliberations is that there is no convincing reason to think that the world can be improved by modification and tinkering. The complaint that the actual world could be improved upon by a replacement world confronts its proponents with the effectively unmeetable challenge that no such putatively superior replacement could ever be identified. And the idea that this world's manifest imperfection stands in the way of its optimality is quite erroneous, since even the best is bound to be imperfect here.

But is optimalism not by its very nature theological and thereby unscientific? Surely not! Water flows downwards; tumbleweeds follow the path of least resistance; entropy increases. All such processes exhibit a directionality in respect of some factor and yet act plan-conformably without any explicit planning. Axiotropism can be seen as just another such phenomenon— albeit one that functions at a more fundamental level. Nature dictates an optimal arrangement for stacking logs and for packaging cannonballs. The most efficient and effective means of reaching specified ends are often dictated by nature's laws. In principle this sort of situation could prevail at the global level as well, with those laws being themselves engendered under the aegis of an axiological mega-law.

In closing, the dialectical purport of the present discussion must be reemphasized. It has not been the object here to argue that this imperfect world of ours is actually the best possible. Instead—and far more modestly—the discussion has tried to show that the standard objections to this idea just do not work. If one is minded to take seriously the Leibnizian view that this is the best of possible worlds, there is no convincing obstacle of general principle to stand in the way.

Chapter 11

CONSCIOUSNESS

WHAT IS CONSCIOUSNESS? THE BASIC ISSUE

Even a denial that consciousness exists commits one to specifying what consciousness is, every bit as much as if it actually did exist. Thus before inquiring where consciousness is present and how it works, one has to begin by asking just exactly what consciousness is. And here it is helpful first to spell out a few things that consciousness is not, which includes such features as being:

— a substance (like air)
— a property of things (like their weight)
— a state of things (like liquidity)

Unlike most of the things that concern us, consciousness is not an object of experience but represents a mode of experiencing. But it is easier to say what consciousness is not than what it is.

The nature of consciousness is a classic metaphysical puzzle. We all know that it exists and yet do not really understand it. We can indicate what it enables us to achieve in the way of an apprehension of things; we know what it does; but we cannot quite manage to say what it is. In addressing the matter, we have "to beat around the bush."

Think of a door contrived to open automatically when a sensor detects an approaching person. We have here an effectively functional stimulus-response system. But there is no consciousness. The sensor detects but does not feel; the device responds appropriately but does not realize it. The system can be said to obtain information (a person's approach) and to initiate appropriate action in response (in arranging for the door's opening), but something crucial is absent. So just what is missing? Clearly it is the intervention of a functioning mind. Only mind-endowed beings can be conscious.

Consciousness is the capacity for awareness of situations. Stuck with a pin, your body will react by withdrawal, but your mind will react by feeling pain. This sort of realization is a gift of evolution. Like arithmetical computation or linguistic communication—or indeed intelligence itself—consciousness emerges at a certain stage of complexity and sophistication in the course of organic evolutionary development. It is present only relatively far up on the ladder of evolutionary development. In this regard, it is in the same boat as various other higher-level mental components, such as intelligence, reason, evaluative affectivity, and (very possibly) conscious choice and free will. Only a conscious being can actually know various facts, but then too, only a conscious being can ever be mistaken about something.

Among humans, factual knowledge (informative knowledge in contrast to performative how-to knowledge) is always verbalized. But consciousness can outrun verbalization and is thereby broader than factual cognition. The information that our consciousness places at our disposal is too extensive, complex, and convoluted for complete, explicit verbalization. Conceivably, any individual item that figures in our consciousness can be verbalized in some way, but neither time nor space is available to deal with the entire lot. (Think here of the game of musical chairs: any one participant is in principle seatable, but one can never seat the whole lot.)

Consciousness is a *disjunctive* conception. To be conscious is to be able to perform any one of a long inventory of consciousness-indicative things. A wide variety of performances are inherently conscious-indicative: one can do them only when (fully) conscious, for example,

— recognize a friend
— categorize something as an instance of a type
— understand a verbal communication
— answer a question
— describe a feeling

— "get" a joke
— solve a puzzle
— make a mistake[1]

A person can be said to function consciously in inconceivable ways: the list cannot be completed.

Consciousness in this regard is much like *employment.* People can be employed, but there is no such "thing" as employment. It is a human condition that can be endlessly diverse and variegated. Its innumerable forms have no common denominator: those who occupy this state or condition need have no identifiable commonality. And there can be no general theory of consciousness any more than there can be a general theory of employment (or of nourishment or of moving). The question "What is consciousness (at large)?" makes as much—or, rather, as little—sense as the question "What is amusement (at large)?" All these are presupposition-laden questions predicated on a flawed commitment to a nonexistent commonality.

Particular modes of conscious activity—doing arithmetic or translating text—may admit of a profitably informative study, but consciousness as such is a delusional mirage. There is as much to consciousness (as such) as there is to furniture as such. To think of consciousness as something with a certain particularity, let alone a fixed identity, is to fall victim to a delusion.

It is one thing to have consciousness—to be *capable* of its exercise—and quite another to be actively engaged therein. (Conscious beings can sleep!) And consciousness-involving performances are interconnected, not invariably but at least statistically: when one can do one of them, one also can do various others. To be a conscious being, one must be able to perform some of them. But the range of the consciousness-indicating operations at the disposal of a consciousness-capable being can be larger or smaller, varying both with individuals and with their species. Both dogs and humans can function consciously, but humans can tell jokes, while dogs cannot. Consciousness is clearly present whenever the mind does any of a considerable variety of things.

Self-consciousness is a particularly sophisticated version of consciousness, a reflexive version that encompasses self-awareness. This is a facility that has certainly evolved in humans but presumably not in lower animals. When you toss bread crumbs to sparrows, you surely come to realize that they are aware of environmental developments. However, as best we can tell, there is no self-consciousness among sparrows. (You would find it hard to embarrass or insult them.)

"I shall now count slowly to ten, and when I reach seven I shall wiggle the fingers of my left hand." Here, there is consciousness of myself as agent, as well as an awareness of certain performatory resources at my command (finger motion) and of my power of engendering conditions that would otherwise not be. These capabilities and capacities are not aspects of my physical makeup or physical nature—they relate not to how I am constituted but to what I can do.

CONSCIOUSNESS IS NOT A PROCESS OR PROCEDURE

A big question arises: Is consciousness a particular sort of common factor or feature (except consciousness itself) that is present throughout the whole range of its occurrences? Or is consciousness something like combustibility—a feature possessed alike by wood, kerosene, oxygen, rubber, and so on, which lack any other fact of unifying commonality? Is there some pervasive linking factor such that consciousness is the effect of its presence, or is consciousness itself the unifier of its occurrences?

By all available indications there is no single specific consciousness-producer: consciousness represents a uniformity of product rather than a uniformity of production. Just as a writing style (of some sort) is present throughout what a person writes, so consciousness (of some sort) is present throughout what a person thinks. The terms at issue are highly generic: there is no single sort of thing to be called "style," and there is no single sort of thing to be called "consciousness." The unity of consciousness is not collective but distributive—a unity not of resulting but of result. The prospect of providing a set of necessary and sufficient indications for the presence of consciousness—apart from the circularly redundant indications of consciousness itself—is a hopeless proposition.

What has to be going on for someone to be conscious of something? There just is no *particular* answer here—the appropriate response is simply: Any one of a considerable variety of things. There is no uniform route to consciousness: its presence is nowise a uniformity of productive process but merely a uniformity of result. Our initial question is like asking, What has to be the case for someone to be wealthy? Once we get beyond tautology—respectively, "He has to be aware of something," and "He has to have a lot of money"—there is nowhere else to go. There are just too many different ways to get there from here. The condition at issue—call it *X*—is such that there is no uniform *X*-making factor or feature. The quest for any single definitive "basis of consciousness" is quixotic and—to put it bluntly—pointless.

Being conscious of something is like being informed by someone. In either case, the end result is somewhat the same—being aware of some fact and/or situation. But information can come in endlessly diverse ways: verbal or written communication, observations, signals and inferential reasoning, memory and recollection, and so forth. And just as there is no such thing as a single process of informativeness, so there is no such thing as a single process of consciousness. Consciousness and awareness are a vast array of modes that has no common core in a single proceeding or process. We lump them together because of an analogy of result, in the same way in which we lump together games or means of communication. But to look for a processual unity of consciousness is as vain as to look for a processual unity of ways of doctoring or of cleaning. There is no unity of operation to being aware, any more than there is with remembering or forgetting.

With respect to its nature as a conception, *mental consciousness* is thus rather akin to *mental illness*. There are numerous and endlessly varied ways of being mentally ill, and they can have very little to do with one another—indeed, they all fail to fit any generally common features apart from qualifying as mental illnesses. And the same goes for consciousness. Tautologies aside—for instance, "having awareness"—there is no uniform mental process that qualifies as "being conscious."

Our conscious-awareness functions sequentially, now this, now that. The result is the conception of a "stream of consciousness." This expression, however, suggests a problematic continuity. What is actually at issue seems more like a set of discrete steps or links than a continuous stream.

There are many things a conscious-capable being can do only when actively conscious. To be sure, breathing and perspiring are not among them, but remembering and joking certainly are. Like feeling, being conscious of something also just happens—without preplanning or prearrangement. One can no more write an instruction book about feeling than one can about being aware of something.

The question "How do I know *that I am aware* that there is a cup on the table?" is a lot like the question "How do I know *that I feel* cold?" or "How do I know *that I don't believe* in the Tooth Fairy?" There simply is no "How I go about securing such knowledge," no process or procedure for verifying that these things are so. I "just realize" these things, and that is the end of it. There is no definite process or procedure I employ to acquire such knowledge and no specifiable procedure I follow for its realization. Awareness of things is not something I *acquire* by doing something, it is something that I *have* in the circumstances. It comes to me automatically as a free gift of my capacities as an intelligent being.

CONSCIOUSNESS REQUIRES CORRELATIVE BRAIN ACTIVITY BUT IS NOT PRODUCED BY IT

Conscious reactions can be *evoked* by physical stimuli, but they are not *constituted* by them. Physical developments may be prominent in their causation, but mental developments are paramount for their constitution.

Without the brain the mind cannot operate, but without the mind the brain is functionally helpless. In providing the brain/mind complex, nature has, through evolution, created a collaborative partnership. Consciousness is an evolved capacity of mind-endowed creatures to become aware of the aspects of their setting. Its most developed form is self-awareness—explicit awareness of oneself. A being with no self-conception can still in principle be conscious of things.

There is no question that consciousness of something is the (invariable) accompaniment of correlative brain activity. But this does not mean that consciousness reduces to brain activity from a causal and productive standpoint.

To coordinate consciousness with brain activity and to hold that beings cannot be conscious without suitable brain activity is not to say that consciousness is the causal result of brain processes. People are coordinated with their fingerprints: different prints belong to different people. But that does not mean that the fingerprints *cause* persons to be the individuals they are. The emotions of a person are coordinate with his facial expressions but not produced by them. ID numbers are coordinate with people, but neither produces the other. Coordination says nothing about the direction (or even existence) of causal efficacy.

Consider a group of ball-bearings spread out on a stretched rubber sheet. Here we have a clearly correlative system—move the ball bearings, and the shape of the sheet changes; alter the shape of the sheet, and the ball bearings will move accordingly. To all visible appearances, the mind and the brain are coordinated in this way. Processual inauguration is a two-way street: sometimes as the mind functions, the brain responds correspondingly; sometimes as the brain functions, the mind responds. There is always coordinative agreement, but sometimes the one potency is in control of change and sometimes the other. Brain activity often controls the mind's thought, but thought sometimes inaugurates brain responses. Either will sometimes produce the other.

Brain activity and thought proceedings are interrelated in a complex way that exhibits the following features:

(1) Every thought process has a corresponding counterpart in brain activity: there are no "spooky" (brain-independent) thought processes.
(2) Some brain activities have no corresponding counterparts at the level of thought at all—neither in conscious nor unconscious thought.
(3) Not every brain activity has a corresponding counterpart at the level of *conscious* thought. There is such a thing as an unconscious thinking.
(4) Some brain activities cause thought responses (thought activities) that would not exist without them. Here, brain activity is the causal inaugurator of thought.
(5) Some thought activities cause brain responses: here, thought is the causal inaugurator of brain activity.

In the operations of the brain/mind complex, the brain is the invariable participant in the overall processuality of what goes on. It is thus the senior partner of the enterprise. But it is not the invariable *inaugurator* of what goes on: the direction of initiative is left open. And this will work sometimes in the one direction and sometimes in the other. (The two factors are interlinked, but which is the free and which the dependent variable will be a matter of case-by-case determination.)

The relation of brain/mind in relation to activity is like the situation of plane/pilot in relation to location. The pilot's location is always coordinate with the plane: he does not go his separate way. But while their location change is generally managed by the plane itself (via its autopilot), it is occasionally managed by the pilot when he happens to take control. The initiative can work both ways. Analogously, it is sometimes mind rather than brain that is the change-initiating operator.

MISTAKES IN AWARENESS

There are certainly abnormal states of consciousness—in dreaming, say, or under the influence of drugs. One can also have the mistaken impression of being aware of things in the ordinary way. Further, unconsciousness is not the only alternative to consciousness; there are states of subconsciousness and mis-consciousness (i.e., faux consciousness) as well. But only for beings capable of authentic consciousness can consciousness possibly malfunction.

As a more or less typical experience, consider a pinprick and its associated withdrawal response. Unless we are numbed by anesthetic or have otherwise lapsed into an "abnormal" condition, we are certainly aware of such a bodily development. Presumably the response can be counterindicated by extraordinary intervention (such as posthypnotic suggestion), so that what ordinarily would be a normal response is evoked in abnormal circumstances. But even an abnormally produced sensation of a pinprick is still a perfectly real sensation, however extraordinary the mechanics by which it is evoked. And—be it authentic or inauthentic—it could certainly not be evoked in a being incapable of feeling, of mental experience, or of consciousness.

There is nothing automatically veridical about consciousness. Misimpressions can occur. We can take ourselves to be aware of a cat on the mat when it is actually a puppy. I can mistake one person as another. That tree we take ourselves to see may be a thing of smoke and mirrors. What we think of the things we are experiencing may fail to reflect their reality. But even being mistaken is a version of mental activity: even misunderstanding is a mode of understanding, and even thinking mistakenly is still thinking.

Ordinarily, cat sightings are produced by cats, pinpricks by pins, shivers by cold. And such responses standardly occur via consciously apprehensible events such as cat-encounters or pinpricks. It is perfectly possible, however, that certain putatively cognitive experiences could be produced in a manner that is unwarranted and systematically inappropriate—for example, in a phantom limb situation, someone feels as though he is receiving the handshake of a muscular friend. This sort of "sensory malfunction" is certainly conceivable in unusual circumstances. But that such malfunctions should prevail systematically—always, unavoidably, and with everyone—is effectively inconceivable, given the way in which human capacities evolve. Sense experience is our ground for action in this world, and if it were to mislead us regularly and systematically, we would not be here to tell the tale.

The question "Can awareness be mistaken?" calls for drawing a crucial distinction. In ascribing to someone an awareness of a particular state of affairs, we automatically concede correctness. In saying "Smith realizes that the cat is on the mat" or "Smith is aware of the cat's being on the mat," I commit myself to the fact that there actually is a cat on the mat. To put this factual commitment into suspension, I would have to say "Smith thinks (or believes) that the cat is on the mat" or "Smith is under the impression that the cat is on the mat." Such statements are commitment-neutral regarding the declarer's own position. And in this regard they differ from the negative extreme: "Smith mistakenly thinks there is a cat on the mat" or "Smith hallucinates a cat on the mat."

The same sort of thing holds in one's own case. The statement "I am aware of the tiger in the room" stakes the dual claim: "There indeed is a tiger in the room, and I realize that this is so." To be epistemically more cautious about it would require saying something like "I am aware that there is a large creature in the room, and I take it to be a tiger" or, even more indefinitely, "Something is going on in the room which I construe as the presence of a large tiger." However, we must thus distinguish between the fact of awareness and the awareness of fact. When I take myself to be aware of a cat on the mat, I cannot be mistaken about the fact of awareness itself—about my belief that there is a cat on the mat. It makes no sense to say "I believe there is a cat on the mat but might be wrong in thinking that I believe it." I might be wrong in thinking what I believe, but I cannot be wrong in thinking that I believe it. Of course, that belief itself may very well be wrong: I could well mistake a small dog for a cat and a towel for a mat. The fact that I claim to be aware of may be all wrong. But the fact of my having this awareness remains untouched by its error.

Language works in such a way that certain experiences are self-certifying. "I am conscious of its raining outside" might well be wrong—that pitter-patter could be a scrabbling squirrel. But "I am conscious of a strong odor" is something else again. Subjectivity stands on secure ground. When I am under the impression that there is a cat on the mat, I can be mistaken about the cat (and indeed the mat as well), but I cannot be mistaken about having the impression. I can mistakenly believe that you are absent, but it is somewhere between difficult and impossible for me to be mistaken about my belief in it. What I am under the impression of may well be amiss, but my being under this impression stands secure, wholly unaffected by the factual mistake.

Two related questions occur here: (1) Can one be *unaware* of a belief one actually has? and (2) Can one be *mistaken* about this? The answer to (1) is certainly affirmative. Think of the innumerable romances whose protagonist did not realize a deep love for a "friend" until it was too late. And the answer to (2) is similarly affirmative. For could I not, in my deep Freudian subconscious, "really" believe in ghosts, while at the level of conscious avowal I reject the very idea?

Insofar as these considerations hold good, one would need to distinguish between persons' *acknowledged* beliefs and their *authentic* beliefs, between those prima facie beliefs they view themselves as having and those they actually have. And then it will only be in respect to the latter, authentic beliefs, outside the realm of "false consciousness," that people cannot be mistaken.

WHY CONSCIOUSNESS SEEMS
PROBLEMATIC OR MYSTERIOUS

There is no public access to the substance of someone's subjectivity. Feelings and impressions are private property. The individual agent is the only person able to experience what is transpiring on the stage of his conscious awareness: anyone else knows this only through inference or by second-hand report. *Brain activity* can be monitored by observers, but the *experiential content of awareness* cannot. One cannot be conscious without being conscious *of* something, any more than one can be afloat without floating *on* something. Feeling pain—one's own pain, a pinprick, for example—is a quintessential mode of awareness. This is not just a matter of an aversion/evasion response: that response does not *constitute* my pain experience but rather *evidentiates* it for all to see.

The observational inaccessibility of a large section of cognition is an awkward reality for "cognitive science." The easy way out for its practitioners is a "fox and grapes" approach—taking the course of denying that it exists. Subjectivity is, however, a "fact of life." I cannot possibly appropriate your experience: experience as such is not interpersonally transferrable.

Consciousness is in many respects like gravity. One experiences gravity, all right, but one certainly doesn't *observe* it. What we observe are its effects, and what one can know of it has to be inferred therefrom. As far as we are concerned, gravity is what it does. And this, of course, does not automatically make us well informed regarding either its nature or its origins. Consciousness is much like this. It manifests itself through its effects: primarily, awareness and lived experience.

Many things are visible; many things are combustible. But they are not so through any across-the-board possession of some shared feature or fact constitutive of visibility or combustibility. There is no initial condition that constitutes this condition, no visibility-producing or combustibility-engendering constituent. The only commonality among all visible (or combustible) things is the fact of this visibility (or combustibility) itself. The only commonality is ex post facto and retrospective. The same is true for consciousness. The only thing common to all items that figure in our consciousness is that very fact of consciousness-involvement itself.

Consciousness is not some type of stuff (like metal) nor even a certain state of things (like magnetic attraction). Instead, it comprises a broad and diverse range of phenomena—phenomena gathered together under a common instance of communicative convenience.

And so, just as there is not and cannot be any uniformly focused science of mental illness, there cannot be any uniformly focused science of consciousness. Just as "abnormal psychology" has to be a disjointed assemblage of diverse specialties, so does "consciousness studies." Neither constitutes a unified science, because both lack a uniform subject-matter.

This or that mode of conscious activity can be studied, but "consciousness studies" has about as much substantial integrity as would "amusement studies." The manifold sorts of conscious activity are clearly open to fruitful scientific study in their distinctive particularity. But consciousness itself is not, given that what is at issue with this idea lacks the thematic focus requisite for such an integrated enterprise. And so, in its deliberations about consciousness, metaphysics has little choice but to "beat around the bush."

NEW HORIZONS

A new dimension of reality emerges in the world with the arrival of conscious and intelligent beings: the realm of thought. Heretofore, there is only the manifold of physical reality, but now the manifold of hypothetical possibility emerges. Heretofore, there are only the discernible features of the things at which one can point. But now there are also the merely suppositional creations of thought, which cannot be identified by pointing; now things come into play that do not exist as such and whose only mode of being is being thought about.

Prominent among these is *knowledge*—the capacity to formulate and process information. After all, knowing, like supposing, is something that only intelligent beings can possibly do. But on the other side of the coin is also its contrary: ignorance. And ignorance even includes the *inevitable ignorance of unknowable fact*. Cognitive access here stands in direct logical conflict with the item-characterizations at issue. For consider the following items:

— a person who has passed into total oblivion
— a question that is never formulated
— an idea that no one ever mentions

A knowledge claim regarding such items will automatically unravel their specifying characterizations.[2] The unknowability of the facts at issue is built into their very specification. Thus no one can answer the question: "What is an example of a question that will never be asked?" Such a challenge defeats the effort of this world's finite intelligences.

But when it is said that a fact about the world is unknown or unknowable, two questions immediately arise: Which world? and By whom?

The answer in both cases is straightforward: The world at issue is of course this world of ours—the one only available to us for factual knowledge rather than conjecture or supposition. And the question "By whom?" is of course to be answered: "By us—the intelligent beings who inhabit this world." World-external super- or supra-natural beings are not in question here. So when we speak of "facts being known" or of "questions being asked," we mean these to be construed with reference to this world's intelligent beings.

But since knowing and unknowing are something that only intelligent beings can manage, it follows that such facts can meaningfully function in the world only after intelligence gains a foothold there. Only then will there be facts about it that are not just *unknown* by those intelligences in the world but actually are even *unknowable* by them. For what intelligence cannot manage to do is to get a comprehensive grip on its own imperfections. Finite minds will always be inadequately informed about their own limits and limitations. And since thinking and thought-guided acting are integral to the functional makeup of the world, there will be aspects of reality regarding which the world's intelligences must always remain imperfectly informed. For, given the integration of thought into nature, an incompleteness of knowledge regarding the former unavoidably carries in its wake an incompleteness of knowledge regarding the latter. Ironically, with the emergence of intelligent consciousness the universe itself becomes (imperfectly) intelligible.

Just how does the emergence of intelligence change the world? The short answer is in a revolutionary way. For there is now a place for self-awareness in the scheme of things—self-awareness in matters of thought and in action through recognizing the limitations that will inevitably afflict the cognitive condition of finite beings. What intelligence cannot do is to get a comprehensive grip on itself, and specifically on its own limits. Significantly, the questions that defy the utmost efforts of intelligence are exactly those that relate to facts concerning the limits of its own operation. The very existence of intelligence in the world is a precondition of its cognitive opacity.

Chapter 12

CONTROL

WHY CONTROL MATTERS

The concept of control has an important role in many contexts. In engineering it is salient in the theory of control systems. In metaphysics it plays a key role in mind-body deliberations and the problem of free will. In ethics and law it figures critically in relation to culpability and responsibility. The issue of control has substantial scientific involvements. What sorts of things can be controlled, how much control can be achieved, how it can be exercised, and what sorts of processes and procedures are needed to do this efficiently and effectively are all quintessentially empirical questions. Moreover, control figures importantly in our very understanding of natural science, seeing that "control over nature" is generally regarded as one of the definitive aims of the scientific enterprise. All in all, it is one of philosophy's most prominent and significant conceptions. And yet the question of just how the conception works in its physical, metaphysical, and ethical involvements is something to which philosophers have given little explicit attention.

VARIOUS MODES OF CONTROL

Control might be exercised not by an intelligent agent but by an inanimate device of some sort—a thermostat, for example, or an autopilot. Control

146

by sensor-activated automata is still control. Today automatic controls are becoming ever more prominent, for example with the self-driving car. Moreover, natural laws can exert control over the condition of physical systems, as in the case of gravity in astrophysics, entropy in thermodynamics, or metabolic operations in organisms.

An agent has positive productive control over an outcome when he can ensure its realization, being able to act so as to guarantee this. An agent has negative or preventive control over an outcome when he can avert its realization, being able to act so as to prevent it. The combination of these modes of control over an outcome constitutes full control over it. Note that positive control over an outcome provides for negative control over all of its alternatives.

Normal people ordinarily have full control over the things they say, although not over the things they think. But in exercising control, the operator need not be an intelligent agent or even an organism. Control via the volitions of a consciously purpose-pursuing controller is only a special case—albeit an especially important one. Control can be exercised by automata and artificial devices. A traffic light can control the flow of traffic; a thermostat can control the functioning of a climate control system; an electronic computer can control the functioning of an automated production line. An operation can be "under control" without its being possible to specify an agency *X* with respect to which it can be said that the operation is under *X*'s control.

Think of a wartime aircraft navigator who, as the plane's sole survivor, is frantically working the controls to get the hang of what they do so as to be able to bring the pilotless aircraft under his control. There is no question that he "is in control of" the aircraft, since whatever the aircraft does is being done in response to his settings and resettings of the control apparatus. But until he masters their workings so as to be able to coordinate this control at his disposal with his purposes, we would not say that he "has control over" the aircraft. There is an important difference between the former mode of "control in the causal order" and the latter mode of "control in the intentional order," to which we must return below.

An agent has partial control over an outcome when he shares full control with others. When you have full control of the cold water faucet of your kitchen sink, but someone else controls the warm water faucet and someone else the outflow, your control over the water levels in the sink is only very partial. You presumably have full control of the trees planted in your apple orchard but only very partial control of the crop yield. Mother Nature also has her share of the control here. This divided control might consist in control over one dimension of a multidimensional outcome. (Think, for example, of an Etch-a-Sketch apparatus, where one operator controls the vertical and the other the horizontal movement.)

Suppose that Smith's survival depends on his securing 100 grubniks. You cannot provide him with more than the 70 you possess. His fate in point of survival or nonsurvival is something you cannot control. And whatever you do may well prove to be irrelevant to the outcome. (For instance, Jones might come along and provide Smith with 120 grubniks.) So you are not really in control of Smith's survival. All you can do here is to exert such partial control as you possess. By giving Smith those 70 grubniks you open the door to other developments involving his possible survival. This is partial—that is, *shared*—control. Casting your vote for a candidate obviously affects his or her prospects of winning (by however small an amount). But it is something that stands worlds apart from actual control.

Even where an agent has only partial control over a certain outcome, there is always *something* (albeit something else) over which he has full control, namely, whether or not actually to exercise that partial control. Partial control over something is always correlated with full control over an associated something else. Even if many votes are needed and you have no control over who gets elected, you still have full control over whom you vote for.

Three sorts of situations can exist with respect to shared or divided control:

(1) Positive productive control can be shared among several parties, with each making a partial contribution. (Think here of several bricklayers all working at parts of a large wall, or of an automobile production line.)

(2) Negative (preventive) control can be shared among several parties, each able by itself to avert a certain outcome. (Think here of a bench of judges each empowered to issue an injunction that blocks some proceeding.)

(3) A mixture of positive (productive) and negative (preventive) control. (Think here of two operators presiding over the water level in a bathtub, the one controlling the inflow and the other the outflow.)

Absolute control over a range of alternatives exists when there is total positive and total negative control over each member of this range. However, absolute control is a matter of exactly how that range is specified. Thus, consider a situation with three possible outcomes, *A*, *B*, and *C*. And let it be that agent *X* can determine whether or not *A* is realized but has no power over whether *B* or *C* should occur when *A* is not the case. Then *X* has absolute control with respect to the range *A* vs. not-*A*, but lacks such control with respect to the range *A*, *B*, *C*.

There is also such a thing as vicarious control: control exercised over other controllers, be it by delegation or by subordination. The pilot controls the aircraft, but the ground controller may control how the pilot goes about it.

PROBABILITY PROBLEMS: CONTROL VS. INFLUENCE

Control in general consists in the capacity to intervene in the course of events so as to create conditions that would not otherwise obtain. And here, those "conditions" may only be that a certain outcome has a certain probability. This involves a contrast between control and influence.

Full productive control puts the controller in a position to determine the outcome with fail-proof assurance. Influence, by contrast, only enables an operator to affect the probability of an outcome. The master of a small vessel in strong seas will have only limited control over the movement of the ship. At best he may exert influence. But even when you can only influence an outcome rather than control it, you are still in full control of how you employ your influence.

An archer fully controls the shooting of his arrow but only probabilistically controls its hitting its mark. You control the pulling of the trigger of a gun and thereby normally also the firing of the gun. However, whether or not the bullet hits its mark and, furthermore, whether the kind of damage that results is what you had envisioned are issues you do not actually control but only (strongly) influence.

You can (presumably) control what you say. But what someone takes you to mean is something that you can, at best, only influence. The thermostat's operation controls the operation of the furnace; but it only influences the temperature of the house, seeing that someone may choose to leave the windows open.

EXERCISING CONTROL

The distinction between *having* control and exercising (asserting) it must be carefully heeded. The driver has control of his car but, when distracted, refrains from exercising it. The pilot has control of the plane but *may* delegate it to the autopilot system. Direct control by an operator is control exercised by this operator himself; indirect control is control delegated by him to subordinates and intermediaries.

The conscious and deliberate exercise of control requires a personal agent, an intelligent being. Many difficult and complex issues are raised by the question of what such beings have or can bring under control.

Here is just one of them: the nature of the agent who exercises control. Under normal circumstances it can certainly be said that I am in control of my bodily movements, and perhaps even to some extent of my thoughts. But what answers to the "I" here? Is it not somehow a specifiable part of myself? Not at all: I do these things, to be sure; they are all "under my control." (Think of the familiar expression "self-control." Where there is control there must be a controller.) But the "I" here is myself, not a part of me, and the controlling self is indivisible. There is surely no homunculus-like "inner man" or "self" that guides my body or thoughts in the way that the helmsman steers a ship (shades of Descartes and the Rylean "ghost in the Machine"!). It might be objected that if such control is indivisible, how does one make sense of the (perfectly meaningful) locution "He lost control of himself"? We reply as follows: Since nobody would question that this locution is meaningful, the only live question is what it means. Surely we are not required to think in terms of a part of him (his so-called "inner self") losing control of the rest. Rather, the point of the locution is simply that he (that entire indivisible controller, as we see it) is simply not in a position to control the things that he usually controls (his words, or body movements, or the like).

A person can not only possess but even *exercise* control without being aware of it. In walking about in sunlight, you control your shadow's movements but without giving the least thought to the matter, quite unaware of it.

But even when control is being exercised consciously, it may not be asserted willingly and voluntarily. Think here of the bank manager who opens the safe under duress.

OUTCOME ISSUES

Control is always control over something: it is by nature always aspectival. Thus, for example, it may address:

— the location of a medical patient
— the position of a door
— the setting of a dial
— the orientation of one's hand
— the pointing of a pencil

Of course a controller may exercise control over several aspects of a controlled object. In this context, we may adopt the idea of "degrees of freedom" in the control over an object to designate the various (independent) respects in which the controlled object is in the controller's power.

Control will accordingly depend critically upon how this outcome range is specified. Thus, in a game of "pick-a-number greater than 23 and less than 29" the agent has control over whether the chosen number is odd or even but not over whether it is a prime or not.

The concept of the outcome of an exercise of control is surprisingly convoluted. Our acts generally set in train a cascade of causal consequences, whose description requires a complex developmental narrative. Consider, for instance, the following sequence:

— the agent pulls the trigger
— the revolver fires
— the bullet flies
— the victim is shot

— the victim is disabled
— the ransom money cannot be delivered by him
— the kidnappers are enraged
— their abductee is killed

All of these events are "outcomes" of the initial act, although only some of them will figure in the agent's awareness, let alone his intentions.

This of course means that causal responsibility and moral responsibility are going to be rather different things.

From this standpoint, the acts of agents will involve different ranges of outcomes:

- the actually *possible* outcomes (for instance, heads or tails with the tossing of a coin).
- the *envisioned* outcomes as the agent sees them. (Some possibilities may never have occurred to the agent. Or he may contemplate an outcome that is not really possible—as when the addressee of his letter is already dead.)
- The *intended* outcomes (ones that the agent has in mind).

RECIPROCAL CONTROL: FREE AND DEPENDENT VARIABLES

Consider two piles of stones, A and B, and suppose a controller exercises control over the relative size of A and B. The controller can thus determine, ex hypothesi, whether A > B, B > A, or A = B. However, this, of course, is not the whole story. It wholly leaves out of account the issue of the modus operandi: the means and manner (processes, procedures, techniques, control devices, etc.) by which the controller effects his selection of one of these alternatively realizable states of the system under his control.

Even after all of the preceding considerations have been settled, the question remains: How are we to suppose the controller exercises his control? There are four basic possibilities for the controller:

(1) add stones to A
(2) take stones from A

(3) add stones to B
(4) take stones from B

These four items spell out alternative modes of operation in control of outcomes by specifying where the "points of control" lie at which the controller intervenes to exercise his mode of control.

At this point another important issue comes to the fore. Only the knowledge of the modus operandi will enable us to specify the independent and the dependent "variables" (i.e., parameters at issue in the control situation).

Consider a money transfer between two parties. As regards overall wealth, there is a situation of stasis: *A*'s wealth increases by a certain amount that is also exactly the amount that *B*'s decreases. They collaborate, as it were, in producing this outcome. But which agent is active and which passive? Is that wealth-conserving transfer the product of *A*'s paying *B* or the result of *B*'s robbing *A*? Is *A*'s fund-diminution the cause or the effect of *B*'s fund-increase? Which agent is the actively controlling factor and which is the passively controlled one? The transfer itself does not answer these questions.

Or again, consider a teeter-totter. The overall total elevation of *A* and *B* is a constant. But is *A*'s going up the cause or the effect of *B*'s going down? Who is pushing up and who is pressing down? Who is the controller and who is the controllee? Again, the basic setup does not answer the questions.

In such interactive cases the issue of directionality in the exercise of control—or in more technical terms, the question of which is the dependent and which the independent variable—remains open. There is—by hypothesis—coordination and collaboration in the production of an outcome, but the issue of the direction of the exercise of control in the face of overall coordination remains open.

(As a side remark: This issue is particularly germane to the problem of mind-brain coordination in studies of the relation between thought activity and brain physiology. For no matter how tight the coordination, the question of the direction of causality in a given case—of which is the dependent and which the independent variable—constitutes an additional and by no means easy problem. For owing to other factors, it is also perfectly possible that the direction of control changes from case to case.)

As these deliberations indicate, clarity regarding the conception of control requires drawing many significant distinctions, including:

— positive vs. negative
— complete vs. partial
— categorical vs. probabilistic
— conscious vs. unconscious
— deliberate vs. automatic
— voluntary vs. involuntary
— intentional vs. unintentional
— direct vs. vicarious (or delegated)
— conceptual vs. causal
— proximate vs. remote

With these matters clarified, let us consider some of the specifically ethical ramifications of the exercise of control. Clearly, the operative detail of a control situation will interact delicately with the ethics of the matter.

A TRANSITION TO ETHICAL ISSUES

Only beings *capable* of conscious and willing control over outcomes—and thus only agents of a certain level of intelligence—fall within the sphere of moral assessment. Machines and lower animals can cause harm but cannot do wrong. But we humans are in another category: we can control outcome by belief, intention, and action.

Even if you are causally responsible for an untoward outcome, you are nevertheless free from moral culpability if

- You had no effective control over the outcome. (E.g., your own inadvertent fall knocked someone over and did him harm.)
- There was no reason for you to think that this outcome would or might ensue from what you did. (E.g., you administered to him medication that, unbeknownst to you, had been poisoned by someone else.)
- While you realized that this outcome might ensue, you neither expected not intended for it to do so. (E.g., you administered a situationally mandated medical procedure, which—you fully realize—may occasionally prove fatal.)

The point is that in all such cases the negative outcome causally produced by you was nevertheless beyond your conscious and intended control.

However, saying that an agent is responsible only for those events that lie within his control is no more than a first approximation, which needs to be qualified in many ways. For one thing, a certain result may be beyond an agent's control only because he himself has conveniently put it there. One could certainly not issue him a moral free pass for that. Or again, think of the intoxicated driver, who is "in control" of his vehicle even though he does not have control of it. The law unhesitatingly holds him responsible for mishaps that arise even when he no longer has control of himself (and a fortiori of his vehicle). Of course, there was likely a "point of control" at an earlier juncture, when he let himself become intoxicated. Even the exercise of mere influence that facilitates a misstep can be reprehensible, for example, by lending a vengeful maniac a gun. Even the mere failure to exercise negative control to avert some mishaps that your control (or even mere influence) should have prevented is a proper occasion for moral reprehension.

Circumstances where there can be moral culpability for an agent without actual control include the following:

- When that lack of control is counterbalanced by the existence of influence that makes the misstep more likely without actually creating it. (E.g., by letting it be known that one's neighbor keeps his house key under the doormat.)
- When that lack of control is caused by the agent himself exactly to avert responsibility. (E.g., by leaving town deliberately to avoid a possible call to duty.)
- When that lack of control exists but the agent thinks otherwise. (E.g., when the antidote has already been administered and the agent's doing so is rendered irrelevant.)
- When that lack of control is the product of irresponsible delegation. (E.g., when a child's parents have left a demonstrably incompetent babysitter in charge.)
- When the agent's action creates an otherwise avoidable negativity for someone else, which—while the agent neither envisioned nor intended it—was such that he should have been aware of it but was improperly negligent.

Thus, overall, the issue of moral culpability is complicated, murky, and situation-sensitive.

Then, too, a negative outcome can be the product of the collaborative agency of several collectively controlling agents. Here the full quota of moral culpability falls upon each and every one of them alike.

Moreover, matters must be handled differently when the fat in the fire is not one's own. You are free to manage your own risks but must be very guarded if those negativities can fall on someone else. (Risky situations are an exception to the rule that one should treat others as one would wish to be treated by them. You might well wish that others would expose you to duly favorable risks, but you are not morally free to do the same to them.)

An interesting situation arises with respect to collective action when a group is responsible for something, without any member bearing individual responsibility for it. Thus, for aught he knows to the contrary, any given member of a firing squad might be only shooting blanks. Distributively, no one member is in full control of the execution. Any particular individual member of the firing squad might be making a zero contribution to the outcome. But collectively, the group is fully in control and accordingly is responsible for the outcome.

Suppose that there are three agents (A, B, C), each of which can turn their switch on (T) or off (N). They act independently, and none of them knows what the others are doing. If exactly two of them set their switches on, then all is well, but otherwise there will be some disaster (recall the example and discussion in chapter 5).

Here every agent is in the same boat. So each can reason as follows: My two companions can produce four possible outcomes, namely, TT, TN, NT, and NN. Now if I choose T, then in two of the four cases all will be well. But if I choose N, then this will be so in only one of these four cases. Hence I must chose T. But by parity of reasoning the other two agents will arrive at the same conclusion, and disaster is then assured.

On the other hand, suppose the agents forego making a definite choice and say to themselves: To maximize the chance of averting disaster, I must use a mixed/problematic approach. And here a bit of calculation shows that if I pick T with probability 2/3 (and so N with probability 1/3)—and if my colleagues do exactly the same—then we will have a chance of 4/9 of averting disaster. In such cases randomization is the best way to proceed (as already discussed in chapter 5 and Display 5.1).

The clear lesson here is that sometimes it is best to forego definitive control over outcomes and simply "roll the dice," and instead of exercising control to decide matters probabilistically. However, delegating a decision to a random device does not cancel responsibility. (The situation of a positive outcome is then debatable.)[1]

And so various qualifying complexities intervene between having control over a bad outcome and bearing responsibility for it. In neither direction is the relationship straightforward. You can be in control of a bad outcome without bearing any moral responsibility for it. And conversely, you can be morally responsible for outcomes you do not control.

The issue of control over improper outcomes poses special difficulties for moral evaluation. Thus, consider a situation where you have to decide between doing something (X) and doing nothing. However, if you do nothing, then something bad will occur, while if you do X, something rather less bad will result (as illustrated in Display 12.1). Accordingly, we here confront a conflict between two plausible moral imperatives.

- Act so as to minimize the bad.
- Act so as to minimize the bad that results from your actions.

In effect, we have here a conflict between two ethical doctrines: on the one hand, a consequentialism of maximizing the good and/or minimizing the bad, and on the other hand, a deontology of dutiful avoidance of deliberately creating negative outcomes.

Display 12.1

A CHOICE DILEMMA

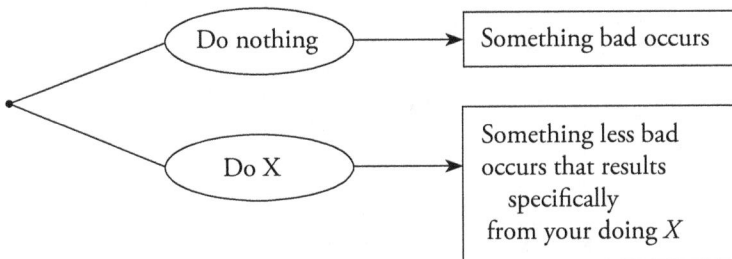

Examples of this sort of illustrate that in moral deliberation there is a place for taking collateral damage in stride and accepting "the lesser of the evils."[2] Thus in the Display 12.1 situation, the agent has to choose between having a clear conscience for himself and keeping people from greater harm. In the circumstances, there is no way to have it all. And this means that a promising case can be made for questioning the otherwise plausible idea that the deliberate production of bad outcomes is always morally reprehensible.

All in all, then, the ethics of control is complex and poses challenging philosophical issues.

Chapter 13

FREE WILL IN THE LIGHT OF PROCESS THEORY

A quintessentially free act, in the philosophical sense here at issue, is one that is carried out by an agent in consequence of a decision made by that agent on the basis of his or her own self-generated wants, wishes, and motives, without externally imposed constraints or "undue influence." A good deal of loose thinking about free will results from insufficient heed to the processual complexities of decision and action. Only careful attention to the nature of the process of decision and its implementation can avert needless problems and difficulties.

Agent control is the crux of the matter. And it is often argued that the prospect of free agency is obliterated by two lines of consideration.

- *The Time-Regress Objection*: The regress of decision-causes to earlier conditions will recede chronologically to conditions existing prior to the agent and so cannot really be ascribed to any active contribution on the agent's part.
- *The Pre-Necessitation Objection*: Any supposedly free decision is not really free because it is the inevitable causal product of earlier conditions.

To see why these seemingly plausible objections do not accomplish their intended mission, we need to take a close look at the relevant complexities of process theory.

DEFEATING THE TIME-REGRESS OBJECTION

Daniel Dennett has formulated the time-regress objection to freedom of the will as follows:

> If determinism is true, then our every deed and decision is the in-exorable outcome, it seems, of the sum of physical forces acting at the moment; which in turn is the inexorable outcome of the forces acting an instant before, *and so on to the beginning of time.* . . . [Thus] if determinism is true, then our acts are the consequences of the laws of nature and events in the remote past. But it is not up to us what went on before we were born, and neither is it up to us what the laws of nature are. Therefore the consequences of these things (including our present acts) are not up to us.[1]

However, this transit from "and so on" to "the beginning of time" commits what one might call the Zenonic fallacy. It overlooks the prospect of back-wards *convergence* as illustrated in the following diagram.

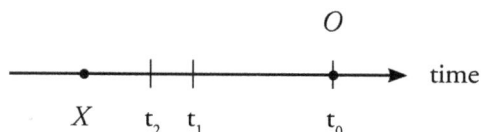

Thus consider an occurrence O at t_0, putatively the result of a free de-cision at X. And let it be that t_{i+1} stands halfway between t_i and X. Then as long as all of the O-preceding events required for O's explanation are pos-terior to t_0, we will have satisfied the demands of the principle of causality without the need for a regress that is not merely *in infinitum* but also *ad infinitum*.

To explain O's occurrence in terms of what precedes it, we certainly need not go back to "the beginning of time." There will be causal *compres-sion* rather than *unending retrogression*. No explanatory recourse to the dis-tant past is necessary. After all, even if a cause must precede its effect, nevertheless, there is no specific timespan, however small, by which it must do so, and hence the causal regression argument against free will loses all of its traction. In Zeno's paradox, Achilles never catches the tortoise because his progress must go on and on before the endpoint is reached. In the present reasoning, an explanation will never reach an initiating choice-point because the regress goes on and on. Such a perspective leaves the principle of causality wholly compatible with freedom because all those causal antecedents of the act remain causally explicable in a way that converges in some past decision-event.

DEFEATING THE PRE-NECESSITATION OBJECTION

In the interests of clarity and cogency, the idea of pre-necessitation has to be contextualized in a wider framework of deliberation. For the issues of predictability and predetermination are more complex than they appear at first view. Thus consider again an occurrence (O) at the temporal juncture t_0:

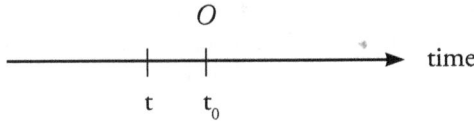

There are in fact two importantly different possibilities:

(1) O is *pre-necessitated*. As of some time $t < t_0$ the course of events *up to and including that earlier point* renders the occurrence of O at t_0 inevitable. Thus t is a point of no return as far as the realization of O is concerned.

(2) O is *predetermined*. Once the *entire* course of occurrences prior to t_0 is given, O is bound to occur at t_0. There need not, however, be an earlier point of no return. At any and every juncture prior to t_0 the issue of O's occurrence remains open. Only *the entire course of earlier developments* is determinative of the occurrence.

An occurrence that is not predetermined—which is never a sure thing in advance but only becomes so upon its actual realization—can be characterized as temporally contingent. Thus, with contingency pre-necessitation fails. By their nature as such, contingent occurrences are never predictable with certainty.

And so as long as a free decision is a temporally contingent event in the presently specified sense of the term, the pre-necessitation objection collapses—*even in the face of its predetermination.*

After all, predetermination is not at odds with freedom as long as the determination functions via the agent's thought processes. As long as the operative factors at work relate to the agent's thought and are matters of what he wants and believes—what he emphasizes and prioritizes—this sort of dependency is not an obstacle to freedom but a precondition for it. The essence of volitional freedom is agent control. As long as the agent remains in control via his thought, as the agent who himself produces those prior act-determinants—his own decisions—then the outcome is free. The processuality of decisions is the crux of freedom.

The crucial difference here is that between being active and being passive, between what someone does and what happens to that individual. When I confront a choice between X and Y and opt for the former, this is something I do rather than something that happens to me. And there is no question here of "agent causation": I do not *cause* the choice to happen, I simply choose. The problematic concept of "agent *causation*" is not in play: the issue is merely one of agent *actions.*

AN AMBIGUITY IN THE LAW OF CAUSALITY

The distinctions between pre-necessitation and predetermination bring to light a significant ambiguity in the principle of causality.

As generally stated, the principle runs as follows:

(PC) Every occurrence in nature is the (inevitable) causal consequence of temporally prior occurrences proceeding under the aegis of natural laws.

But this formulation admits of two very different constructions, according as the causal dependence at issue is deemed to be a matter of pre-necessitation or predetermination. For with this differentiation in view, we arrive at two very different principles.

(PC-Weak) Every occurrence in nature is the (inevitable) causal consequence of *the entire course* of prior occurrences proceeding under the aegis of natural laws.

(PC-Strong) Every occurrence in nature is the (inevitable) causal consequence of *a finite number* of prior occurrences proceeding under the aegis of natural laws.

The difference between these versions becomes critical in the present context. The strong version is indeed incompatible with free decision. For it would mean that at some time antecedent to the point of decision, the outcome becomes settled and a point of no return arrives that moves the matter beyond the agent's control. However, the first, weaker version of the principle is perfectly compatible with leaving matters in the agent's hands. Free will is entirely compatible with this version of the principle.

The preceding deliberations speak for what has been called "compatibilism." A decision is *metaphysically free* if it issues from the agent's course of deliberation without antecedent causal pre-necessitation, and thereby is not subject to any temporally antecedent point of no return. It may well be predetermined in the aforementioned sense, but this is wholly compatible with the agent's retention of control over the outcome up to the very moment of decision.[2]

However, the distinction between free action and free decision is important here. A decision that is pre-necessitated is not free. But a pre-necessitated action can be free. Thus if I freely decide to take a sleeping potion, my going to sleep becomes pre-necessitated but is nevertheless done freely. And so, freedom of the will is not at odds with the principle of causality as long as the locus of causal determination is the thought-process of the agent—that is, as long as causal determination is channeled through the mediation of the choices and decisions emerging from the agent's deliberations. And there is consequently no opposition between freedom and causal determination so long as that determination is effected by what transpires in the proceedings of agents—by what they do.

THE PROCESS ASPECT

It is of interest to note that even predetermined events need not be predictable with certainty. For as far as we humans are concerned, prediction is always based on available information that is finite in scope. To be predictable with certainty, an event must therefore be pre-necessitated in the sense just discussed. There will have to be a last time, prior to the time of occurrence, with respect to which all of the predictively requisite information is available. And this will make for pre-necessitation.

Free *actions* are events, and as such they are always explainable in terms of earlier events. But this regress does not go back endlessly: it converges to a fixed point, the point of decision. And free decisions have a unique status of their own. From a process point of view, it is necessary to distinguish between two different modes of occurrence:

- *Events*, namely, occurrences that have duration and occur over a time interval that can be represented on a linear time axis by time segments, however small.
- *Eventuations*, namely, occurrences that are effectively and temporally instantaneous.

On this basis, natural processes are temporally structured sequences of events.

Properly understood, an event is not just an occurrence on the stage of nature's history but an occurrence of a particular sort, namely, a process or mini-process that has a beginning, a middle, and an end, and accordingly unfolds over a period of time. The move of a chess piece from one point to another is a typical event. Events are in principle observable.

By contrast, an *eventuation* is an occurrence that takes place in time but does not itself take time. The move of a chess piece to effect a checkmate is an event, but its termination—the checkmate in which it results—is not: it is, rather, an occurrence at the start of an event. Eventuations are unobservable: only their consequences can be observed. (Eventuations are temporally punctiform occurrences, which as such may, but need not, admit of any temporally geared explanation, and whose indeterminacy—should it exist—would be perfectly consistent with the principle of causality, which deals only with events.)

The difference between events and eventuations, such as "beginning" or "ending," is clearly marked in linguistic usage. When you ask someone what they are doing, they can tell you that they are preparing to run a race or that they are engaged in running it, but they cannot say that they are starting or beginning to run it. There is no present continuous "I am beginning" or "I am starting" (over and above indicating that one is in the entry stages of a process). And the same holds for "I am completing" (or ending) the race, and also for "I am changing direction." Beginnings, endings, and redirections are not themselves activities in which one engages but modification in the activities one engages in. Eventuations as such are not observable: they can only be discerned with the wisdom of hindsight. The critically important point for our present deliberations is that eventuations as such are not themselves events but simply structural features thereof: startings, endings, and redirections.

The initiation of a process is not an event but an eventuation. It is not a part of the process but simply its start. The historical timeline of a process is an interval that is open to the left (so to speak). A process is a succession of events, but there is no first event at its beginning. It bursts into time. It has the structure "$\bullet \to$" where the initiating dot is neither an event nor even a part of the process, but simply its start. And the situation with the ending of a process is analogous: it is not a part of the process but is an interval that is open to the right (so to speak). A process is a succession of events, but there is no last event at its ending. It peters out in time. It has a structure "$\leftarrow \bullet$" where the terminating dot is neither an event nor a part of the process, but simply its termination.

Decisions, then, are terminations to courses of deliberations. They are not events but eventuations. They are not observable; they are only informative for the shaping of events, shifting the cause of occurrence from what it would otherwise be. Strictly speaking, if the principle of causality is taken to apply to observable events in nature, then eventuations as such fall outside its scope—and decisions as such accordingly do so as well.

A free decision, then, is not the sort of occurrence that is necessitated by entire events. From the standpoint of the principle of causality, it is a discontinuity in the causal order. It admits of no determination by prior events. It is, like any other inaugurating start, an eventuation rather than an event proper.

Like all eventuations, decisions admit of prediction on the basis of what goes before. But these predictions are not categorical and are probabilistic in nature. I can explain your free choices of a book to read or a film to see on the basis of your motivating tastes and inclinations. But such explanations are matters of probability and not causal inevitability.

And from the angle of free will, such predictability is simply no problem. If I offer you the choice between a hundred dollar bill and an unnecessary root canal operation, there is no difficulty in predicting which you will choose. But your choice is nevertheless perfectly free. What matters for freedom is not predictability as such—which can be based on probabilities, not only on for-certain predictability. If and when the prediction rests on the agent's tastes, dispositions, preferences, and the like, then that decision is free.

"But we do not choose our tastes, dispositions, and so forth." Perfectly true. But this is also quite beside the point. The objection rests on an erroneous premise: "Choices are free only if their motivating inclinations are freely chosen." But this requirement is inappropriate. By their very nature, motives, tastes, and the like are not themselves objects of choice at all. Nor are they somehow forced on the agent by constraints from without. They are not externally *imposed* on the agent but rather are internally constituted—a part of what makes an agent into the individual he or she is. They are components of the individual's very nature.

The predictability of free decisions is not, however, simply stochastic and driven purely by randomness and chance. Rather, it is motivational, inherent in telic factors that (in Leibniz's terminology) *incline* rather than *necessitate*. They inhere in the autonomously developed motivational makeup of the decider. And to say that an agent decided "autonomously" is to say that he is deciding on his own account. Autonomy is the default when there is no externally managed undue influence. When all agent-oriented questions of the type "Was he forced?" "Was he subjected to threats and pressures?" or "Was he subject to post-hypnotic influence?" are answered negatively, then autonomous agency becomes the default.

It is exactly this—being determined by the internal composition of the agent's autonomous makeup rather than being heteronomously imposed upon the agent by factors operating *ab extra*—in which the freedom of a free decision consists.[3]

FREE AGENCY AS AN EVOLUTIONARY GIFT

One often hears it said that "the very idea of free will is antithetical to science because free will is something occult that cannot possibly be scientifically naturalized." But surely any sensible exponent of free will could (and should) be happy to see it as part of the natural course of things. For if free will exists—if *Homo sapiens* can indeed make free choices and decisions—then this should ideally be part of the natural order. And in fact if we indeed are free, then this has to be so for roughly the same reason that we are intelligent—that is, because the evolution of our species worked out that way. The objection above is thus fallacious in that it rests on the presupposition that free will must be super- or preternatural. The mind-engendered decisions of intelligent agents on the basis of motivational deliberation are themselves a mode of causal determination characteristic of the modus operandi of such beings. Deliberative choosing and deciding must be as much a capacity developed through evolutionary emergence as are the capacities of speaking or of imagining possibilities. If free will exists, it can and will be an aspect of how naturally evolved beings operate on nature's stage.

The elaborate present-day studies of brain physiology do not invalidate free will. Consider what happens when two people look at a page written in Mandarin, one of whom knows Mandarin and the other does not. Both "see" the same thing in one sense but not in another. One sees squiggles; one sees ideas. Only when physical processes impinge upon a suitably prepared mind—a mind duly schooled for thinking—is there an apprehension of meaning and a basis for understanding. The brain processes may be essential to thought, but thought goes above and beyond them. To be sure, brain physiology is always connected with thought. But in matters of understanding, the mind is the crucial player in its own right, and in matters of choice and decision, it is thought that is the ultimate controller of outcomes. Brain and mind may work in lock-step coordination, but, as with a teeter-totter, sometimes the one side is the agent and the other the responder, and sometimes the reverse. (The situation is akin to that of independent and dependent variables in physics.)

These deliberations point to a further salient point, namely, *the patent utility of free will as an evolutionary resource*. For what lies at the heart and core of free will is up-to-the-last-moment thought-control by a rational agent of his or her deliberation-produced choices and decision in the light of continually updated information and evaluation. Recognizing that such a capacity is advantageous in matters of survival is not a matter of rocket science. And so, the explanatory rationale for this innovation would be substantially the same as that for any other sort of evolution-emergent capability, namely, that it contributes positively to the business of natural selection. A free will is clearly an efficient and effective way for agents to function successfully in a complex environment. It gives them the power to adjust their decisions and choices to the detail of their conditions up to the moment of resolution. Such an arrangement puts the agent into an optimal position to provide for his operative needs and wants. It affords the agent a flexible, continually updated harmonization of information and the satisfaction of needs and desires. After all, if *Homo sapiens* indeed has free will, surely we come to have it because evolution put it there for our advantage.

In the final analysis, the realization of free will hinges on its status as an instrument of survival advantage. There are, of course, many different ways for a creature to shape its activities to meet its needs and wants, including sheer biochemical automatism, pure instinct, and even random groping about. But intelligently managed free agency—the alignment of behavior with desire satisfaction via thought, based on information secured through inquiry—is also one of these. And experience and theory alike indicate that only the flexibility of free decision and choice can most efficiently deliver the goods here.

The ancient Greeks divided reality into the works of nature (*phusis*) and the contrivances of artifice (*nomos*). And this was a wise step. For with the developmental emergence of intelligent beings in the world, all sorts of new things came into existence. Beings capable of intelligence-guided agency will be capable, among other things, of

— symbol use (and thus linguistic communication)
— conjecture and hypothesis entertainment (and thus reasoning and mathematics)
— value commitment (and thereby also romantic love)
— rule adoption (and thus social interaction with rights and obligations and duties)

And a prominent addition to this register is overt control for the exercise of reasoned choice—the essence of free will. After all, deliberative choice is basic to our being what we are—even in matters of cognition, in contrast to overt action, since knowing something involves accepting it as true and rejecting its denial as false. Evaluation—the discrimination of positive and negative, plus and minus—is crucial here and pervasive as well, since it can appertain both to the doings and eventuations of nature (good/bad, pleasant/unpleasant, true/false) and the doings and actions of mankind (right/wrong, correct/incorrect, appropriate/inappropriate). And such opposites are the poles of an axis stretching between them as matters of degree, be it in nature (*phusis*) or human affairs (*nomos*). And just here, of course, "the will" enters in, since alternative proceedings are always in prospect and call for choice, be it wisely and properly or not.

Our capacity for rational choice—the ability not only to choose but to do so on the basis of mind-contemplated reasons—is what distinguishes man from the lower animals on this planet. To be sure, subhuman creatures can also act, but they cannot act wisely or unwisely since they do not act rationally (i.e., for deliberative reasons); for them the evaluative dimension of good versus bad is missing. Acts of will—choices and decisions—are eventuations of a special sort produced in, by, and for minds. They are a critical part of what developed minds do as they emerge within nature in the wake of evolution's evolving complexity. It is thus only sensible to view free will, along with the emergence of intelligence, as one of evolution's crowning glories. For free agency is an optimally useful evolutionary resource for intelligent agents, and if this arrangement did not already exist in the world, evolutionary pressures would militate for its emergence.

Free agency is therefore inherently bound up with rationality. Specifically, (1) cognitive rationality calls for the control of belief by thought, and (2) practical rationality calls for the control of action by belief. Put together, these two considerations mean that with the development of rational creatures, there will be beings who can control action by thought. But just exactly this idea—that with the evolution of intelligent agents upon the world's stage there will be creatures that are able to control their actions by means of thought—is the heart and core of the doctrine of free will.

In principle, a perfectly "naturalistic" case can thus be made on behalf of the freedom of the will through evolutionary considerations. Charles Darwin thought that he had to negate free will to make room for the evolution of mind. But here he was being uncharacteristically nearsighted. For there is no good reason to refrain from acknowledging that free will, rather than being an impediment to survival, is like intelligence itself in providing a survival advantage. Rather than being a problem for evolution, freedom of the will should be regarded as one of its greatest achievements.

For if free will exists, it will have to be an aspect of how naturally evolved beings operate on nature's stage. The fact that we humans get here by evolution does not mean that we cannot make free decisions any more than it means that we cannot solve calculus problems or play chess. There simply is no decisive reason for denying that, just as intelligent beings can evolve, similarly, intelligent agents can evolve—creatures whose actions are the product of thought-determined decisions.

Only a being capable of choice-resolution about alternative actions on the basis of a conscious evaluation of their assumed outcomes in relation to this being's motivating affinities and aversions will qualify as a free agent. Whether the deliberations at issue are well or ill managed is ultimately irrelevant: what matters is that they are determinate of the outcome and within the control of the agent. What lies at the heart and core of free will is up-to-the-last-moment control by a rational agent over his or her deliberation-produced choices and decisions in the light of cognitions and evaluations. Freedom, then, is a matter of having cognitive endowments provided by evolutionary development, supplemented by a "software" of cognitive acclamation. There is nothing mysterious or supernatural about it: it is an altogether natural course of biological and cultural evolution.

With the development of minds in the course of evolution, new capacities and capabilities come upon the scene, expanding the repertoire of beings—remembering past occurrences, for example, or imagining future ones. And one of these developmental innovations is the capacity of the mind to take the initiative in effecting changes in the course of events.

And so, the present fallacy rests on a failure of imagination. It is predicated on an unwillingness to acknowledge that with the evolution of intelligent agents, there arises the prospect of intelligence-guided agency decided through the deliberations of these intelligent agents. And only in the setting of a process theory can we make the distinctions—between decision and action, determination and necessitation, events and eventuations, and so forth—that are necessary to articulate a cogent analysis of the nature and possibility of volitional freedom. By its very nature, volitional freedom inheres in the nature of the processes of deliberation, decision, and supplementation. The basics of process theory serve to show that there is no clash between the principle of causality and free will, and that the standard objections to free agency supposedly rooted in such a conflict cannot prevail.[4]

Admittedly, the sort of free will now at issue admits of a determinism of sorts, namely, a determination of actions by the decisions and choices of an agent. As long as those decisions and choices are made in the normal way—determined autonomously and without undue external influence and interference—the action qualifies as free on the current conception of freedom. If this position is deemed to be compatibilistic, then the present view of free will is a compatibilism between determinism and freedom.

Chapter 14

PERSONHOOD

HUMANS VERSUS PERSONS

To be human is to belong to a particular animal species through the operations of biological and physiological evolution. As such, humans exist only here on earth. However, to be a *person* is something quite different and far broader, something determined by one's capacities and possibilities for action. Persons are beings that make their way in the world by means of thought, acting on the basis of their beliefs and choices. In principle, alien creatures very different from humans could be persons. Thought-implementation—the capacity to act in response to and under the direction of thought—is the crux of personhood. Being human is a purely biological category: it defines one's place in the organic scheme of things. Being a person is different from that: it involves the capacity for modes of thought and action that can—in theory—function outside the biological realm as usually understood. There is no reason in principle why non-human organisms (aliens) or purely spiritual beings (angels) or purely mechanical beings (robots) could not have the abilities needed to qualify as persons. Personhood is not a biological but a metaphysical category.

The concept of a "person" is accordingly a complex one that involves many constituent components—both descriptive and normative. However, one cannot be more or less of a person. Being a person turns simply on whether or not certain specific requirements are met. Personhood is a matter of yes or no, and not one of degrees: a given creature either is or is not qualified to count as a person.

But while personhood is a decisive classification and being a person is a binary matter—one either is or is not a person—nevertheless one can certainly honor the obligations and harness the opportunities that being a person puts at one's disposal to a greater or lesser extent. So while one cannot be more or less of a person, one can be a better or worse person. In this regard, personhood is like kingship: a matter of better or worse, even if not of more or less.

Interestingly, it does not lie in the concept of a person that one must necessarily have a body. To be sure, one must be able to act, but this agency could in theory be purely mental—involving solely, say, the direct communication between minds through a sympathetic resonance of some sort. Only agents for whom the transmission of information requires sending and receiving physical signals and thus a physical depository will need to be embodied—as persons, their embodiment is contingent.

Persons are first and foremost cognitive agents, beings who act on the basis of information and thought. For such beings, radical skepticism is not an option: a systemic refusal to accept contentions creates a 100 percent certainty of lacking the information needed to guide action. A person can reasonably be a *mild* sceptic, denying the prospect of settling factual issues with 100 percent certainty. But a person cannot reasonably be a *radical* sceptic who holds that all factual claims are equally meritorious and that none deserves greater credence that any other. For rational decision and thereby rational action then become impossible, and persons will no longer function as rational beings.

Persons are bound to have beliefs about how matters stand in the world, creating for themselves some sort of mental thought-model about its arrangements. And they have various needs and wants that give them an interest in what goes on. On this basis—their beliefs and their interests—they make choices. This capacity to deploy beliefs, evaluations, and choices into conjoint operation in an endeavor to produce results is what defines them as persons. Agency guided by cognition, evaluation, and choice constitutes the heart of the matter. And to be fully a person, a being should not only preside over the aforementioned capabilities of cognitive and practical intelligence (belief, desire, choice) but be conscious and indeed self-conscious thereof.

Persons as thus conceived are intelligent beings who see themselves—reciprocally—as having the capacity for self-controlled choice-implementation and who insist on viewing themselves as something other than robots or mere naturally evolved mechanisms without the ability of choice or self-inaugurated agency. They regard themselves as free and responsible agents who, when they act, generally "*could* have acted otherwise" in the sense that they *would* have acted otherwise if some difference in the circumstances would have motivated them to do so.

The explanatory unraveling of this "if" clause is a very long story. For being a *person* requires seeing oneself as capable of acting in the light of values appropriately deemed valid. Specifically, this means that one must value personhood itself, seeing that reason demands respect: it is a requirement imposed by one's own reason that rationality should be valued. As long as personhood is not valued for what it is, the conception of it still remains unachieved. Accordingly, the evaluative dimension is crucial to the full-fledged conception of a person. To have this conception of oneself is not only to function as a being of a certain kind but to *value* oneself for it—that is, to deem oneself a bearer of value for this very reason.

To be a person is thus to regard oneself as a unit of worth and a bearer of rights. And this is something that generalizes to others as well. A full-fledged conception of personhood can develop only in a social context. To regard oneself as a possessor of worth and a bearer of rights *in virtue of being a person* is thereby to accord a certain status to persons in general. It is to see persons-in-general as occupying a special place in the scheme of things—as constituting a special category of beings with whom one has a particular kinship and toward whom one consequently bears particular responsibilities. When others treat me as an object rather than a person, this may possibly diminish my self-image but is far more likely to diminish my image of them.

Granted, evolution has not made us humans into persons. That was too much to ask for. But what it did is to give us the resources—the facilities and capacities—needed for us to be able to function as such. We have made ourselves into persons through the way in which we make use of our evolutionary endowments.

The capabilities that define our human personhood are the product of evolution. They include:

- intelligence and rationality
- agency that is reason-guided (and thus free)
- consciousness and especially self-consciousness

And all this, like Rome, was not made in a day. Animals, and especially higher primates, possess some of these characteristics: certainly intelligence (at a lower level) and possibly free agency (or one that is lower yet). Self-consciousness did not emerge until humanoid evolution was well along the way to our present form. In all these matters, exact boundaries are difficult to determine and may well not exist, given the conceptual complexity of the transitions involved.

THE SOCIAL AND ETHICAL DIMENSION

We are born *humans* (members of the species *Homo sapiens*) but become *persons*. Only as we progress through childhood and learn to think of ourselves as responsible agents—intelligent, free individuals interacting with others as such—do we become full-fledged persons. (No doubt this communal development reflects a tendency that evolutionary processes have programmed into our developmental history, so that personhood is de facto more closely affixed to humanity than abstract theory alone suggests.)

In seeing ourselves as persons we lay claim to a special status defined by the capacities involved. We profoundly value our personhood and would rather lose our right arm than our personality. To cease being the persons we are is a version of annihilation. We naturally regard our personhood as a possession of paramount value. And because we make this claim for ourselves—if our personhood is to count as having paramount value—then we must also concede this special status to others similarly endowed. And in conceding them such status we stand committed to a special responsibility for care and concern. If personhood is a condition of paramount value that we prize greatly in ourselves, than it has to be prized in itself—whenever it is encountered.

In demanding respect and care for ourselves as persons, we thus acknowledge a responsibility to care for the personhood of others. We commit to a special responsibility toward them. In short, our self-classification as persons involves us in a social solidarity that has a moral agenda of rights and responsibilities. Personhood thus has an inextricably social dimension. The conception of a (full-fledged) person is subject to a principle of reciprocity-expectation. To qualify as a person oneself involves acknowledging and accepting as such the other creatures who seem plausibly qualified as being persons. And it involves the expectation that they will reciprocate. In deeming others to be persons and thereby entitled to being valued as such—qualified to have me treat *their* interests, rights, and concerns as deserving *my* respect—I also expect them to see me in exactly this same light. Consequently, if others whom I recognize as persons treat me as a mere thing and not as a person, it injures my own personhood; it undermines my ability to see myself as a person.

William James wrote somewhere that we become moral beings only when we believe that we are free agents, because only then will we deliberate about our actions with a view to reasons and thereby function as morally responsible for them. But the real point here is a more fundamental one. It is precisely because persons as such form part of a mutually recognizant community of rational agents that persons are ipso facto beings who fall within the domain of morality. (Morality is not inherently rooted in a social compact. If extraneous persons were to come upon the scene, perhaps from outer space, we would at once have certain moral obligations to one another—to respect one another's "rights" as persons, and the like—which would certainly not need to be products of a prior "agreement," real or tacit.)

On this basis, personhood carries in its wake a moral sense of right—of obligation, fairness, and justice in relation to other persons. Personhood is thus a condition of profound ethical involvement including due care for the interest of other persons. Morality, in short, takes root in personhood itself. For if one is a person who recognizes and prizes this very fact, then one ought for that very reason to behave morally by taking the interests of other such beings into account. If I am (rationally) to pride myself on being a rational agent, then I must stand ready to value in other rational agents what I value in myself—that is, I must deem them *worthy* of respect, care, and so on in virtue of their status as such. What is at issue is not so much a matter of *reciprocity* as one of *rational coherence* with claims that one does—or, rather, should—stake for oneself. To see myself in a certain normative light I must, if rational, stand ready to view others in the same light. And clearly, if personhood is something of paramount value in and to me, I must (as a rational being) acknowledge its value as such and thereby consequently in others as well. (After all, if I deem myself the better person for being truthful and honest, how could I consistently refrain from thinking well of truthfulness and honesty in others?) In seeing ourselves as *persons*—as free and responsible rational agents—we thereby rationally bind ourselves to a care for one another's interests insofar as those others, too, are seen as having this status.[1]

THE GROUND OF OBLIGATION

Only persons can have obligations. The bearer of an obligation must be a self-conscious decider, a rational agent, someone who can—in principle at least—act out of a realization that honoring this obligation is the appropriate thing to do. A being who cannot be aware of having a duty or who, even when so aware, is unable to have this circumstance constitute an impelling nisus to action is thereby outside the range where duty and obligation can function. There are no obligations that are not "toward" some person or persons. These obligations will either be toward other people (individuals or groups) in the case of other-directed obligations, or they will be toward the obligatee him- or herself (in the case of self-directed obligations).

Obligations thus always have debtors in the sense of being owed to someone, and this is invariably the case with the bearer. We owe it to ourselves to be people who meet their obligations. We owe meeting an obligation to others most clearly in the case of contractual obligations, but also in the case of quasi-contractual obligations linking us to the wider community in such matters as obeying the law. Sometimes, however, there are no external debtors. The obligation to treat animals humanely is not something we owe to them, but only to ourselves. And the same is true for the obligation to preserve and conserve nature's assets. (Some would argue that we owe this obligation to future generations via a strange kind of social contract.)

Obligations also always have beneficiaries: there is always someone who benefits from someone's meeting an obligation. This is, again, invariably the case with the bearer: he always benefits from meeting his obligation through making himself into a better person thereby. Typically others also benefit when an obligation is met, for example, when I honor my promise to aid you in some way.

Only in the case of agents themselves are the beneficiaries and debtors of obligation one and the same. Collateral beneficiaries need not be debtors:

nor need the debtors themselves necessarily benefit by the discharge of an obligation. (It is possible, for example, that in honoring my promise to keep an appointment with you, I could cause you considerable inconvenience in the light of changed circumstances.)

Other-directed obligations are generally contractual (as with promises) or quasi-contractual, as with our "social contract" with society-at-large. However, obligations we have to ourselves are not contractual. All of them are subordinate to the paramount obligation inherent in the primary injunction: "Act so as to produce the best realizable version of yourself by endeavoring to maximize your opportunities for the good." This is the overarching obligation we have to ourselves. Its basis is inherent in the ontological reality of our existence in this world as a rational being. Even our supposed obligations toward animals and toward our natural environment ultimately fall within the scope of this primary injunction. Thus the obligation to treat animals humanely does not rest in a right on their part but in our obligations to avoid making ourselves into the sort of persons who abuse animals. It is one of our self-directed obligations.

Obligations arise in two different ways. Some are assumed voluntarily; others become incumbent upon us willy-nilly, in view of the circumstances in which we find ourselves. The former category of *voluntarily assumed* obligations includes those of one spouse toward the other, of the captain of a ship toward its passengers, or of an employee toward his employer (and vice versa). These are *ex efficio* obligations arising through someone's voluntary undertakings: they are assumed duties, as it were. The second category of *circumstantially involuntary* obligations includes those of a person to oneself, of a child to the parents, of a citizen to the law of the land, of a passerby to an injured person on the wayside, of the finder of someone's wallet to that owner, and the like. These are *ex conditio* obligations arising through someone's happenstance connection to others— relationships that are not in some way of their own making.

In relation to our willingly assumed obligations, we are active: they are in a way contractual. Through our entry into a certain role (as spouse, physician, employer, etc.), we voluntarily "sign on" to a certain range of duties, within which these obligations are inviolate. Involuntary obligations, by contrast, are inherent in circumstances that are in no way of our own making. Take the obligation we automatically have toward our fellow beings—for example, my duty to regard and treat you as a fellow human being. Neither am I a human being by choice, nor do I by choice exist in a world in which you too are present. At no point did I volunteer to be born into this world by certain parents, yet here we are, and I have duties toward them. Again, I have a duty not to be unduly burdensome to those around me, but this duty does not issue from some voluntary arrangement between us. Then, too, I have various obligations to myself—among others, to avoid pointless harm, heedless negligence of needs, pointless wastage of opportunities for the good, and so on. These are also entirely noncontractual and involuntary.

All of the voluntarily assumed obligations are based in and issue from one fundamental imperative: "Honor your commitments: where the interests of others are engaged, perform as you have undertaken with them. Do as you have freely undertaken." And there is a yet more fundamental and deep-rooted imperative that underlies obligation: "Act as it is proper and appropriate for a rational human agent to do. Be an honorable human being (a *Mensch*). Do what is required of you to qualify as a self-respecting person." All obligatory action is self-enhancing. Throughout their entire range, obligatory actions are governed by the principle that in doing them, we automatically make ourselves into better people than we otherwise would be.

To be sure, the question "Why should I honor my obligations?" has a certain oddity. Clearly if something indeed is one of my obligations, then I should for that very reason do it. That is built tautologically into the very concept of an obligation. Instead, what the question presumably means is not this triviality but rather something like: "What is it that makes something into an obligation for me?" And the answer that this question demands will have to proceed along the lines of:

In failing to do A in the circumstances at issue, I would become X.

where X would have to be something like:

— diminished as a person
— less deserving of self-respect
— less entitled to see myself as a decent human being

One way or another, what makes a certain action (morally) obligatory and incumbent upon me is that by not acting in this regard, I would do myself an injury by diminishing my moral stature in the sight of any reasonable person—myself, presumably, included. The ground of obligation is our claim to personhood.

ONTOLOGICAL OBLIGATION AS THE SOURCE OF THE DEONTIC FORCE OF MORALITY

In a classic paper of pre–World War I vintage, the Oxford philosopher H. A. Prichard argued that it makes no real sense to ask "Why should I be moral?"[2] For once an act is recognized as being the morally appropriate thing to do, there is really no room for any *further* question about why it should be done. "Because it's the moral thing to do" is automatically, by its very nature, a satisfactorily reason-presenting response. The question "Why *do* the *right* thing?" is akin to the question "Why *believe* the *true* thing?" On both sides the answer is simply: "Just exactly because it is, by hypothesis, right/true." When rightness or truth have once been conceded, the matter is closed. According to Prichard, then, the question "Why should one's duty be done?" is simply obtuse—or perverse. For duty as such constitutes a cogent moral imperative to action—automatically, as it were, of itself and by its very nature. To grant that it is one's duty to do something and then go on to ask why one should do it is simply to manifest one's failure to understand what the conception of "duty" involves. Duty as such constitutes a reason for action—albeit a *moral* reason.

But clearly, this line of reflection, though quite correct, is probatively unhelpful. Self-support has its limitations as a justificatory rationale. The questions still remain: What makes reasons of moral appropriateness into good reasons? Why should I be the sort of person who accepts moral grounds as validly compelling for his own deliberations? If being moral indeed is the appropriate thing to do, there must be some sort of reason for it—that is, there must be some line of consideration, not *wholly* internal to morality itself, that renders it reasonable for people to be moral. We must probe further for a satisfactory resolution to the question "Why be moral?"—one that improves on the true but unhelpful answer, "Because it is the (morally) right thing to do." There has to be more to it than that. But where are we to look?

The answer is that we must look into the very core of our being—our status as rational agents. For with us, obligation is coordinate with rationality.

Rationality is inherent in the ontology of what we are: we are *Homo sapiens*, implanted in the world's scheme of things as conscious, knowing, rational agents. And rationality is promoted in our evaluative scheme of things. We would rather lose a limb or two than lose our reason.

The obligation to morality, like the obligation to rationality itself, is rooted in considerations of reason. If one is in a position to see oneself as in fact rational, then once one recognizes the value of this rationality, one must also acknowledge the obligation to make use of one's rationality. And if one is a rational free agent who recognizes and prizes this very fact, then one ought for that very reason to behave morally by taking the interests of other such agents into account. For if I am (rationally) to pride myself on being a rational agent, then I must stand ready to value in other rational agents what I value in myself—that is, I must deem them *worthy* of respect, care, and so on in virtue of their status as rational agents. What is at issue is not so much a matter of *reciprocity* as one of *rational coherence* with claims that one stakes (and should stake) for oneself. To see myself in a certain normative light, I must, if rational, stand ready to view others in the same light. If we indeed are the sort of intelligent creature whose worth in its own sight is a matter of prizing something (reflective self-respect, for example), then this item by virtue of this very fact assumes the status of something we are bound to recognize as valuable—as deserving of being valued. In seeing ourselves as *persons*—as free and responsible rational agents—we thereby rationally bind ourselves to a care for one another's interests insofar as those others are seen as having the same status.

In holding that something (life, liberty, opportunity) is of value—that it is not just something one *wants* but something one is *rationally well advised* to pursue—we rational agents must recognize its generic value and acknowledge that others, too, are well-advised to pursue it. And if the capacity to be a rational agent—to act for reasons I myself think to be good and sufficient—is something I respect and value in me, then I am rationally bound, out of simple consistency, to respect and value it in others as well. In seeing our own rationality as deserving their recognition and respect, we must extend the same privilege to them. In sum, we must proceed as moral agents in our interactions with others.

Rational agents are accordingly bound, by virtue of that very rationality, to the view that valuing something commits one to seeing it as worthy of being valued by themselves or anyone like them in the relevant respects. One can, quite properly, *like* things without reasons, but for a rational agent to *value* them involves seeing them as having value by generalized standards. And thus to see value in my status and my actions as a rational agent, I must be prepared to recognize this value in others as well. For reason is inherently impersonal (objective) in the sense that what constitutes a good reason for X to believe or to do or to value something is automatically also a good reason for anyone else who stands in X's shoes (in the relevant regards). So if I am to be justified in valuing my rationality (in prizing my status as a rational agent) and in seeing it as a basis for demanding the respect of other agents, then I must also—from simple rational self-consistency—stand prepared to value and respect rationality in others. In degrading other rational persons in thought or in treatment, we automatically degrade ourselves, while in doing them honor, we thereby honor ourselves.

When someone acts immorally toward me—cheats me or deceives me or the like—I am not merely angry and upset because my personal interests have been impaired, but I am also "righteously indignant." Not only has the offender failed to acknowledge me as a person (a fellow rational being with rights and interests of his own), but he has, by his very act, marked himself as someone who, though (to my mind) a compatriot of mine as a rational agent, nevertheless does not give rational agents their proper due, thereby degrading the entire group to which he and I both belong. He has added insult to injury. And this holds more generally. One is also indignant at witnessing someone act immorally toward a third party. One is disturbed in a way somewhat like what one feels when a serious gaffe or worse is committed by a member of one's own family. For one's own sense of self and self-worth is mediated by membership in such a group, and this worth becomes compromised by *their* behavior. As rational agents, we are entitled and committed to be indignant at the wicked actions of our fellows who do not act as rational agents ought to act, because our own self-respect is inextricably bound up with their behavior. They have "let down the side."

The upshot of such considerations is that to fail to be moral is to defeat our own proper purposes and to lose out on our ontological opportunities. Only by acknowledging the worth of others—and thus the appropriateness of a due heed of *their* interests—can we maintain our own claims to self-respect and self-worth. And so, we realize that we *should* act morally in each and every case, even where deviations are otherwise advantageous, because insofar as we do not, we can no longer look upon ourselves in a certain sort of light—one that is crucial to our own self-respect in the most fundamental way. Moral agency is an essential requisite for the proper self-esteem of a rational being. To fail in this regard is to injure oneself where it does and should hurt the most—in one's own sight.

In basing the commitment to morality on such an ontological obligation, its ultimate rationale comes to be located outside the moral project itself—where it must be located, as observed above. In *this* regard, the present ontological validation of morality indeed resembles that of the various theorists who base morality on a morality-external factor, such as custom, social utility, or individual advantage. But the crucial difference is that the ontological appeal to the value of personhood is itself altogether consonant with the inherent nature of moral concerns, whereas the alternatives are not. There is no problem about locating the ultimate impetus to morality in an inherent obligation of responsible rational agents as such. On the other hand, there is a deep problem in locating it in blind custom or social advantage or crass self-interest. For morality would be utterly compromised (nay, destroyed as the sort of thing it is) if its ultimate grounding were based on values that are wholly disjoint from those at issue in morality itself. Its "validation" would ultimately be incoherent. But this is clearly not the case with an account that locates the rationale of morality in the ontology of personhood and the rational commitment that personhood involves.

The ontological imperative to capitalize on our opportunities for the good carries us back to the salient issue of philosophical anthropology: the visualization of what man can and should be. "Be an authentic human being!" comes down to this: Do your utmost to become the sort of rational and responsible creature that a human person, at best or most, is capable of being.[3] The moral project of treating other people as we ourselves would want to be treated is part and parcel of this.[4] What we have here is in fact an evaluative metaphysic of morals.

MORALITY AND RATIONALITY

To clarify the connection between personhood and obligation, the most promising prospect is to probe into the nature of personhood itself, to *the ontological duty of self-realization* that appertains to any rational agent whatsoever—the fundamental obligation of endeavoring to make the most of one's opportunities for realizing oneself as fully as possible, a duty that, insofar as one "owes" it to anyone at all, one owes no less to the world at large than to oneself. For any reason-endowed agent is thereby under an obligation to use its reason to capitalize on its potentialities for the good. The impetus of such an ontological obligation is predicated on the principle that someone who systematically wastes his opportunities for the realization of potential—say, by having too low a self-image and too low a level of expectation for himself—is being less than he can and should be and thus fails in that most fundamental of all duties, the ontological obligation to make the most of one's opportunities for the good. The dutifulness of obligation is inextricably connected with its rationality. To say that X ought (morally) to do A is to commit oneself to the claim that there are good reasons of the appropriate sort—that is, good *moral* reasons—for X to do A. The moral enterprise is an inherently rational one that pivots on reasons of a characteristic sort, those grounded in the inherent value of personhood. Such an ontological obligation is not an *ex officio* obligation (like that of a sea captain or a husband) that one takes on in assuming a role, but an *ex conditione* obligation (like that of a son or sister); it inheres in what one *is* rather than in what one has undertaken. It is an obligation that is rooted in personhood itself. And in deliberately violating this ontological obligation for self-development, one is doing something that is not just ill-advised but somehow perverse and actually wicked.[5]

What matters for us rational agents is not simply the sort of creature we are, but the sort of creature we conceive and believe ourselves to be called upon to be—and thereby the sort of creature we purport ourselves to be. Now as Kant maintained, we *take ourselves to be* free rational agents and, in consequence, must assume the inherent commitments and obligations of such beings.[6] As intelligent beings, we rational agents have no adequate excuse for avoiding the questions: "What sort of creature am I? What possibilities and opportunities does this engender? What should I do to make of myself that which I ought to be? How can I realize my highest potential?" By its very nature as such, an intelligent agent who has the capacity and opportunity for value-realization ought to realize it. The principle at issue is a conceptual one, implicit in the very idea of value. One could not appropriately call something a value if it were not of such a sort that a rational agent ought to opt for it whenever it is available at a manageable cost.

Of course, the relation between morality and self-interest is complex. It is certainly true that people's true self-interest is best served by moral comportment. But doing the morally appropriate thing for reasons of self-advantage defeats the very purpose of morality. Kant was right in insisting that authentic morality is a matter not just of behavior (doing the morally appropriate thing) but also of motivation (doing so for morally appropriate reasons, among which self-advantage assuredly does not figure).

Such a position aligns closely with that which Plato ascribes to Socrates in the *Republic*: that being unjust and immoral—regardless of what immediate benefits it may yield—is always ultimately disadvantageous because of the damage it does to our character (or *psyche*) by making us into the sort of person we ourselves cannot really respect.[7] ("What profiteth it a man if he should gain the whole world, but lose his own soul?") On such a view, it is not the case that the rationale of morality consists in its *rewards*—either intrinsic ("virtue is its own reward") or prudential. The justificatory impetus is of a very different sort. We should be moral not because of its benefits for what we *have*, but because of its benefits for what we *are*—the sort of creature we can then appropriately see ourselves as being.[8]

THE END OF THE LINE: THE DEMANDS OF PERSONHOOD

Hume may well be right: perhaps the universe does not care about us.[9] But this, of course, is no reason why *we* should not care about ourselves—or about the universe, for that matter.

Accordingly, morality and rational self-interest can and should live in peaceful coexistence. For morality itself has a perfectly sound rationale, via the argument:

> The intelligent cultivation of one's *real* self-interest is quintessentially rational.
> Given that we are free rational agents, it is to our real self-interest to act morally—even when doing so goes against our immediate selfish desires.
> *Therefore*: It is rational to be moral.

The *rational* person will thus also be morally good—conscientious, compassionate, kind, and so on—because his own real and best interests are served thereby. He has a real and sizeable personal stake in maintaining the worth and dignity of rational agents. For in trampling the just claims of other rational agents underfoot, we undermine the very factor on which our own claim to value and consideration is ultimately based.

Morality, in other words, is a part of rationality and specifically of practical and thus judgmental/evaluative rationality. In failing to care for your real interests you are being irrational, but by way of poor judgment rather than poor inferential reasoning. An immoral person errs, not (necessarily) in *calculation* but certainly in *evaluation*, in failing to assess at their proper value the ends that people ought (metaphysically or otherwise) to set for themselves. And so whether or not you actually care about your best interests, you ought (qua rational agent) to care about them as a matter of your ontological obligations. The point is best put in normative terms: every rational (reason-possessing) creature *should* and every fully reason-exercising creature *does* have such a tendency toward realizing its opportunities for the good. This normative impetus creates the bridge leading from rationality to morality and grounds the deontological force of appropriate moral injunctions in an ontological aspect of the human condition, namely, in our self-claimed (and self-image essential) status as free rational agents.[10]

The fundamental injunction of rationality is this:

[Insofar as possible] do the best you can to realize your opportunities for the good.

Making the most and best that one can realistically manage in the circumstances is what rationality demands of those who fall within its purview. It is the rational thing to do. And in view of our ontological status as rationality-purporting beings, this fundamental obligation is incumbent upon us, like it or not. It means that in matters of inquiry we should seek the actual truth, and in matters of action the authentically beneficial. Whether or not we succeed in these projects is certainly not up to us. But what is up to us as salient beings is to make the effort.

One of the corollaries that flow from this basic imperative is a commitment to the effort to produce the best version of oneself that is practicable in the circumstances. And all the rest of our obligations follow from this. The exchange at issue runs as follows: "Why is it that I stand obligated to do *X*?" The answer: "If I failed to so do—or at least to try to do so—then I would not be the person I ought to be as a rational being who endeavors to make the most and best of himself."

But is this in fact the end of the line? Or is there some other, yet more fundamental principle in which the mandate of rationality itself is encompassed?

But what further consideration could possibly validate the injunction "Be rational in how you act: try to do what is rationally appropriate: heed the 'voice of reason'"? The answer is that there just is nothing further. The only thing that could possibly be asked for here is a rationally cogent answer. When this question is posed, it is too late, and the commitment to rationality has already been acknowledged. Rationality is self-justifying. It is the end of the line. And morality is part and parcel of it.

Only someone who mistakenly thinks that selfish reasons alone can qualify as good reasons can see an irreconcilable conflict between morality and rationality. And this would indeed be a gross mistake. For a rational commitment to morality inheres in the (ontologically mediated) circumstance that other-concerned reasons for action constitute perfectly good *rational* reasons because of their unseverable link to the real interests of the agent himself. The coordination of morality with rationality is established through the fact that the *intelligent* thing to do and the *right* thing to do will ultimately agree, because acting morally *is* the intelligent thing to do for those who have a proper concern for their real self-interest. There is nothing irrational about being moral, and there is nothing imprudent about it either, as long as we understand "true prudence" aright. However, this is emphatically not to say that the validation of morality should be sought in its consonance with prudence. Prudential gain is merely a collateral benefit of the moral propriety of doing what is right and proper, and neither is or should be its rationale.[11]

Chapter 15

THE METAPHYSICS OF
MORAL OBLIGATION

IS OBLIGATION ALWAYS CONTRACTUAL?

Philosophers often maintain that our obligations toward others are grounded in a tacit agreement of some sort. And they incline to the idea that this agreement is something that those obligated have entered upon voluntarily. The obligations of a husband to his wife or a sea captain toward his passengers are seen as paradigmatic models.

In fact, however, there is no neat fit between obligation and contract-making, and adjustments of doctrine will have to be made accordingly. Parents have not made an agreement with their children, nor has the bus driver made an agreement with the passengers. So here the agreement might be seen as inherent in and derivative from other agreements that have been made. However, even this step from overt to implicitly derivable agreements does not quite do the job. For what about the obligations of children to parents or of a citizen to his fellow citizens and their common country? At this point, many philosophers have resorted to the ingenious idea of a fictional social contract. The idea is that by affiliation to a society and by participation in its system of polity, an individual subscribes to a tacit agreement of sorts. And in this way, the initial idea of obligation via agreement has been extended by moving from explicit agreements to derivative and tacitly implicit agreements.

The aim of the present discussion, however, is to maintain that even this approach is not adequate to the task at hand because it leaves out of account obligations that have nothing to do with voluntarily actual contracts of agreements, be they formal or informal, basic or derivative, explicit or tacit. For it must be acknowledged that certain obligations are wholly nonconsensual and entirely involuntary.

Some clear examples of obligations toward others that do not fit the contractual-origination models are:

- people's obligations to siblings
- people's obligations toward their neighbors
- people's obligations to their fellows in need
- people's obligations toward their posterity and future generations
- people's obligations toward animals

The first of these, inherent in the age-old question "Am I my brother's keeper?," is typical here. But perhaps the principal category of involuntary obligations consists of those inherent in the acknowledgment of due gratitude for unasked-for but needed benefits. Typical cases of such noncontractually responsive obligations are the obligations of children to parents, victims to rescuers, and, generally, beneficiaries to benefactors. This sort of obligation, issuing from reciprocity/gratitude, can be owed not just to known individuals but to unknown benefactors as well—and not only to persons but also to institutions (such as public hospitals or the emergency services).

Or again, consider our obligation "to take care of ourselves" and not become a problem for or burden to others. It would clearly be an unrealistic flight of fancy to see this as a matter of some sort of quasi-compactual agreement with our fellows. We are doubtless obligated "to do unto others as we would have them do unto us." But this is clearly not a matter of some sort of negotiated understanding.

In such cases the agreement-origination model does not fit for one reason or another—in particular because the aspect of voluntary agreement is entirely absent. A different account is required, and distinct factors are at issue here. For in such cases there is no *making* an obligation-engendering commitment to others, but only a matter of *having* a commitment on account of one's relational connection to them. It is a matter not of what one *does* but of what one *is*: a brother, a neighbor, a fellow pas-senger, or some such. As expressed by the dictum *noblesse oblige*, it is one's condition in relation to other persons or factors, rather than one's agree-ments, that grounds obligations of the sort now at issue.

The point is simply that there are two distinct routes to obligations toward others:

- the *contractual*, which results from and inheres in making an agree-ment regarding the interests of people
- the *relational*, resulting from and inherent in having a certain rela-tionship of affinity toward others

In both cases, obligation is rooted in a connectivity to other people, be it by some sort of agreement or compact, or through a natural rather than artificial linkage.

Valid obligation is grounded in general principles. If it is appropriate for Smith to be grateful to Jones for doing A, then it is also appropriate for anyone (x) to be grateful to another (y) for doing what is, *mutatis mutandis*, the same sort of thing. And this holds for both contractual and relational, or situational, obligations.

But how do such relations go about creating duties and obligations?

With contractual matters, obligation issues from the universally ap-propriate basic principle that people have an obligation (duty and respon-sibility) to keep their promises and honor their agreements; they *ought*. Is there anything comparable on the side of the relational obligations that inhere in situational affinity?

Indeed there is. For people also have an obligation to acknowledge the responsibilities and to discharge the duties inherent in their place in the world's scheme of things. In being related to others in certain modes of affinity, we thereby incur the obligations inherent in this relationship.

A somewhat desperate last-ditch effort might be made to contractu-alize all obligations. It leads to the idea of a cosmic supercompact—a deal with reality at large. On this line of thought, I accept the validity of my noncontractual obligations because when others do so, I myself become a potential beneficiary. We thus all become caught up together in one vast mutual aid arrangement, a massive fiction based on the idea that I might be (or might have been) the brother who profits, the future individual who benefits, perhaps even the animal that is spared pain or worse. But if the contract model can be rescued only by so massive an exercise of disbelief, it hardly remains worth saving.

It is clear that the rationale for honoring relational/situational obligations will be different from that for contractual obligations. The latter fall under the rule that agreements must be kept—that when one binds oneself to doing something, one is honor- and duty-bound to keep one's word.

Contractual obligation pivots on the interests of others; relational obligations, however, pivot on our own best and true interests. Their binding force inheres in what deserves to be seen as the ultimate human imperative of self-optimization, of realizing oneself as a human being and achieving the real and true benefit, that is, of realizing one's potential for being what one should be: a decent and honorable human being. The root of the matter is ontological rather than contractual: it pivots on what we *are* rather than on something we explicitly *do*. One has only a single life at one's disposal, and realizing the opportunities for the good that this resource affords us is the paramount obligation that we have in this world. And this imperative is the ultimate basis for all of the other obligations that are incumbent upon us.

The ultimate basis of our situational obligations is thus ontological. As indicated above, it inheres in the nature of our place within the world. Once we enter this world, we incur, like it or not, willy-nilly, the obligation to make the best and the most of the opportunities for the good that such existence affords us. And this obligation to self-optimization underlies a vast host of others. To be sure, this obligation—like any other—is one that we may thoughtlessly ignore or willingly reject. But that fact, of course, does not undo its status as an obligation.

DOES OUGHT IMPLY CAN?

In addition to the *ought of obligation*, there is also the *ought of idealization*. Here, *ought* certainly does not imply practicable possibility. There ought to be—and ideally would be—no injustice, no unmerited suffering, no poverty, and no toothaches in the world. But realistically, this state of affairs simply cannot be. Ideally, all children ought to be healthy, happy, and well-mannered, but this is little more than an impossible pipe-dream.

The *ought* of idealization simply does not imply the *can* of realizable possibility. And of course the *ought* of obligation and duty is something else again.

Ethical theorists since Immanuel Kant have commonly held that "ought implies can." And of course if this is true, then by contraposition, "cannot implies need not"—what is not possible cannot be required. The limits of possibility set limits to obligation, and ethics in general conforms to the Roman legal dictum, *ultra posse nemo obligatur*.

But is it really true that impossibility absolves one from an obligation? In deliberating about this issue, the first thing is to look closely at the idea of incapacity at issue in that "cannot." There can be very different sorts of reasons why someone cannot do something:

(1) reasons of *logical* impossibility (e.g., demonstrably one cannot square the circle)
(2) reasons of *physical* impossibility (e.g., one cannot squeeze blood from a turnip)
(3) reasons of *situational* impossibility (e.g., one cannot keep secret something that has already been revealed)

The crucial issue for obligation lies in the question of why the impossibility at issue obtains. Clearly, what is logically impossible cannot plausibly be deemed obligatory. But with other modes of impossibility a crucial question of rationale arises. If something becomes physically or situationally impossible due to the agent's own manipulation, then obligation is still very much upon the scene. It does not undo my obligation—and accordingly remove blame for defaulting—if I am unable to repay my debt to you because I have become impoverished by betting on the ponies.

The salient point is that a moral *ought* does not entail an implementational *can* because people's duties can outrun the practicalities of implementation. I ought to be able to discharge all of my duties and meet all of my obligations, but the circumstances of limited time and resources may prevent this. And when this occurs—and does so entirely for reasons above and beyond my control—I am absolved from the requirement of meeting those obligations.

But even here there are problems and complications. Suppose that I owe $100 to each of Smith and Jones under an agreement to make repayment at a certain time. En route to the place of repayment with my entire fortune of $200, I am mugged and the villains make off with $100. I now can meet one of my obligations, but I simply cannot (for reasons outside my control) meet both of them, Here, *ought* certainly does not imply *can*. (Nor yet does the *can* for each and any imply the *can* of all and every.)

This repayment example carries a significant lesson with regard to the idea of what *can* be done. On the one side is the *distributive can* of performance over a certain range of possibilities, where each and every one is *individually* realizable. On the other is the *collective can* over the range, where the totality of alternatives is *concurrently* realizable. And it must be stressed that even if you can fulfill your obligations individually and distributively, you may yet be unable to do so conjointly and collectively—though of course you clearly *ought* to do so. And then, you are in default of obligation, by definition, as it were.

It deserves to be stressed that (1) a deliberate and avoidable failure to honor a contractual obligation and (2) a deliberate and avoidable default in matters of positivity realization are both alike in that they are not just unfortunate and regrettable but actually inappropriate and reprehensible. Throughout, failure deserves not just pity but censure: we have to do not only with unhappy negativities but with outright wrongs. These two modes of default, however, are independent and detached. The former does not absorb the latter owing to some sort of contract with reality. Nor does the latter absorb the former because of some inherent positivity of contract fulfillment.

One concluding observation is in order. The present deliberations cry out for a comment on methodology relating to the role of distinctions. For the considerations canvassed above do—or should—make clear that a sensible treatment of the ought/can problem will depend on a manifold of critical distinctions, specifically those between

- the logical, physical , and situational sense of *can* (i.e., different modes of possibilities)
- the *ought* of idealization and the *ought* of obligation
- the *distributive* and the *collective* modes of multiple obligation

Without careful attention to these distinctions, there is no way to rescue the problem of the ought/can relationship from incomprehensibility.

WHAT VALIDATES ETHICAL INJUNCTIONS?

How can an ethical claim—or for that matter any philosophical contention—be validated?

There are basically two ways, based on what comes before or what goes after, that is: (1) by inferential *derivation* from other, already preestablished claims; and (2) by *consequentiation* either in the positive mode (acceptance conduces to the realization of advantages) or in the negative mode (acceptance averts disadvantages). Only consequentiation affords a way of getting started: on the positive side it looks to the cognitive gains of acceptance, and on the negative side to the losses sustained through non-acceptance.

Against this background it is clear that ethical injunctions, in the final analysis, must be validated by consequentiation.

Like most areas of human endeavor, ethics and morality constitute a functional enterprise that has a purposive reason for being. The aim is to make human actions systemically congenial—to channel actions into modes that are generally beneficial and advantageous. And accordingly, the validation of an ethical injunction will pivot on the extent to which the mode of action it enjoins conduces to the general benefit.

This issue of benefit leads to the question of just what it is that conduces to the realization of human interests. The issue of benefit and positivity now comes to the forefront. Exactly where do those "best interests" and "authentic positivities" characteristic of the human condition lie? The answer is provided by what may be characterized as an *unquestionably positive* aspect of the human condition. Thus consider such factors as

- *health*   in contrast to   *illness*
- *happiness*   in contrast to   *unhappiness*
- *well being*   in contrast to   *misery*
- *understanding* in contrast to   *confusion*
- *contentment*   in contrast to   *discontent*
- *joy*   in contrast to   *distress*

All of the factors in the first column are unquestionably positive, and their contraries unquestionably negative. The desirability and advantages of these conditions may or may not be self-evident, but they are in any event undeniable. Their positivity is a matter of elemental common sense, and their denial would be a matter of patent absurdity.

Consider a contention on the order of "Health is an unquestionable positivity and, with other things anything like equal, is categorically preferable to illness." The point is not that such a contention does not admit of some sort of demonstration, but rather that it does not require any demonstration. It is not that demonstration is altogether impossible, but rather that it is altogether unnecessary. The thesis at issue is probatively patent: in an augment for its tenability, no premise could be more obvious and acceptable than the thesis itself. Such contentions are not self-evident, but nevertheless evidence can be dispensed with.

With these considerations in view, we can now turn to the question before us. How can we validate our ethical claims for the appropriateness of truth-telling or promise-honoring? Is the validation simply that people generally favor such practices, or is something deeper and more objectively grounded at stake?

Even to pose this question clearly is virtually to answer it. Ethics is not a matter of "the customs of the tribe": morals are not mores. Ethical comportment has a rationale—a rational basis of validation. Insofar as ethical claims are valid, they achieve their validity via considerations of efficacy in fostering the best interests of the community at large and thereby of the individuals that constitute that community. They are validated through promoting conditions of life that conduce to people's best interests in realizing the unquestionable positivities of the human condition.

The validation at issue is accordingly not so much logical as teleological: it is grounded not just in general principles but in considerations of functional efficacy. It lies in the very nature of the idea of ethics as a functional enterprise designed for the realization of certain objectives— objectives whose legitimacy and appropriateness as such are inherent in the very nature of the benefits at stake.

To be sure, it is one thing to identify what the injunctions of ethics and morality are, and quite another to determine why it is that we should obey them (and this is itself a dual question in asking not just why it is *advantageous* to do so—if indeed it is—but also why it is *obligatory* to do so). But all of these issues, although different, have to harmonize. And in the end, both the advantages of moral comportment and its obligatory nature lie in our best (real and true) interests individually and collectively.

But ethical norms often require us to do something that goes against the grain. Is it ever rational to do something one does not want to do? At first glance, the answer looks to be an obvious yes. We are constantly doing things that we would rather not do: go to the dentist, pay taxes, take out the garbage.

But a clever critic might say that for such things, the statement that we don't want to do them is really only a surface disclaimer. Deep down, we really do want to do all those things, exactly because we want to avert the even more unwelcome alternatives: serious tooth issues later on, dealing with IRS offenses in court, living with piles of rotting garbage. The things we actually do—even under duress—are things we ultimately want to do because they avert yet more unpleasant developments.

And so the lesson seems to be that the things we actually and actively do (unlike tripping on a banana peel, which is not something we do but rather something that happens to us) are all things that we ultimately want and choose to do. They may not be done *gladly*, but they are nevertheless done *voluntarily*, because in the final analysis we choose to do them, however forced that choice may be.

But now comes the tricky bit. Consider such plausible contentions as:

All voluntary actions are want-driven.
All of our choices issue from wants.

Supposing that such claims are indeed true, what is it that makes them so? Just what is the linkage between volition and wants?

Clearly the above theses are not *logico-conceptual* truths, whose status as such inheres in the meaning of the terms "voluntary," "authentic choice," "want-determinants," "want-driven," and the like—that is, they are not *semantical* truths based on the established usage of terms (as in "forks have tines"). Nor are they *empirical* truths, for example, based on opinion surveys of how people respond. Rather, like the ethical injunctions contemplated at the start of this section, their validation lies in the consideration of what is incontestably in our best and real interests as the sort of beings we are. For *appropriate* decisions and choices go in the direction of what we *should* (albeit not necessarily *do*) want, while our *actual* decisions and choices may well be entirely detached from what we desire or want under the pressure of extreme circumstances.

Chapter 16

EMPATHY, SHARED EXPERIENCE, AND OTHER MINDS

TYPE-AFFILIATION AS THE BASIS OF EMPATHY

Our natural human capacity for taxonomic type-affiliation with others is the basis of an empathy grounded in the apprehension of kind-kinship. For in accepting suitable others as our type-mates—as we all readily do—one imputes to them a manifold of attributes and capacities that one takes oneself to possess. Once that classification is in place, there is no question of further evidence for their type-characteristic features and capacities—all this "comes with the territory." A particularly important instance of such taxonomic affiliation is the ability to see others as being "of our own sort," to view others as conjoined with us in the nature-engendered family of human beings.

A sense of affinity and affiliation is a reaction we already have in relation to domesticated animals but which is far more powerful in relation to other members of our species. We have a keen sense of "identification" with them and naturally endow them with the same sorts of cognitive and affective capacities we experience in ourselves. (Think here of the I-thou relationship that lies at the core of Martin Buber's anthropology.) When you flinch with pain or cry for joy, then, seeing myself as your partner and type-mate, I can not only *think* "If that were me, I would be hurting (or joyful)" but can actually to some extent be pained (or happy) myself. I can not only think about your joy or pain but participatorily share in it. Thus, on the line of thought being unfolded here, the expression "I feel your pain" is not really a contradiction in terms.

The capacity to group things into kinds is a basic human talent without which we could not exist as intelligent beings who guide their actions by thought. For an intelligent creature determines its action on the basis of its beliefs and objectives (needs and wants). And it cannot so guide its present actions without resort to classificatory grouping that assimilates present situations to those encountered in past experience. Without the capacity to sort and to group into kinds, such an agent would become immobilized. Unable to meet the conditions for evolutionary survival, it simply could not come into existence or reproduce itself.

Even property attribution is itself a mode of taxonomic-kind apprehension. When I say that this grass is green or this liquid has a pungent odor, I in effect classify the item at issue (the color of the grass or the odor of the liquid) in a way that assimilates it to other kindred experiences.

Such sorting or classifying is pervasive: Taxonomic talent—the capacity to class things into kinds—is an innate human endowment. Even small children do not take long to learn to sort things into natural kinds— and even when these things are substantially dissimilar, like the various species of dogs or birds.

To belong to a kind is to function as things of this kind do. To be a duck is to swim, waddle, and quack like a duck. Things of a given kind behave alike in being able to do the sorts of things characteristic of their kind. This holds for ducks and elm trees and iron ore; and it holds for people as well. And especially notable and significant in this regard is that the capacity for self-classification—for classing oneself as a human being along with others—is one of our most salient classification capacities.

This sorting capacity is not learned but innate, a gift of evolution. The basic idea at work here was marked accordingly by C. S. Peirce, for whom the validation of human cognition lies in the fact that under the pressure of evolutionary forces, the human mind has come to be "co-natured" with physical reality:

> It is certain that the only hope of retroductive reasoning ever reaching the truth is that there may be some natural tendency toward an

agreement between the ideas which suggest themselves to the human mind and those which are concerned in the laws of nature.[1]

We shall do better to abandon the whole attempt to learn the truth, however urgent may be our need of ascertaining it, unless we can trust to the human mind's having such a power of guessing right that before very many hypotheses shall have been tried, intelligent guessing may be expected to lead us to the one which will support all tests, leaving the vast majority of possible hypotheses unexamined.[2]

And this capacity is not super- or supra-natural but must be seen from a naturalistic standpoint as a gift of evolution—as part of the unfolding development of the mental rudiments of beings of our sort. It is simply yet another aspect of the kind-distinguishing capacity without which we intelligent agents could not function.

The commonality at issue is not something learned by inductive reasoning but rather a sympathetic coordination based on the apprehension of type-commonality: the kind-affiliation in question is—or at any rate can be—noninductively immediate. When you see the letter A in print here, you do not infer that it is a letter A from the apparent character of the lines involved; instead you apprehend it immediately in the experience of seeing it. And some sort of immediacy is also at work in apprehending the thought—and thereby the mediating—of others. I do not infer that you have a mind; I apprehend it directly in my experiential interactions with you.

The immediacy of type-affiliation apprehension reflects the fact that this apprehension is not a product of induction but a prerequisite for it. For inductive reasonings are standardly designed to establish generalizations of the form "All items of kind K have the feature F" and to draw such conclusions from particular cases, as per the argument:

Many items of kind K have been determined to have the feature F.
No instance of a kind K item without the feature F has as yet even been encountered.
Therefore: All items of kind K have the feature F.

But this sort of reasoning always presupposes the feasibility of sorting by kind. If such sorting into natural kinds were not noninductively obtainable, then induction itself would become impracticable and scientific understanding would be immobilized.

Without taxonomic type-groupings, any sort of rational explanation of phenomena would become impossible. For explanation is by its very nature subsumptive. Explaining why *this* elm sheds its leaves in the autumn is achieved by identifying some features of it such that all or nearly all things that have this feature are comparably deciduous. The classificatory demands of any such explanatory project are evident.

TYPE-AFFILIATION AMONG HUMANS BY
NONINDUCTIVE IMMEDIACY

We do not learn by inference from observations that our fellow humans are mind-endowed people, who have beliefs and feelings and come equipped with the full spectrum of mental capabilities that we experience in ourselves. This knowledge comes, rather, via the capacity for the direct taxonomic apprehension of natural kinds. That you are an intelligent being reading a novel to keep boredom at bay is not something I infer from your behavior. On the contrary, I interpret your behavior on the basis of a preconceived supposition that you are an intelligent being functioning to keep boredom at bay. It is not because I realize that you too have thoughts and feelings that I credit you with a mind. It is because I acknowledge that you have a mind that I credit you with thoughts and feelings.

In understanding other people, we do not move indirectly from the nature of observed actions to a conjectural mentality, but rather from a postulated and presupposed mentality to the nature of observed actions. The inferential picture of mind puts the cart before the horse. The real picture is not inferential but presuppositional. Accordingly, when I accept others as type-mates, I postulate that we share a functional commonality in respect to object-typical modes of comportment—assuming from the very outset that we all can and do perform the standard range of type-characteristic things. I do not require further evidence to substantiate this—I presume it from the very outset, when the type classification is made. And this type-affiliation is of course a matter of reciprocity. In classing myself with others, I class them with me. Naturally, and without the least hesitation, I group myself with those others as constituting a special kind of being—a human person. And this is automatically a matter of reciprocity and recognizance—I am like them, they are like me.

How is it that I have unqualified assurance of other minds? We clearly do not have unmediated observational insight into the thoughts and feelings of others. Their outer expressions in talking or their gestures or facial contortions provide an observational basis for what I know. However, I do not proceed by inductive reasoning from observational data. The joy or sorrow you feel is something I may be able to apprehend directly within your various expressions. As with the example given above of seeing the letter *A*, when I look at a printed word like *CAT*, I see its meaning directly; I do not infer it from an examination of shapes. The investment I place on such physical manifestations is a matter of direct and immediate apprehension. And this also holds in the case of my observation of your talk or gestures or facial movement. In both cases alike, of reading text and of "reading" people, we have a cognitive capacity for immediate symbolic insight into the significance of observational experience, which is the product of the evolutionary development of intelligence. In observing *CAT*, we realize (immediately and inferentially) that it symbolically betokens the correlative sort of animal. And in looking at your agonized expression when injured, we realize (immediately and inferentially) that it betokens the correlative sort of (painful) feeling.

When I look at a *3*, I do not see an ink configuration but a number. When I see you wince, I see not a bodily contraction but a pain experience. When I see you cry, I directly apprehend your dismay; in hearing you laugh, I directly feel your gleefulness. I apprehend—immediately and noninferentially—what you feel in the circumstances. I do (or at least can) immediately share your feelings in such cases.

To be sure, it would be possible for me to reason

You are crying.
Whenever I cry, I am dismayed about something.
You are like me in the relevant ways.
Therefore: You are dismayed about something.

But while I could indeed reason in this way to reach that conclusion, I certainly *need* not do so. The pathway can be one of immediate apprehension rather than inference.

Seeing is a matter of seeing-as, and the "as" at issue can be either descriptive/taxonomic or affective. In neither case need the conclusion be reached by a mediating inference.

If it were otherwise, we could in fact be embarked upon an infinite regress. For consider the inference:

> You exhibit feature F.
> Anyone who exhibits F will meet condition C.
> *Therefore*: You meet condition C.

But what of that initial premise? How are we to come by it? Would this also require a mediating influence, as in the following?

> You exhibit feature G.
> Anyone who exhibits G will meet the condition of F-exhibition.
> *Therefore*: You meet the condition of F-exhibition.

If it did, we would embark on an infinite regress. And so a premise of that initial sort must be available directly. And this obtains whether the feature is descriptive or classificatory or affective.

Contrast the line of thought at issue in the statement

(1) He has mental experiences like mine, therefore I must acknowledge him as a fellow intelligent being.

The fact is that I could not realize the antecedent of (1) without presupposing its consequent. In practice we have to operate instead with:

(2) I must acknowledge him as a fully intelligent being, therefore I can claim that he too has mental experiences like mine.

We certainly cannot get by with inferential reasoning alone. For all our reasoning has to proceed via language use, and language is something that has to be learned through observational experience. —It does not and cannot come to us through reasoning. If one does not accept people with informative intent—and thus with minds, thoughts, and intentions—language acquisition becomes impossible.

FROM AFFINITY TO EMPATHY

In order to come to grips with "the problem of other minds," one must understand the terms and concepts by whose means alone the problem can be posed. At this stage, however, one already has the answer to it.

It is natural and, as it were, automatic that I would accept you as an intelligent being of my own sort, and vice versa. But am I right in doing so? Is what I take to be the case here really true? Not only is it ingenuous to raise this question but it is foolish. For at this point, what I should be asking for is not evidence for a presumptive fact (that other minds exist) but rather for validation of a practice of presumption (that they do). And what validates this practice is exactly the sort of thing that validates any practice, namely, that its condition leads to success in our endeavors. The proof of the pudding here lies not in the making but in the eating.

Cognitive acceptance can properly be based on utility. We need or want an issue to be resolved, and we accept a resolution that answers to our purposes provided that no direct counterevidence speaks against it. Acceptance is here based on trust: trust in our fellows, our sensory facilities, our instruments.

There are two pathways to the rational acceptance of propositions. In either case the contentions we accept make factual claims. But the warranting credentials for acceptance are substantially different. The one is cognitive and evidential, the other pragmatic and prudential. The expert's basis for his or her claims is of the former sort; our basis for accepting them is of the latter sort.

In both cases there are claims to truth: acceptance and truth are interconnected. But in the one (cognitive) case, we deem the contention acceptable because we think it to be true. In the other (prudential) case, we think it to be true because we deem it acceptable. In both cases alike, acceptance and truth are seen as linked, but the basis of the linkage is effectively reversed. In the cognitive case truth is the independent variable and acceptance the dependent variable; in the pragmatic case the situation is reversed.

I cannot tell you what is true independently of what I think to be so. Of course, I cannot establish the equivalence

What I take to be true about something = the actual truth of the matter

From an evidential point of view, this equivalence only holds most of the time, and I cannot insist on its tenability in the particular case before us. Yet I have no real choice but to accept it as fact. And in the nature of the case, this acceptance is pragmatic and not evidential.

The line of thought at work in these deliberations is constituted by a stepwise cascade of conceptual transitions along the following lines:

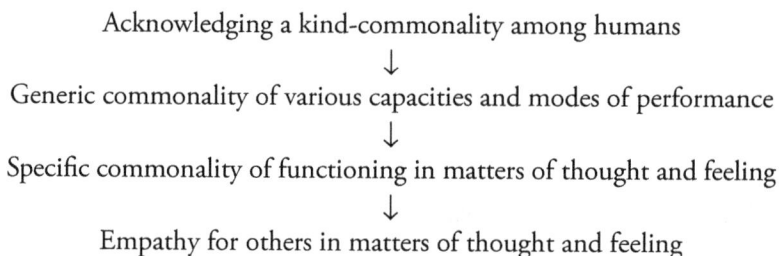

Acknowledging a kind-commonality among humans
↓
Generic commonality of various capacities and modes of performance
↓
Specific commonality of functioning in matters of thought and feeling
↓
Empathy for others in matters of thought and feeling

The stepwise transit illustrated here moves from a cognitive acknowledgment (kind commonality) to an affective performance (shared empathetic performance). At the top we "identify with" others in points of taxonomic classification, and at the bottom we "identify with them" in their manifestations of cognitive acknowledgment and affective emotion.

Although this cascade has been described as a transition from thought to feeling, this description actually confuses the situation somewhat, because the idea of a separation of thought and feeling is somewhat unrealistic. The two are inseparately intertwined in a single process. One cannot think of certain occurrences (a lost opportunity, say) without feeling pleased or dismayed. Often the two (thought/feeling) are aspects of a single unified experience. In these matters an affective feeling stands in inherent coordination with a given thought.

SHARED EXPERIENCE

Imputing to others the same kind of mental operations we experience in ourselves is the crux of empathy. In exercising this practice, we ascribe to others various kinds of our own mind-involving operations (having beliefs, distrust, annoyance, dislike, etc.) in consequence of their verbal or other behavior (facial contortions, tone of voice, gestures, and the like). Throughout, we take such overt manifestations to be expressions of what others think.

There is nothing mysterious or supernatural about empathy. Its basis in our developed talent for the apprehension of kinship is as much a product of evolutionary development as is our talent for the exercise of other modes of intelligence—language, say, or arithmetic. It issues from the developed understanding that "this is how beings of my/our sort behave."

Empathy between persons, accordingly, involves two components: (1) having the same thoughts or feelings about something that another individual also has, and (2) accepting this as being the case, out of a recognition that the other person must do so too. Empathy thus requires a certain degree of sympathy. However, one can empathize not only with people but with other creatures as well. As Jeremy Bentham insisted, the principal question is not, Can other creatures reason? but rather, Can they suffer?

In matters of empathy—both of cognitions or affections—the stance I take is effectively that of answering the question "What would I feel (or think) if I were in your shoes?" But the pathway to this distinction is homogenous with the matter at issue: with respect to cognitive matters of belief it is the path of ratiocination, but with regard to matters of feeling it is the path of affective sympathy. There is no disharmony here: I do not think my way into feelings, nor do I feel my way into convictions. The thematic homogeneity at issue means that empathy is a two-track process.

Suppose you see a person or even an animal who is injured and obviously in pain. You then do not only see *that* the victim is suffering, you see and indeed to some extent emphatically feel this suffering. And it is no longer just this creature's suffering; the painfulness is no longer just the victim's because you to some extent share it. It is present not just in your thought but in your feelings: you do not merely "know how he feels" but in some degree you share his feelings. This degree of sharing can become so acute as to be almost unbearable. The realization that you are not dealing with a mechanism—an automaton—but a being who is mind-equipped, at least to the extent of having some thoughts and feelings, is in such circumstances the only available option. And its basis lies not in some sort of inferentially mediated inducting but in the immediacy of affective experience. When I see you suffering, I actually share your agony to some degree.

EXPERIENTIAL ACCESS AND "INTERIORITY"

Granted, I cannot feel *your* sorrow or your pain. But then I cannot own *your* umbrella, either, for were I to do so it would not be *your* umbrella. To be sure, I could get to own the same umbrella that was once yours. And there is no reason why I could not feel sorrow that is exactly the same as that which you once did. (Of course, the sorrow would not be *physically* the same—sorrow isn't that kind of thing. But it could certainly be *descriptively* the same throughout the range of our communication. It is, in fact, exactly this sort of thing that is at issue with the common expression "I feel your pain.")

All experience is personal and, as it were, owned: it must be somebody's experience. Many philosophers have been entranced by the idea of a unique access to experience. They make much of the idea of the "interiority" inherent in the fact that my experience is accessible to me alone, since you cannot have *my* experiences. However, the limitation at issue is not unique to experience. Thus consider the distinction between my ownership of a rug and the rug itself. My ownership of the rug is unique to me; unlike the rug itself, it is something I cannot transfer to you—were I to do so, it would no longer be my ownership that is at issue. And similarly with my thoughts of something. I cannot transfer to you my thoughts of the Eiffel Tower, though in principle you can certainly come to share everything and anything that I think of the Eiffel Tower.

In general, we have to distinguish between what is done and the doing of it. You too can guarantee something that I guarantee, or write something that I write. But you cannot produce my guarantee of it or my writing of it. My producing something (a declaration, say) is inalienably mine, but the producing of it is something someone else can do as well.

But in this regard experience is like thought. You cannot think my thinking, but you can certainly think as I do. And analogously, while you cannot suffer my sea-sickness, you certainly can—if you have ever been sea-sick yourself—also experience what it is that I am experiencing when I am sea-sick. You cannot feel my feelings, but you can certainly have the same feelings about things that I do.

You cannot believe *my* believings or recall *my* recollectings, but that does not mean that you cannot share my beliefs or my recollections. Exclusivity of acting does not carry exclusivity of action in its wake. What it is that I believe or recollect is available to you as well. And the same is true of what I experience.

Just as you too can have a bite of my apple but cannot have my biting of it, so also you too can have the headache or the heartache from which I suffer but cannot have my suffering of it. But this is not so because of the aches at issue, but rather because they are explicitly *my* aches. My ownership of my feelings is not a deep fact about these feelings but only a surface feature of the grammar of ownership. You cannot sign another person's signature, for if you forge it, it is no longer his. You cannot own another person's farm, for when you buy it it is no longer his. When another person has a headache or toothache, you too can have a headache or toothache of precisely the same nature, but of course it is then yours, not his. But that is just how ownership works all of the time. "Interiority" is not a feature of one's experience; it is an artifact of ownership. My belief in Aristotle's intelligence or in Kant's honesty are inherently mine: I cannot turn them over to you. But there is nothing exclusive about these beliefs; you too can have exactly the same beliefs.

There is no significant "interiority" here, but only a linguistic deficit—a failure to draw the due distinction between what it is that is done by me and my doing of it. What is personal is the action (the performing) but not the acting (the performance).

And so, the answer to the question whether I can have your thoughts or your feelings can only be reached on the basis of disambiguation. For on the one hand, I certainly cannot manage to do your feeling or your thinking. But this does not mean—and must not be construed as meaning—that I cannot think what you think or feel what you feel. I cannot perform your acts, but I can act as you do.

Experience has two aspects. There is the *informative* aspect of what is experienced (the roar of the engine) and the *affective* aspect of the experiencing of it (the apprehending of that roar). The latter alone is a matter of interiority—it alone is a matter of personal possession. Usually, and in general, the former is something accessible to many. It is thus important not to conflate these two aspects. The fact that the experience is mine does nothing to establish the exclusivity of what is experienced. The idea of the interiority of experience is built on a house of cards, in that it is based on a confusion—a failure to heed due distinctions—between a certain relationship to an object and the object itself, between the experiencing and what is experienced. Different people can have the same experiences: what they cannot do is to have the same experiencings. Experiencing is clearly a matter of exclusivity: only I can have *my* experiences.

For that which is experienced—the content of the experience—is in principle public. One has to heed the distinction between *privileged* (i.e., ready and unalienable) access to the substance of one's experiences and *exclusive* access. The former clearly affords no ground for postulating the latter. But this is no reason for denying that you too can experience what I do as I experience it.

Of course, I have easier access to my experiences than you do. Indeed there may be aspects of my experiences that you will never learn unless I tell you about them. But ease of access does not entail exclusivity. And there is nothing about my experiences that you cannot in principle come to know. The fact that the experiencings are mine does not make what is experienced so—any more than the fact that the recollections are mine means that what is recollected is so.

There clearly is a crucial difference between privileged access to experience and exclusive access. No doubt the individual who actually *has* a certain experience enjoys privileged access—ready and unmediated access—to its nature. But this does not mean that there is ever a single feature of it that is exclusive and unavailable to others. There is nothing about the substance of my experience in which you cannot in principle share: you too can experience the same anger or surprise at certain developments that I do. The *experiencings* are, to be sure, different, but the *experiences* are not.

You cannot have my stutter, but you can stutter as I do. You cannot have my headache, but you can suffer as I do. You can recite the same poem I do, but of course you cannot give my recital of it. And experiencing is in the same boat. The experiencing of something (say a thunderclap) can be done by many, though each person's experience belongs unquestionably to the individual. My experiencing is mine, and you cannot have it. You too can have an aversion to spiders, but you cannot have my aversion to them. You can have my dislikes but not my dislikings.

There is nothing deep and portentous about the "interiority" of my experiences any more than there is about the "interiority" of my physical possessions. In either case, what it is that I experience or own is potentially available to others. It is just that my own particular relationship to these items is, by hypothesis, inseparably bound to me. Experience simply has no significant sort of "interiority" because that aspect of it which is personal and individualistic is substantively trivial—embodied in the language of ownership rather than in the nature of what is owned.

And so, in the final analysis, one's conviction that other people are intelligent agents much like oneself is rooted in the acknowledgment of a taxonomic commonality with them as fellow "birds of a feather," in whose thoughts and feelings one also shares.

Chapter 17

PHILOSOPHY AS AN
INEXACT SCIENCE

OVER-REACHING AND OVERSIMPLIFICATION
IN PHILOSOPHY

By custom and tradition, philosophy ideally seeks to maintain doctrines and propound theses that hold with universal and strict generality. But in actual practice, we find that philosophers often propound theses that do not hold without exception but instead are no more that rough approximations to the facts. Examples of this phenomenon abound. Philosophers often say, for instance: *An agent does not act freely when he could not have acted otherwise*. But this is only the case usually and ordinarily. There are clear counterexamples, one of which was already given by John Locke in the seventeenth century. Thus suppose that someone is in a room where—wholly without his knowledge and even suspicion—all of the doors have been locked. And now suppose that our agent deliberates about whether to leave or stay and decides—freely and without the least interference or compulsion—that he is going to stay. Then (by hypothesis) he freely decides to stay. Yet even if he wants to leave, he cannot do otherwise than stay. In the face of such examples, the thesis above is true only in the generality of cases—in ordinary circumstances, so to speak. It is not more than an approximation.

Again, consider a contention that is not uncommonly found in philosophical discussions of causality: *The cause of an event is another, earlier event without which the former could not possibly occur.* This seems plausible on first view, but it is clearly inadequate. You cannot turn off the bulb of the light fixture if it has not earlier been turned on, but that does not make the turning on the cause of the subsequent turning off. The one end of the teeter-totter could not go up without the other going down, but that does not make the one the cause of the other. The direction of causality remains altogether indeterminate.

Moral philosophers not infrequently say: *A person is morally responsible for a harm only if he has caused it.* But again, this contention is not literally and strictly correct. The careless homeowner who fails to lock the door that provides the burglar with easy entry does not produce that bad outcome but simply renders it more likely: he does not cause the theft but nevertheless bears some moral responsibility for it. The person who fails to act preventively—say, by not alerting someone of an impending danger—plays no causal role but is nevertheless morally culpable when disaster ensues.

Metaphysicians sometimes have it that: *A part of a part is a part.* This seeming tautology does not actually hold. For consider:

— a chapter is part of a book
— a paragraph is part of a chapter
— a sentence is part of a paragraph
— a word is part of a sentence
— a letter is part of a word

But nevertheless it could not be said that a letter is part of a book.

This handful of illustrations should suffice to illustrate that philosophical generalizations all too often do not convey the exact truth but only a rough approximation to it. They are often committed to an overreaching that stands in need of qualification and emendation.

WHY MERE APPROXIMATION?

An assertion may be said to *approximate* to the truth if the amount of emendation, qualification, and correction required to render it correct and true is small and insignificant. But why should so many of the contentions of philosophers be merely approximately true, and hold only subject to qualifications, caveats, and emendations? How is the frequent philosophical over-simplification to be accounted for?

A combination of two considerations comes into play here.

- Philosophy aims at generality: it ideally seeks for truths that hold always and everywhere and not merely generally and for the most part.
- The philosophically relevant situations and phenomena are complex and wide-ranging: they cover a vast and highly differentiated landscape that resists the reduction to total uniformity.

Philosophers have to explain and develop their doctrines by generalizations. But when the material one deals with is almost unendingly variegated and complex, every generalization will have its exceptions and be approximate at best because the complexity of the issue and the diversity of the phenomena preclude unexceptionable generalizations. Consider an analogy, that of describing the makeup of a town you know. There are streets and buildings. But some of those streets aren't exactly streets but alleys or highways. And some of those buildings aren't exactly buildings but industrial structures such as power plants or water towers. And what of lakes, rivers, or inlets? Bridges and cell phone transmission towers? Such complications can be endless and will make difficulties for generalization. Or consider what can truly be said about all (and only) chairs or about all (and only) eating utensils—let alone all (and only) virtuous actions.

The importance in human affairs of regularities that do not hold always and everywhere but only *ceteris paribus*, that is, "when other things are equal"—as they occasionally are not—has long been noted.[1] With such approximate generalizations one can reduce the number of exceptions only at the cost of increasing the volume of necessary caveats, qualifications, and restrictions. To illustrate this situation, suppose that the first 80 percent of certain kinds of events will indeed follow the rule set by an approximate generalization. But to catch the next 10 percent we must amend, complicate, and qualify the generalizations. And then to catch the next 5 percent we must carry this process a great deal further. And so we here encounter a law of diminishing returns. More and more complexity is required to gain increasingly diminished coverage. And so the ideal of transforming inexact into exact generalizations by the addition of qualifying clauses becomes unrealizable. For there simply is no limit to "the things that can go wrong"—as is also the case with the potential side-effects of medications. The modes of potential anomaly simply cannot be detailed in advance. We can always spread the net out more widely and cover more cases or situations. But we cannot manage to encompass them all, because what we claim holds only "when all goes well."

NORMALISTIC GENERALIZATIONS

Much in our cognitive proceedings is subject to the "presumption of normalcy," to the effect that our claims are usually directed at the typical, general, common-garden-variety versions of things. Thus when we say that *X*s are *Y*s, we mean *X*s of the ordinary normal kind. When we say "Chairs have legs" we are for the present keeping plastic balloon chairs out of contention. They are "exceptions to the rule" that emerged when interior designers engaged in a quest for quirky modernity.

With normalistic generalizations we do not have unrestricted generality. Rather, we have something along the lines of:

Ordinary (normally, typically) *X*s are *Y*s

Two aspects of the situation are critical: the existence of exceptions and the infeasibility of specifying these exceptions in toto. We doubtless have it that

For every exception there is a (case specific) explanation why it does not conform to the rule—a cogent rationale that accounts for the exception's arising *in this instance.*

But we will not have it that:

There is a general explanation for exceptions failing to conform to the rule via an explicit marking of exceptional cases that can be articulated from the very outset.

Three types of generalizations must accordingly be distinguished:

- *Universally valid generalizations*, which hold strictly in all cases (e.g., copper wires conduct electricity)
- *Stochastic generalizations*, which hold probabilistically in most cases (e.g., people live less than a hundred years)
- *Normalistic generalizations*, which hold universally in normal conditions that exclude certain exception categories (e.g., free actions result from free decisions)

Strict generalizations admit of no exceptions. Stochastic generalizations have exceptions, but these occur fortuitously, without a rationale of grounding in specifiable exception categories. Normative generalizations also admit of exceptions, but these can ultimately be accepted and "explained away" in terms of their special conditions and circumstances.

EXPLANATORY POWER

There is a crucial difference, however, between statistical or stochastic explanations and normalistic explanations in point of their explanatory power. With statistical explanation we have something along the lines of:

Most *A*s are *B*s.
This is an *A*.
Therefore: This *A* (likely) is a *B*.

Here we do not explain occurrences as such but only their likelihoods. However with normalistic explanations we can proceed along lines such as:

*A*s are normally *B*s.
This is an *A*.
There is no reason to think of *A* as extraordinary, that is, as belonging to an exception category in relation to *B*.
Therefore: This *A* is a *B*.

This reasoning results in a definite conclusion, albeit proceeding by a *via negativa*.

The distinction between strictly universal and standard normalistic generalizations in turn grounds the distinction between an exact and inexact science. An exact science is one that is able to conduct its explanatory business by means of strict and universal generalizations. An inexact science, by contrast, has recourse to standard normalistic generalizations. And accordingly, a significant part of its work has to be devoted to identifying exception categories and "explaining away" the exceptions that its generalizations admit.

PHILOSOPHY AND INEXACTNESS

What does the inherent imperfection of the generalizations in philosophy mean for the nature of the discipline?

It means that the ideal aspirations of philosophy as a scientific enterprise cannot be realized in a straightforward way.

In circumstances where no categorical generalizations are possible and where "always and invariably" is unattainable, the most one can have is a qualified generalization relating to what is typical, usual, normal, or the like. But this of course is not how modern science works. Aristotle was willing to hone science to deal in what was the case ordinarily and for the most part, but we are not. Precision has come to be the demand of science, and it combines to function vestigially as the ruling aspiration of philosophy.

And yet those aspirations are not totally defeated: the philosopher does not have to confront fortuitous randomness. In philosophy, what we have is an *inexact* science. It is a discipline that has explanatory power because its generalizations are exception-admitting.

Philosophy is an inherently normative enterprise. Immanuel Kant rightly observed that the history of philosophy is different from philosophy itself. Philosophy is not a venture in describing what people say on the issues, and not even one of describing the grounds on which they base these contentions. Its characteristic assertions do not (and should not) take the form:

With respect to a certain philosophically relevant issue, X maintains that p because he thinks that T.

Instead the only sort of philosophically appropriate contention will (and should) take the form

> With respect to a certain philosophically relevant issue, T is a good (or bad) reason for maintaining p.

Properly conducted, philosophically appropriate contentions should (1) focus impersonally on the issue and (2) focus normatively on the matter of good and appropriate (or poor and inappropriate) reasons for accepting a certain position.

Thus philosophy is a normative enterprise concerned with the rationale of the contentions at issue. The philosopher is more than a historian. He is (or should be) concerned not with describing what people have maintained and explaining *their* reasons for maintaining this. Rather, his primary focus should be the (impersonally cogent) reasons for the maintained positions. His concern for X's or Y's reasons is not why those people accounted them as reasons, but rather with the question of whether they were well advised in so doing: whether *their* reasons were good reasons.

As a fundamentally normative (evaluative) enterprise, philosophy's task is to identify problems, to canvas possible solutions to them, and to assess the comparative merit of these solutions. Looking at the history of the debate can be very informative. It can enable us to see more clearly just what the problems are and what sorts of solutions are available. And it can help us to see what can be said for and against these solutions. But all of this is no more than preliminary with respect to the task: that of assessing the comparative merits (and demerits) of the possible issue-resolutions at our disposal.

The proper role of philosophy is thus the task of comparative assessment: of normative evaluation in the context of problem-solving. The assessment of reasons is the crux.

Philosophy seeks to clarify and resolve the big questions about ourselves and our place in the world's scheme of things. But questions about truth, justice, beauty, and similar idealizations pose issues of unsurpassed scope and complexity. The generalizations we need in order to define and address the issues are never more than rough approximations based on normalistic commitments.

The salient role of normalistic generalizations means, again, that philosophy is in effect an inexact rather than an exact science. And this role thereby accounts for further aspects of philosophical deliberation. The first is the prominence of apparent paradoxes arising when exceptions need to be made from what would otherwise be general rules. And the second is the prominence of distinctions in philosophy—specifically, of the distinctions needed to provide a cogent account of these exceptions via the special considerations that distinguish their specific circumstances from the general run of things.

However reluctantly, the philosopher must heed Aristotle's deeply wise admonition that one must not ask for more precision than can possibly be had.

The abandonment of strict universality makes philosophy much more akin to the common sense knowledge of everyday life than the exactitudes of natural science. Thus, in saying "Chairs have legs" we only mean that they normally and typically do so without insisting that this will invariably hold. Communicative convenience is the objective in our ordinary discourse, and trying to be exact would be simply too cumbersome. A presumption of normalcy obtains.

Consider, for example, the epistemological thesis that propositional knowledge consists in justified true belief. This contention that *someone knows something when it is true and they believe it to be so* is not strictly accurate. For let it be that

- X believes p-or-q
- X does this because he believes p (which is false)
- p-or-q is true, because q is true (although p is false)

Here we cannot say that X *knows* p-or-q even though the specified conditions are all satisfied. That initial claim is again not more than a rough first approximation, which holds in the usual run of cases where truth-reasons and belief-reasons are in proper alignment. Bertrand Russell and Edmund Gettier are theorists who have sought to repair the flaws of this contention by adding additional clauses to provide for counterexamples. But there appears to be no achievable end to this process. No matter how elaborate the process and the qualifications, further counterexamples manage to slip through the projected safety net.[2]

The point that emerges from these deliberations is that the view that knowledge is true justified belief is inadequate. For when the considerations that ground the belief in question are out of synch with the facts that ensure the truth of this belief—as is sometimes, albeit not *normally*, the case—then it no longer makes any sense to speak of knowledge. Knowing is not just a matter of having *some* grounds or reasons for accepting a truth: it requires *appropriate* grounds. Knowledge is not merely belief that is true and justifiably accepted, but rather true belief that is justifiably accepted *as such.*[3]

Philosophical understanding is in large measure a matter of explaining exceptions to rules. As a rule, promises must be true. But what if, having promised to meet a friend for a meal, you witness an accident where a victim desperately requires your aid? Does not this greater demand upon you override and thereby cancel out that earlier obligation? Here we have embarked on the sort of deliberation that figures on philosophy's agenda. Elucidating the rationale of the exceptions to its generalizations forms the key mission of any inexact science. When, as so often in philosophy, a generalization holds only approximately, then we confront something of a paradox. For on the one hand, we want to maintain the thesis "The Xs are Ys," but we are forced to confront an exception: "This x is an X that is not a Y."

For example, a typical philosophical deliberation would proceed somewhat as follows. Take Kant's thesis:

Ought implies can: people are indeed able to do the things that are morally required of them.

In considering this thesis, it becomes clear (by simple logic via the principle of contraposition) that it effectively comes to: *Cannot implies need not*. The idea is that people are free from obligation—and thereby from blame—if they fail to do something that they simply cannot do. But this view of the matter is decidedly dubious. For consider the following situation:

You have promised to lend me the money that I will need to pay my rent next month. But as the hour draws near, you go to the casino and gamble all your money away. So when the time comes, you cannot give me the loan: without funds it is impossible. But nevertheless one would not say that you do not have that obligation and are free from blame.

So clearly the rule has exceptions and needs to be qualified. And in this case the exception arises through the circumstance that the inability to satisfy the obligation is self-created, and indeed self-created as a convenience for excusing lack of performance.

So what we have here is

- a general rule of normalcy
- a cogent exception to that rule in a particular case
- a specification of a general category to which this exception belongs
- a philosophical account of why this sort of case—one belonging to that particular category—should qualify as an exception to the rule

It is this sort of analysis that constitutes part of the normal, day-to-day work of philosophical inquiry. A not inconsiderable part of philosophical endeavor must accordingly be devoted to the identification and validation of exceptions to rules and the consequent drawing of distinctions to provide for the requisite justificatory rationale.

Such an approach carries in its wake the prospect of a more modestly conceived philosophy—one prepared to make its claims not with a view to how things must necessarily stand always and universally, but rather with a view to how things generally stand in the normal, ordinary, usual course of things. In its methodological stance, such a philosophy accordingly carries philosophical empiricism in its wake: what is standard (normal, accustomed) is only determinable as such in a way that does—and must—reflect our limited experience in a realm of complex and almost endlessly variegated phenomena.

Chapter 18

PHILOSOPHY'S INVOLVEMENT
WITH TRANSCENDENTAL ISSUES

ULTIMATE QUESTIONS AND
TRANSCENDENTAL ISSUES

One of the most fundamental issues of metaphysics is the "ultimate question" of G. W. Leibniz: "Why is there anything at all?" And other examples are readily available, for example,

Why does what exists have the nature it does?
Why should humans cultivate knowledge, beauty, or justice?
What is it that can make a product of human creativity important?

All such questions go beyond the resources of standard direction-based inquiry.

Virtually by definition the issues characterized as "transcendental" resist resolution by the standard methods and resources of factual inquiry. The reason for this lies largely in the very modality of the matter. Standard inquiry is designed to deal with *what is*, whereas these issues extend beyond what is discernable about things.

To characterize a thesis as transcendental is not to describe the nature of its substantive content but to characterize its mode of cognitive validation: it does not address what the thesis says but the nature of the considerations that can validate its acceptance. And in this regard, the matter is of a negative bearing, in that the usual means of "inductive" substantiation on the basis of observational evidence are insufficient to achieve the requisite result.

Thus consider the following array:

1	1	1
0	0	1
1	0	1

Its descriptive character lies open to inspection by all. But that the corner position *must* be occupied by a 1 or that the center position *could* be occupied by a 0 is not observationally discernable. Such modal issues are transcendental—as are issues of significance, value, or priority. And for better or worse, philosophy is full of "transcendental" questions that lie beyond the realm of the standard or normal, and in particular beyond the realm of scientific inquiry. Why should this be so? Three lines of consideration come to the fore.

Existence Problems

Standard inquiry as we have it in science addresses the what and how of things. Science concerns itself with observable phenomena and the patterns that indicate their lawful modus operandi. But the issue of the ultimate why of these things—why the phenomena and the laws are as they are—is not and cannot figure in the observation-based agenda.

Thus science can address *how* we humans get to be here—and answer it very effectively in terms of evolutionary development. But the question of *why* we are here is something else again, and science has really nothing to say on the subject.

Value Problems

Another of the factors that puts philosophical issues beyond the range of strictly empirical investigations is their *normative* dimension. Consider an analogy: a strictly empirical investigation might show that the English word *deceit* is in fact spelled as follows:

- as *deceit* by 98 percent of writers
- as *deciet* by 1.75 percent of writers
- as *deceet* by 0.20 percent of writers
- other variations by 0.05 percent of writers

But this leaves the normative question: what is the right (proper, appropriate) way of spelling this word? And this normative issue goes beyond the observable facts. Something of the same situation obtains in philosophy. For here too, the problem is not what people *do* think about the issues but what is the *right* (proper, appropriate) way of thinking about them. And this normativity carries over to matters outside the observational domain.

We can, of course, bring the normative into alignment with the determinable facts by such small plausible suppositions as (in the present case) a principle of common sense to the effect that people predominantly incline to doing the right and proper thing. And in our orthographic example, this seems plausible enough. But in the case of the transcendental issues of philosophy, this tactic is largely unavailable because the relevant phenomena (wholly unlike those of language use) lie far removed from the domain of common experience, so that the alignment between what people do and what they should do becomes problematic, and we cannot expect common sense to get matters on the right track.

Scope and Scale Problems

Transcendental questions deal with matters on a scale of comprehensiveness and ultimacy that is not encountered with questions of limited scope and mundane routine.

In explaining nature's pleasure, our recourse is to nature's laws. But questions about those laws themselves, their risks and evidence, move transcendentally outside the usual domain. Why is there anything at all? Why does natural existence have the character it does? Why are there laws of nature, and what explains their nature?

Explanation generally proceeds to explain one fact on the basis of others—it deploys explaining input considerations to account for problematic outputs. Standard explanation cannot proceed ex nihilo.

Accordingly, the standard explanatory modes are not suited to handle issues of the comprehensiveness of ultimate questions, where not only the fact to be explained but the explanatory material itself falls within the relevantly problematic range.

ON ADDRESSING TRANSCENDENTAL ISSUES:
EVIDENTIATION VS. HARMONIZATION

Evidentiation proceeds in the manner of logic: it moves inferentially from premises to conclusions, using given (or assumed) inputs to produce duly validated outputs. Its structure is thus essentially linear, moving from what is probatively more basic and fundamental to what is less so. And with such linear reasoning, the chain of support is no stronger than the weakest link.

Harmonization is something very different. It is a matter of the reciprocal relation of analogy and interconnections of kinship and affinity. It provides not a chain but a rope whose strands cohere together; the overall structure is not a line but rather a spider's web of intermediary components. These components form a part of such a harmonic structure not because they are joined to others by ties of inference, but because they fit together to yield a coherent structure. They come together not as the linked parts of a linear progression, like the cars of a railway train, but as the reciprocally attuned components of a well-designed garden or building. The unity at issue is not inferential but architectonic.

The proper and most practicable way of addressing these questions consists of three steps:

(1) To seek out the spectrum of possible answers.
(2) To spell out in each case exactly what the answer involves in its commitments.

(3) To determine what alternatives best harmonize the totality of our commitments in the sense of achieving the best realizable balance of advantages over disadvantages and cognitive assets over liabilities.

Given that comparative *evidentiation* is not practicable here, we have to turn to a decidedly different procedure, namely, comparative *harmonization*. This harmonization is a matter of assessing those various issue resolutions in the light of considerations of rational economy—of weighing the cognitive benefit gains afforded by those various rival issue resolutions against the costs and liabilities incurred by adopting the correlative commitments.

What is at issue here is a recourse to the principle of rational economy (also commonly known as the principle of least effort). To begin with, we need to look to the economy of cognitive resources afforded by analogies with what we have already determined by the standard evidential proceedings. In bringing to light uniform problems of understanding, analogies economize on explanatory effort.

And moving beyond this, we need to assess which mode of issue resolution raises the least number of other avoidable new problems—new issues, questions, and difficulties. The issue in effect becomes one of cognitive cost-accounting—a compromise of old questions answered and issues resolved in relation to new questions posed and new issues raised.

The point, of course, is that *ex nihilo nihil fit*—nothing comes from nothing; each possible mode of issue resolution carries along more cognitive dichotomies and risks, and none comes free of cost. But in each case, what matters is the overall balance of gain versus cost, the net advantage of the particular issue resolution.

But it is just here, with the issue of cost-benefit assessment, that we come to the core difficulty of the process of speculation involved in rational philosophizing.

In addressing transcendental issues it is very useful to look for analogous ideas and arguments from the empirical (i.e., non-transcendental) side of things, the aim here being to see whether the processes and principles at work might also be put to use with respect to transcendental issues. (For example, insofar as the principle of causality proves useful with respect to empirical norms, one might put the analogous principle of sufficient reason to work on the transcendental side.) And the recourse to matters of analogy becomes critical here; such recourse is justified by the consideration that there is no reason to think that because experience cannot *provide* an answer, it cannot *suggest* one.

WHY PHILOSOPHICAL DISCORD?

Consider the following group of contentions:

(1) Transcendental philosophical propositions cannot be settled by means of standard factual inquiry.
(2) Philosophical theses are inappropriate and meaningless because they cannot be settled by means of standard factual inquiry.
(3) Transcendental philosophical contentions are significant and meaningful (rather than inappropriate and meaningless).

What we have here is the philosophically common paradox where several individually plausible theses are collectively inconsistent.

In view of the logical incompatibility of those contentions, at least one of them must be rejected. This logically inevitable circumstance leads to three prospective, doctrinal "rejection" propositions:

(1) *Deflationism*: Those transcendental philosophical propositions are ordinary factual theses in disguise.
(2) *Conservatism*: Philosophical propositions are appropriate and meaningful despite the fact that they cannot be settled by the procedures of standard factual inquiry.
(3) *Positivism*: Transcendental philosophical contentions are inappropriate and meaningless.

The logic of the situation is such that one or the other of these must be endorsed. The problem comes down to: Which one?

Deflationism is hardly a plausible candidate. For frequently, the facts do not reach beyond themselves but merely inform us about the existing condition of things and remain silent about the nature and promise of alternative possibilities.

For better or for worse, the matter becomes one of comparative assessment and evaluation. What points of analogy (of similarity and difference) are important and which are evidential? Exactly how much weight should be accorded to the various aspects of similarity and difference?

A philosopher is bound to accord different degrees of certainty, importance, and interest on the basis of how matters at issue figure within the manifold of his or her own experience. And in this regard, different individuals are bound to differ. Further, different philosophers will differ in belief (in cognition) because their situation in the domain of personal experience endows them with different views regarding matters of value.

DOES PHILOSOPHICAL DISCORD
INVALIDATE THE ENTERPRISE?

Transcendental issues are empirically irresolvable—a circumstance that led the logical positivists of the mid-twentieth century to leap to the conclusion that they are "empirically meaningless." They adopted the strong idea that a question that someone cannot answer is for that very reason meaningless for them.

The question of our place and role in reality's scheme of things, of the importance and significance of actual or possible conditions, and of the value of our opportunities for intervening in the course of occurrence so as to bring about conditions that would not otherwise exist are of such obvious importance for us that we naturally would—and should—be reluctant to dismiss them as improper.

People often see it as a reproach to philosophy that its practitioners—substantially unlike the practitioners of natural science—fail to reach agreement, commonality, and consensus. But this complaint runs roughshod over the fundamental differences between the fields of inquiry at issue.

As Aristotle already sagaciously put it:

It is the mark of an educated man to look for precision in each class of things just so far as the nature of the subject admits. It is evidently equally foolish to accept probable reasoning from a mathematician as to demand strict demonstration from a rhetorician.[1]

But if transcendental issues indeed are irresolvable by procedures conducted along traditional evidential lines, then should they not thereby simply be dismissed as inappropriate and rejected as "empirically meaningless" in just that way that the early logical positivists of the pre–World War II era proposed to do? (They really ought to be called "logical negativists"!)

What makes positivism an unappealing stance is reflected in its feature of calling a spade a spade. For positivism is in reality simply a negativism toward the traditional philosophical enterprise. It proposes to consign all of those traditional philosophical questions regarding reality at large and our place within it to the trash heaps of meaninglessness. The circumstance that standard modes of factual inquiry prove insufficient for such questions is taken as a basis for rejection—exactly as with Aesop's parable of the fox and the grapes. Rather than looking to different methods and new approaches, the positivist simply abandons the enterprise. One can doubtless understand such a reaction, but it is less easy to endorse it.

A SELF-APPLICATION OF EVALUATIVE RESOLUTION

One good reason for not taking this rejectionist line is that the very question it addresses—namely, "Are transcendental questions meaningless?"—is itself a patently transcendental question. It clearly cannot be resolved by the standard means of factual inquiry; we can at most embark on the question of what various people *think* to be so.

At this point we have three basic alternatives:

(1) *Rejectionism*: To reject transcendental questions as vacuous and somehow inappropriate.
(2) *Agnosticism*: To accept transcendental questions as cognitively appropriate but effectively (i.e., practically) irresolvable.
(3) *Harmonization*: To accept transcendental questions as (non-standardly) tractable and seek to resolve them along the harmonistic lines outlined above.

Viewed in this light, the issue we face here is itself a patently transcendental one, and the perspective for addressing it is itself of the sort typical for the sensible treatment of transcendental questions.

Accordingly, we should carry out a cost-benefit comparison of the three rival approaches. On this proceeding, we arrive at the situation shown in Display 18.1. Given that only in the last case does the magnitude of the benefits significantly outrank that of the costs—at any rate in the present writer's opinion—it is this third proceeding that affords the best option. Insofar as proceeding in this manner is deemed acceptable, harmonization will emerge as the best policy.

Display 18.1

COSTS AND BENEFITS OF RIVAL APPROACHES

Approach	Cost	Benefit
REJECTIONISM	A cognitive vacuum [S]	A cognately inexpensive and risk-free issue resolution [S]
AGNOSTICISM	Conceding ignorance about questions acknowledged as meaningful [M]	Avoiding cognitive risks [M]
HARMONIZATION	Adopting a nonstandard cognitive approach [M]	Cogent answer to a question accepted as meaningful [L]

Note: The magnitude of costs and benefits can be graded as small (S), middling (M), or large (L). The author's own evaluations are as indicated, so that, in his view, harmonization wins out.

A fundamental theorem of epistemology is that there is a teeter-totter relationship between cognitive risks and cognitive range. The higher one sets the bar for evidence that is acceptable, the fewer questions one can answer; the less one demands in the way of probative substantiation, the ampler the range of putative knowledge at one's disposal; the less tolerance for error, the smaller our store of information.

This pivotal tradeoff between cognitive risk and cognitive range divides people into two distinctive classes. For in matters of both action and thought, people divide into the cautious and the daring, the risk-avoiders and the risk-takers.

Nature and nurture, endowment and experience, have molded people into distinctive categories that manifest themselves in contrasting philosophical attitudes:

curious vs. sceptical
daring vs. cautious
speculative vs. scientific

In philosophy, such traits appear in the duality of metaphysical receptiveness contrasted with the scientific scepticism. And in the end, there is no right or wrong here. People are what nature and nurture have made them. Some are prepared to take metaphysical speculation in stride and view its deliberations with sympathetic tolerance; others will view the entire project with aversive distaste. (The reader who has persevered to this point will likely belong to the former category.)

Chapter 19

RELIGIOUS VARIATION AND THE RATIONALE OF BELIEF

ON RELIGIOUS VARIATION

We find ourselves in a world that is neither of our making nor significantly within our control, and we indispensably require information to guide our actions. Evolution has inserted us into the world's scheme of things as intelligent beings equipped with resources to meet our many needs—material and conceptual alike. In this light, evolution is seen as an ultimately creative process (to invoke Henri Bergson's illuminating perspective) that has brought into existence intelligent beings with capacities for increasingly sophisticated thought-orientation encompassing not only consciousness but also self-consciousness, rationality, affectivity, and spirituality. Obviously, not all of these capacities are cultivated by everyone, but all normally developed humans have at least the capability of their exercise.

Religiosity is deeply rooted in the makeup of *Homo sapiens*. It is one of the key formative components of an individual's belief system: one can—and from various points of view should—regard the world itself in relation to a larger, world-transcendent context of consideration. Even the irreligiosity of atheism is a religious position of sorts.

It is certainly not necessary to conceptualize God as the father figure of the Sistine Chapel. There is no good reason why a creatively productive force whose rational agency has brought the world into being should be describable in terms of the concepts needed to address the material in which our sensory apparatus provides us humans with an experiential access to physical reality.

Pascal was doubtless right: religious belief can provide substantial benefits. But one should not, of course, adopt a religion because this somehow "pays off." Religious pragmatism is not quite so simple and crude. But nevertheless there are—or should be—pragmatic benefits to religious faith. But a faith that does not give its exponent a more coherent, harmonious, and meaningful view of the world and his or her place within it is simply not worth the price of admission.

Faith in the sense here at issue is a matter of what might be called reasonable supposition. To have faith is thus not a matter of going *against* the evidence, but rather of going *beyond* it. It does not call for throwing rational conviction to the winds, but it does call for taking prudent risks in transcending the evidence by cautious conjecture in the interests of achieving a more harmonious and intelligible cognitive whole. With the textual interpretation of classical inscriptions, to take one example, we have a small-scale exercise in faith: with the principle of sufficient reason we have a larger-scale exercise. In neither case is what we do evidentially necessitated, but in both cases it is cognitively constructive. In the final analysis, such faith is a matter of practical rather than theoretical rationality. It is not irrational in *violating* the demands of reason, but it is not inert in *limiting* itself to those demands alone.

It is, to be sure, possible for a religion to require its practitioners to do things that even they may see as conflicting with morality or common sense or even established fact. But such a situation can, and should, undermine their confidence that they have "got it right" in regard to religious matters; it should give them second thoughts.

TAKING A STAND

The philosophy of religion is a domain of intimidating scope, scale, and complexity. The whole of the space available for the present discussion could easily be filled by simply listing questions belonging to the field. What is a religion? What sorts of religions are possible? What is it to have or to belong to a religion? Why it is that people should (or perhaps even need) to belong to a religion? Is having a religion a matter purely of accepting beliefs, or are behavioral ramifications (such as prayer or ritual) necessary? Can the existence of God be demonstrable? And if not, can belief in God possibly be validated by other, nondemonstrative means? The list goes on and on.

But one has to make a beginning, and it seems proper to set out from one undeniably salient question: Does the availability of different and discordant bodies of religious belief and practice—the absence of a single, rationally mandated, universal consensus in matters of religion—constitute a cogent reason against committing oneself to one of them?

Can a believer appropriately adopt a particular religion despite the fact that a different commitment is available to—and conceivably appropriate for—someone else? After all, the very existence of different religions is often itself seen as an obstacle to understanding any religious commitment whatsoever.

Yet why should this be? Clearly, the existence of different alternative *professions* need not be an obstacle to committing oneself to one of them, so why should this be so with *religion*? Yet perhaps the analogy does not hold, seeing that professions are spheres of action and not belief systems of the sort involved in religions. But then, consider scientists. There is no reason why the physicists or the physicians of one era need be in agreement with those of others. Different conditions and circumstances render differences in belief not only acceptable but virtually mandatory. There is no consensus or consistency across historical states of science; there is no consensus or consistency across the views of contemporary economists. The cognitive state of the art at different times and in different circumstances provides for different premises. And where the fundamental premises differ, the rationally implied conclusions must differ as well. Why should it be otherwise in matters of religion?

In fact there is no good reason to see religious variation as harmful to the project. It is, after all, only right and proper to align one's beliefs with the evidence at one's disposal. And it will, of course, transpire that different people have to proceed differently in different evidential settings. And so with regard to those who adhere to a religion that is different from ours, we can and should be prepared to say: "If the world is such as their experience indicates it to be, then their particular religious view is only plausible *in the circumstances.*"

After all, viewing one and the same landscape will have very different meanings for the agronomist, the tartillery gunner, or the landscape painter.

It must be emphasized that the resulting situation is definitely not that of an indifferent relativism of matters of taste—*chacun à son goût*. It is rather a matter of a rational contextualism of situation—*chacun à son circonstance*.

Accordingly, a position regarding religion is propounded here that, while indeed pluralistic in the acknowledgment of available alternatives, is nevertheless implacably at odds with indifferentist *relativism*. It has instead come down emphatically on the side of a rationalistic *contextualism*. For an indifferent relativism claims that it just doesn't matter which alternative you select. Given your experiential context, it does matter—those alternatives are not available for a random selection. Given your experience, there is only one proper optimally experience-aligned choice for you. To be sure, apparently equally reasonable people raised in apparently equally reasonable cultures can come to different conclusions about which religion—if any—it is appropriate to adopt. Even members of the same family raised by the same parents in the same environment can differ in this regard. But experience is highly personalized, and thus different interactions and involvement will issue in differences not only in information but in priorities in matters of credibility, plausibility, expectability, and the like. There may be alternatives out there in relation to others, but such impersonality is not an option for the individual.

The difference is important. Indifferentism makes no room for interpersonal convergence: contextualism enforces it, at least insofar as a strict commonality of conditions prevails. In the contemporary world, real factors such as global warming, intercommunal strife, demographic anomalies, and the specter of atomic warfare create conditions shared by all alike and also create a pressure toward doctrinally transcendent commonalities of interests. Such conditions of shared life create pressure for the acknowledgment of shared interests that can and should soften the edges of ethical and religious disagreement, perhaps ultimately, one day, prioritizing existential commonalities over doctrinal divergences.

CHOICE

The question "Which religion—if any—is right for me?" does not generally arise for people. For by the time one is sufficiently mature to have concerns about the matter, fate—that is, the unasked-for circumstances of one's cultural and social context—has generally resolved the issue. The individual—be he Jew or Catholic, atheist or Hindu— has by then almost invariably become embedded in a state of commitment where the otherwise available alternatives no longer qualify as what William James called "live options." With most mature individuals, concern for "the one true religion" is a fait accompli, settled by life's conditions and circumstances.

As matters stand, people only rarely confront an open and unfettered choice among alternative religions. For one thing, the realities of place and time provide limits. Homer could not have chosen to be a Buddhist. And cultural accessibility also comes into play. The Parisians of Napoleon's day could hardly become Muslims. Once one has "seen the light" and adopted a religion, moreover, one cannot but take the view that there is "one true religion." To do otherwise would indicate a lack of seriousness. This is not to say that there are not alternatives. But in such matters, they are usually blocked by the realities of personal background and disposition. Benjamin Disraeli could hardly have become a Mormon. Authoritativeness must be something underpinned by a basis of personal experience.

There is no more a "religion within the limits of reason alone" than there is a "science within the limits of reasons alone," for both religion and science require more than mere reason—namely, experience. (In the case of science this is observational experience, and in the case of religion, life-experience; but in either case, experience.)

For most people a change of religion is not a live option: the impact of nature and nurture make the change from Christianity to Islam infeasible for them. Far more common in the present era is the change from one's parental affiliation with some organized religion to an indifferentist agnosticism or atheism. The latter sort of shift is almost the predominant fashion in the Western world, with irreligion as the predominant religion of the day and the creedal detail of any particular organized religion rejected virtually out of hand. Here, as ever, the affiliation or lack thereof functions by way of cultural conformity rather than rational deliberation. And so, there is no "one size fits all" across different historical and cultural settings. In the end the choice among religions (irreligion included)— insofar as it is rational—is a matter of harmonizing belief with experience. And where deliberation leads a person depends on the available premises. Here, as elsewhere, there is no compelling, evidence-independent resolution. And the rationality of the matter depends not on where one ends up but on the nature of the route by which one gets there.

Still, just which religion are people well advised to deem authoritative for themselves? Granted, there are always alternatives, and it may seem plausible to think of them as being spread out before us as a matter of choice. But this is quite wrong. The fact of it is that in matters of religion, the issue of reasonable choice is in general not something people face prospectively by overtly deciding upon a religious affiliation. On the contrary, it is something they can and generally will do only retrospectively, in the wake of an already established commitment. Perhaps ironically, the very fact that a commitment is already in place as a fait accompli itself forms a significant part of what constitutes a reason for continuing it. If you don't learn a language early on in life, you will never speak it as a native speaker does. If you don't learn to play the violin as a child, you are unlikely to achieve virtuoso mastery. Something like this holds for religion as well. If you are Polish, you will probably feel no more at home with Buddhism than you would feel at home in Delhi. Once we have reached the age of reflection, where we worry about the rationale of things, it is almost always too late to start over. By the time one is sufficiently mature to have concerns about the matter, fate (that is, the unasked-for circumstances of one's life) has generally resolved the issue. Abstractly and irrespectively considered, one can say—and think—that one religion is as available as any other, but in fact they are no longer equally available *to us*. At that stage our circumstances have circumscribed our choice in the matter.

And so in the end there is no sensible alternative to a tolerance of "live and let live." Intolerance is a boomerang; it will almost certainly return back to the thrower. In failing to accord to others a freedom to go their own way in such matters, we create a situation bound to cause problems for all of us alike. It is clearly best for people to go on their own journeys. But in the end, it is not the case with religion, any more than with politics and much else, that the existence of alternatives undermines the appropriateness of one particular resolution for oneself.

NOTES

Chapter 1.   Ultimate Questions

1. William L. Rowe, "Two Criticisms of the Cosmological Argument," *The Monist* 54 (1970); reprinted in *Philosophy of Religion: Selective Readings*, 2nd ed., ed. W. L. Rowe and W. Wainwright (New York: Harcourt Brace Jovanovich, 1989), 142–56 (see 153). On this principle in its relation to the cosmological argument for the existence of God, see William L. Rowe, *The Cosmological Argument* (Princeton: Princeton University Press, 1975). See also Richard M. Gale, *On the Nature and Existence of God* (Cambridge: Cambridge University Press, 1991), and Alexander R. Pruss, "The Hume-Edwards Principle and the Cosmological Argument," *International Journal for Philosophy of Religion* 434 (1988): 149–65.

2. Note that neither of these is the same as $(\exists p)(p @ (\forall x)E!x)$, which obtains trivially given the symbolic conventions adopted here.

3. G. W. Leibniz, *Philosophical Papers and Letters*, trans. and ed. L. E. Loemker (Dordrecht: Reidel, 1969), 487.

4. Ibid., 488.

5. See Arthur Conan Doyle's story "The Adventures of the Beryl Coronet," originally published in *Strand Magazine*, 1892.

6. After all, there is no reason of the nature of a logico-theoretical principle why propositions cannot be self-certifying. Nothing vicious need be involved in self-substantiation. Think of "Some statements are true" or "This statement stakes a particular rather than universal claim."

7. Optimalism is closely related to optimism. The optimist holds that "Whatever exists is for the best," whereas the optimalist maintains the converse, "Whatever is for the best exists." However, when we are dealing with exclusive and exhaustive alternatives, the two theses come to the same thing. If one of the

alternatives A, A_1, ... A_n must be the case, then if what is realized is for the best, it follows automatically that the best is realized (and conversely).

Chapter 2.   *World Views*

1. Wilhelm Dilthey, *Weltanschauungslehre*, vol. 8 of *Gesammelte Schriften* (Stuttgart: Teubner; Göttingen: Vandenhoeck & Ruprecht, 1961), 86–87. My translation.

2. See Stephen C. Pepper, *World Hypotheses: A Study in Evidence* (Berkeley and Los Angeles: University of California Press, 1942).

3. For example, Friedrich Paulsen, Richard Müller-Freienfels, and Karl Jaspers.

Chapter 3.   *Terminological Contextuality*

1. Bertrand Russell, *Our Knowledge of the External World* (London: Allen & Unwin, 1922), 107–8.

2. Arthur Eddington, *The Nature of the Physical World* (New York: Macmillan; Cambridge: Cambridge University Press, 1929), 126. Wilfrid Sellars' oft-cited distinction between "the scientific image" and "the manifest image" of things comes straight out of Russell via Eddington.

Chapter 5.   *Randomness and Reason*

This chapter draws upon a paper of the same title published in *Symposion: Journal of the Romanian Academy of Science* 2 (2015): 11–18.

1. See Rebecca Goldstein, *Incompleteness: The Proof and Paradox of Kurt Gödel* (New York: W. W. Norton, 2005). This was a favorite saying of Einstein's. In Ronald W. Clark's *Einstein: The Life and Times* (New York: World Publishing Company, 1971), it is quoted four times (pp. 19, 69, 113, and 340).

2. Letter to David Bohm of 24 November 1954. See Jeroen van Dongen, *Einstein's Unification* (Cambridge: Cambridge University Press, 2010), 181.

3. Actually, a way of developing relativity theory within the framework of rational mechanics can be found in Arnold Sommerfeld's *Electrodynamics: Lectures in Theoretical Physics*, vol. 3, trans. E. G. Ramberg (New York: Academic Press,

1964); German original, *Vorlesungen über theoretische Physik* (Wiesbaden: Klemm Verlag, 1945). I owe this reference to my colleague Kenneth Schaffner.

4. Alice Calaprice, ed., *The Expanded Quotable Einstein* (Princeton: Princeton University Press, 2000), 260.

5. John Norton has reminded me that search problems such as that of the traveling salesman will often be solved most efficiently by probabilistically geared algorithms.

6. David Bodanis, *Einstein's Greatest Mistake* (Boston: Little, Brown and Co., 2016), 206.

7. I revert here to the title of John Rawls' classic paper "Justice as Fairness." Is it fair that in American presidential elections the candidate who carries a state by .01 percent of the vote should get 100 percent of that state's representation in the Electoral College? The answer is an emphatic *yes*—exactly because the claims at issue are legal claims, and just this is what the law provides for. But the question "Is it just?" is something else again.

Chapter 6.   *Issues of Self-Reference and Paradox*

1. See Aristotle, *Soph. Elen.* 180a35 and *Nicomachaean Ethics* 1146a71. See also Carl Prantl, *Geschichte der Logik im Abendlande*, 4 vols. (Graz: Akademische Druck- und Verlagsanstalt, 1955), 1:50–51. According to Cicero, "Si dicis te mentiri verumque dicis, mentiris" (*Academica priora*, II, 30.95–96; and compare *De divinatione*, II, 11).

2. Eubulides' riddle was discussed not only by Aristotle and Cicero (see the preceding note) but by the Stoics (Prantl, *Geschichte*, 1:490). In medieval times it was a staple in the extensive discussions of *insolubilia*. See Prantl, *Geschichte*, 4:19, 41.

3. Several Greek philosophers, preeminently the Aristotelian Theophrastus and the Stoic Chrysippus, wrote treatises about the Liar Paradox. See Diogenes Laertius, *Lives of Eminent Philosophers*, V.49 and VII.196. The poet Phietas of Cos is said to have worried himself into an early grave by fretting over it, and its notoriety was such that even St. Paul adverted to it in *Titus* 1:12–13. The history of the Liar Paradox is discussed in substantial detail in Alexander Rüstow's *Der Lügner: Theorie, Geschichte und Auflösung* (Leipzig: B. G. Treubner, 1910; reprinted, New York & London: Garland Publishing Co., 1987).

4. Paul of Venice, in Prantl, *Geschichte*, 4:139 n. 569.

5. Prantl, *Geschichte*, 4:37 n. 146.

6. "Socrates dicens, se ipsum dicere falsum, nihil dicit" (Prantl, *Geschichte*, 4:139 n. 569). A doctrine commonly endorsed in late medieval times was that paradoxical statements are not propositions and for this reason cannot be classified as true or false but must be deemed meaningless. See J. E. Ashworth, *Language and Logic in the Post-Medieval Period* (Boston: Reidel, 1974), 115, for later endorsements of this approach. Thus later writers dismissed *insolubilia* as not propositions at all but rather "imperfect assertions" (*orationes imperfectae*). See again Ashworth, *Language and Logic*, 116.

7. Paul of Venice, in Prantl, *Geschichte*, 4:138–39.

8. Ibid., 4:139 n. 539.

Chapter 7. Explanation and the Principle of Sufficient Reason

1. On the principle of sufficient reason, see the book of this title by Alexander R. Pruss (New York: Cambridge University Press, 2006), whose bibliography gives ample references.

Chapter 8. Intelligent Design Revisited in the Light of Evolutionary Neoplatonism

1. St. Thomas Aquinas characterized this hypostasis as "quod sumatur pro individuo rationalis naturae, ratione suae excellentiae" (*Summa Theologiae*, I, q. 29, art. 2, ad 1).

2. The literature on intelligent design theory is vast. Some representative works include Robert Dawkins, *The Blind Watchmaker: Why the Evidence of Evolution Reveals a Universe without Design* (New York: Norton Publishing Co., 1986); William A. Dembski, *Mere Creation: Science, Faith, and Intelligent Design* (Downers Grove, IL: InterVarsity Press, 1998); William A. Dembski, *The Design Inference: Eliminating Chance through Small Probabilities* (Cambridge: Cambridge University Press, 1998); Ronald L. Numbers, *The Creationists: From Scientific Creationism to Intelligent Design* (Cambridge, MA: Harvard University Press, 2006); Robert T. Pennock, *Tower of Babel: Evidence against the New Creationism* (Cambridge, MA: MIT Press, 1998); Robert T. Pennock, ed., *Intelligent Design Creationism and Its Critics: Philosophical, Theological, and Scientific Perspectives* (Cambridge, MA: MIT Press, 2001); and Del Ratzsch, *Nature, Design, and Science: The Status of Design in Natural Science* (Albany: State University of New York Press, 2001).

3. Radek Chlup, *Proclus: An Introduction* (Cambridge: Cambridge University Press, 2016), 48.

4. On this perspective, see Michael Heller, *Ultimate Explanations of the Universe*, trans. Teresa Baluk-Ulewiczowa (Berlin: Springer, 2009).

Chapter 9. *What If Things Were Different?*

1. Sometimes what looks like a counterfactual conditional is only so in appearance. Thus consider: "If Napoleon and Alexander the Great were fused into a single individual, what a great general that would be!" What is at issue here is not really a counterfactual based on the weird hypothesis of a fusion of two people into one. Rather, it is merely a rhetorically striking reformulation of the truism, "Anybody with all of the military talents of Napoleon and of Alexander combined is certainly a great general."

2. Compare Roderick M. Chisholm, "Law Statements and Counterfactual Inferences," *Analysis* 15 (1955): 97–105, esp. 102–5.

3. But why should thing-type characterizations be taken as more fundamental than mode-of-behavior characterizations? The answer lies in the processual perspective that to be an X is to behave as X's do: that to be wooden, for example, is to behave as wooden things do. Since such systemic comportment encompasses the whole range of relevant lawful behavior, it is inherently more general than a specific item—and one particular mode of behavior. The prioritization at issue is thus provided for by the standard policy of giving precedence to what is more general, pervasive, and fundamental.

4. In the setting of our present approach, we have the following accepted propositions:

(1) Four is *not* greater than five.
(2) The consistency of arithmetic [as we know it] entails (1).
(3) Arithmetic is—and ought to be—consistent.

If not-(1) were to be assumed, then we would be forced into an abandonment of either (2) or (3), seeing that the trio not-(1), (2), and (3) is logically inconsistent. Since there is no viable way around (2), this means that we would have to give up (3) and treat arithmetic as involved in contradiction. And this validates the counterfactual under consideration.

5. On possible worlds in literary theory in their interrelationship with philosophical issues, see Calin-Andrei Mihailescu and Walid Hamarneh, eds., *Fiction*

Updated: Theories of Fictionality, Narratology, and Poetics (Toronto: University of Toronto Press, 1977).

6. On this feature of concrete worlds, see the author's "Leibniz and Possible Worlds," *Studia Leibnitiana* 28 (1995): 129–62.

7. See, for example, Alvin Plantinga, *The Nature of Necessity* (Oxford: Clarendon Press, 1974). An alternative perspective could be mereological: a possible world now being seen as simply the sum-total of the possible individuals that exist within it. (The two approaches come to the same thing if we adopt a theory of reductive particularism—or "methodological individualism," as it is sometimes called—according to which every state of affairs regarding things-in-general reduces to a collection of facts about some set of individuals.)

8. "A possible world, then, is a possible state of affairs—one that is possible in the broadly logical sense." Plantinga, *The Nature of Necessity*, 44.

9. Some logicians regard possible worlds as collections of statements rather than objects. But while there is much to be said for such an approach, it faces two major obstacles: (1) not every collection of (compatible) statements can plausibly be said to constitute a world, but rather (2) only those that satisfy an appropriate manifold of special conditions: any "world-characterizing" set of propositions must be both inferentially closed and descriptively complete, to ensure that any possible contention about an object is either true or false. And such macro-sets of statements lie beyond our grasp.

10. Authentic *worlds* thus differ from the schematic "worlds" often contemplated by modal logicians. The latter are not possible worlds as all, but conceptual constructs, which, insofar as we can provide them, are inadequate to the needs of the situation.

11. W. V. Quine, "On What There Is," *Review of Metaphysics* 2 (1948): 21–38; reprinted in his *From a Logical Point of View* (Cambridge, MA: Harvard University Press, 1953), 1–19.

12. Just this was the approach of the author's *A Theory of Possibility* (Oxford: Blackwell, 1975). To question the appropriateness of *possible worlds* is not automatically to gainsay the semantical utility of *scenarios* in semantical analysis—i.e., fictions that characterize possible courses of events in ways that are fragmentary and incomplete in their overall bearing. Compare, for example, the analysis of imperatives in the author's *The Logic of Commands* (London: Routledge, 1969). Moreover, such scenarios could, in theory, be coordinated with descriptively incomplete worlds along the lines of the theory of inconsistent and incomplete possible world semantics expounded in Nicholas Rescher and Robert Brandom, *The Logic of Inconsistency* (Oxford: Blackwell, 1980). Such an approach would have to

trade on the important distinction between a complete picture of an incomplete world and an incomplete picture of a complete world. The point of the above critique is that complete pictures of complete worlds are unavailable, so an explanatory recourse to standard possible worlds is thus vitiated.

13. Leibniz, to be sure, was entitled to compare alternative possible worlds because they were, for him, theoretical resources as instances of God's *entia rationis*. Were one to ask him where possible worlds are to come from, he would answer "Only God knows." And that is exactly correct—only God does so. We feeble humans have no way to get there from here.

Chapter 10. On the Improvability of the World

1. Albert Einstein may be viewed as the thinker who sought to turn back the clock here. See Calaprice, *The Expanded Quotable Einstein*.

2. Some of the classical texts on this issue are presented in Mark Larrimore, ed., *The Problem of Evil* (Oxford: Blackwell, 2001). The religious dimension of the problem is the subject of a vast literature. On its history and (very extensive) bibliography, see Friedrich Billicsich, *Das Problem des Übels in der Philosophie des Abendlandes*, 3 vols. (Wien: Verlag A. Sexl, 1952–59). However, this classic study of the history of the problem of evil devotes only one, somewhat perfunctory, chapter (3:195–205) to the issue of evil in nature. And even here, its focus is the negative aspect of the struggle of organic existence inherent in the Darwinian survival of the fittest. The issue of imperfect design of the physical order of nature does not figure in this otherwise monumental work.

3. *Timaeus*, 29A–30B. My translation, emphasis supplied.

4. Bertrand Russell, *Religion and Science* (London: Oxford University Press, 1935), 222.

5. Ibid., 194.

6. David Hume, *Dialogues Concerning Natural Religion*, Part 11.

7. Ibid. For a modern perspective on the issues, see John Hick, *Philosophy of Religion*, 4th ed. (Englewood Cliffs, NJ: Prentice-Hall, 1990).

8. Alvin Plantinga, *God, Freedom, and Evil* (New Haven: Harper Torch Books, 1974). See also Roderick M. Chisholm, "The Defeat of Good and Evil," *Proceedings and Addresses of the American Philosophical Association* 42 (1968–69): 26–38.

9. See, for example, R. K. Perkins, Jr., "An Atheistic Argument from the Improvability of the Universe," *Nous* 17 (1983): 239–50.

10. Russell, *Religion and Science*, 132.

11. This also provides an objection to some versions of a doctrine of intelligent design. On intelligent design theory, see J. H. Davis and H. L. Poe, *Chance and Dance: The Evolution of Design* (West Conshohocken, PA: Templeton Foundation, 2008); William A. Dembski, *Intelligent Design: The Bridge between Science and Theology* (Downers Grove, IL: InterVarsity Press, 1999); Ernan McMullin, ed., *Evolution and Creation* (Notre Dame: University of Notre Dame Press, 1985); Pennock, *Tower of Babel*; Ratzsch, *Nature, Design, and Sciences*; Michael Ruse, *The Evolution-Creation Struggle* (Cambridge, MA: Harvard University Press, 2000); and Elliot Sober, *Philosophy of Biology*, 2nd ed. (Boulder, CO: Westview Press, 2000), as well as other works cited in note 2 of chapter 8 above.

12. Admittedly, cashing in this loose reference to "the condition of intelligent beings" will need a good deal of fleshing out. Is one to be a Rawlsian maximin theorist, for whom the standard is set by the condition of the worst (the least well-off)? Is one to be an elitist, for whom the standard is the condition of the best, the most able, and most highly developed? Or is one to be a democrat, whose standard is the preponderant condition of those in the middle? And is the standard—however otherwise construed—to be applied at the level of individuals or at the level of species? Clearly, larger and deeper issues lurk behind these questions. But we need not pursue them here because the thrust of the present deliberations will apply across the board—mutatis mutandis—no matter which standard is chosen.

13. See Nicholas Rescher, *Conditionals* (Cambridge, MA: MIT Press, 2007), 77–83.

14. This condition of things is old news, as already noted in the influential *Treatise on Obligations* by the medieval scholastic philosopher Walter Burley (ca. 1275–ca. 1345), who laid down the rule: *When a false contingent proposition is posited, one can prove any other false proposition that is compatible with it.* Translated in part in N. Kretzmann and E. Stump, eds., *The Cambridge Translations of Medieval Philosophical Texts*, vol. 1, *Logic and Philosophy of Language* (Cambridge: Cambridge University Press, 1988). See pp. 389–412

15. Lorenz's discussion gave rise to New Line Cinema's 2004 feature film *The Butterfly Effect*, starring Ashton Kutcher and Amy Smart.

16. Think here of the fine-tuning of the initial conditions of cosmic evolution that plays a prominent role in the anthropic hypothesis.

17. An intriguing example of the adverse consequences of "improving" matters in the world is afforded in Kenneth Boulding's study of the unhappy consequences of significant life prolongation: "The Menace of Methusalah," *Journal of the Washington Academy of Sciences* 55, no. 7 (March 1965): 171–79.

18. F. R. Tennant, *Philosophical Theology*, 2 vols. (Cambridge: Cambridge University Press, 1928), 2:201.

19. Bruce Reichenbach, *Evil and a Good God* (New York: Fordham University Press, 1982), 106. I myself would amend the passage to read "the inevitable consequences." The issue is one of the collateral damage that is unavoidable in pursuing the greatest achievable measure of the good.

20. *Politikos* 273B. See Plato's *Timaeus* 28Cff., 35A, and 50Dff.

21. Even—indeed especially—in the sunlight, will material objects cast a shadow? Cf. Plotinus, *Enneads*, III, 2.5.

22. "Totum et perfectum sunt quasi idem," Duns Scotus maintained. Quoted from W. Tatarkiewicz, *On Perfection* (Warsaw: Warsaw University Press, 1992), 47. St. Thomas maintained that "perfectum dicitur cui nilil deest secundum modum suae perfectionis" (*Summa Theologiae* I, 4.1, ad resp.). The substantial study of R. N. Flew, *The Idea of Perfection in Christian Theology* (London: Oxford University Press, 1934), addresses the issue of human imperfection only; the idea of imperfection in physical reality is not considered. On larger aspects of the concept of perfection, see again Tatarkiewicz, *On Perfection*, as well as M. Foss, *The Idea of Perfection in the Western World* (Princeton: Princeton University Press, 1946).

23. St. Thomas Aquinas, *Summa theologiae*, I, 4.1.

24. Some physicists hold that the world's lawful makeup is such that if things were even slightly different, there could be no world at all. Then this would be the only *physically* possible world. See Heller, *Ultimate Explanations of the Universe*, 92–93. This is not Spinozism: Heller wants to trade in *logical-theoretical* possibility.

25. Even the ontological argument for God's existence—controversial as it is—does not rest on considerations of mere logic, but involves a "creative definition," namely, a substantively laden specification of the nature of the deity.

26. This line of objection to Spinoza's argumentation is admittedly sketchy and in need of a great deal of development. But in any case, its potentially controversial nature inheres in the consideration that it is effectively identical with St. Anselm's proof of God's existence, save only for the substitution of *natura* for *deus*.

27. See Sven K. Knebel, "Necessitas moralis ad optimum," *Studia Leibnitiana* 23 (1991): 3–24 and 78–92, and 24 (1992): 182–251. See also Stefan Lorenz, *De mundo optimo*, Studia Leibnitiana Supplementa 31 (Stuttgart: Steiner Verlag, 1997).

28. See Leibniz, "Discourse on Metaphysics," §6. Cf. ibid., §5, and also his "Principles of Nature and of Grace," §10; *Theodicy*, §208.

Chapter 11. Consciousness

1. One can certainly make a mistake without being conscious of it. But unless one is a conscious being who can adopt a purpose (and thereby fail in its realization), one cannot make a mistake.

2. To be sure, one could plausibly say something like the following: "The individual who prepared Caesar's breakfast on the fatal Ides of March is now totally unknown." But is this true? After all, we have just taken note of this very individual. This seeming anomaly needs to be removed by a distinction. The individual has been alluded to but not specified—individuated but not concretely identified. So I cannot appropriately claim to know *who* the individual at issue is but only at best *that* a certain individual is at issue.

Chapter 12. Control

1. Suppose the trustee for an orphan's legacy bets the whole amount on the ponies. If he loses, the full share of blame is his. If he wins—and perhaps wins big—does he get any credit? Is there any diminution of the obvious moral reprehension of having put his charge's interest at risk? A messy question, this.

2. The situation is reminiscent of the principle of double effect in moral theology. For in the choice of "doing X" the agent accepts the doing of something bad to avoid a greater evil. Of course the issue of how far this goes—of how bad an action can prove acceptable—still remains untouched. The comparative determination of which evil is the lesser is far from straightforward.

Chapter 13. Free Will in the Light of Process Theory

1. Daniel C. Dennett, "I Could not Have Done Otherwise—So What," *Journal of Philosophy* 81 (1984): 554 (my emphasis). Compare Dennett, *Elbow Room: The Varieties of Free Will Worth Wanting* (Cambridge, MA: MIT Press, 1984), 16.

2. For *moral* freedom there is the additional factor that the agent's deliberations must proceed autonomously, issuing from the wants and desires that are authentically his own, without undue influence of any sort.

3. On this situation, see the classic essay by R. E. Hobart (= Dickinson S. Miller), "Free Will as Involving Determinism and Inconceivable without It," *Mind* 43 (1934): 1–27.

4. For the background of the topic, see Nicholas Rescher and Estelle Burris, *Free Will: An Extensive Bibliography* (Frankfurt: ONTOS Verlag, 2010).

Chapter 14. Personhood

1. To be sure, someone may ask: "Why think of ourselves in this way—why see ourselves as free rational agents?" But of course, to ask this is to ask for a good rational reason and is thus already to take a stance within the framework of rationality. In theory, one can "resign" from the community of rational beings, abandoning all claims to being more than "mere animals." But this is a step one cannot *justify*—there are no satisfactory rational grounds for taking it. And this is something most of us realize instinctively. The appropriateness of acknowledging others as responsible agents whenever possible holds in our own case as well.

2. H. A. Prichard, "Does Moral Philosophy Rest on a Mistake?" *Mind* 21 (1912): 21–37.

3. Immanuel Kant portrayed the obligation at issue in the following terms: "First, it is one's duty to raise himself out of the crudity of his nature—out of his animality (*quoad actum*) more and more to humanity, by which alone he is capable of setting himself ends. It is man's [paramount] duty to . . . supply by instruction what is lacking in his knowledge, and to correct his mistakes. . . . This end [is] his duty in order that he may . . . be worthy of the humanity dwelling within him." (*Metaphysics of Morals, Akademie Ausgabe* edition, vol. 6, p. 387, my translation.)

4. A good treatment of relevant issues is given in Herbert Morris, "Persons and Punishment," *The Monist* 52 (1968): 475–501. See also R. S. Downie and Elizabeth Telfer, *Respect for Persons* (London: Allen & Unwin, 1969).

5. Note that such an analysis is reductive but not eliminative. It does not, like utilitarianism, try to achieve the impossible aim of extracting duties from something other than duties (i.e., considerations of advantage). Rather, it derives duties of one sort (moral duties) from those of another (those ontological duties of self-enhancement through the realization of positive potential).

6. Immanuel Kant, *Critique of Pure Reason*, A814/B842.

7. Francis Hutcheson saw morality as a matter of so acting that we can reflectively approve of our own *character*. See L. A. Selby-Bigge, ed., *British Moralists*, vol. 1 (Oxford: Clarendon Press, 1897), which contains Hutcheson's *Inquiry Concerning Moral Good and Evil* (London: J. Darby in Bartholomew-Close, 1725). But even more fundamental is the matter of so acting that we can reflectively approve of our own *nature*, in prizing the kind of creatures we are—or see ourselves

as being. And this requires one to act in such a way that one can reflectively approve of oneself. To maintain my sense of self-worth, I must act in such a way that I need make no excuses for myself toward myself. (The linkage of morality to self-respect—the maintenance of a positive self-image and a proper sense of self-worth—shows why limiting the scope of "real persons" to an in-group of some sort is so conducive to moral wickedness. If slaves or barbarians or enemies in war are not seen as being persons just like oneself, then their maltreatment is not impeded by any threats to self-respect.)

8. Even David Hume is drawn toward such a view. As he sees it, even those "sensible knaves" whom he imagines as taking improper advantage of their opportunities for selfish gains in a moral society would, "were they ever so secret and successful," nevertheless still emerge as "in the end, the greatest dupes," because they have "sacrificed the invaluable enjoyment of a character, with themselves at least, for the acquisition of worthless toys and gewgaws." ("An Enquiry Concerning the Principles of Morals," in *Enquiries Concerning Human Understanding and Concerning the Principles of Morals*, ed. L. A. Selby-Bigge [Oxford: Clarendon Press, 1985], Pt. II, p. 283.) The sensible knave automatically foregoes the pleasure of "peaceful reflection on one's own conduct" (ibid.). Moreover, because he cannot then sustain even his own critical scrutiny, the knave also renders himself unable to enjoy membership in an organized society (which, as Hume sees it, is perhaps no lesser loss). Prudence here reinforces self-respect.

9. "But the life of man," Hume wrote, "is of no greater importance to the universe than that of an oyster" ("Of Suicide," in *Essays: Moral, Political, and Literary*, ed. Eugene F. Miller [Indianapolis: Hackett, 1985]). To be sure, one may wonder how the universe conveyed this information to him.

10. The ontological-obligation response to the question "Why be moral?" exactly parallels the similar responses given in chapter 1 to the question "Why be rational?" And this is only fitting and proper, seeing that morality is simply one sector or subdomain of rationality.

11. The general line of these deliberations has been to ground morality in rationality, while at the same time denying that it is appropriate to ground morality in prudence. For simple self-consistency, then, a validation of rationality that proceeds wholly in terms of prudential self-interest is automatically denied us. Instead, consonance and consistency require a validation of rationality that is itself ultimately ontological and axiological (value-oriented), validating rationality too in terms of its ontological fitness. And this is indeed the line taken in the author's book *Rationality* (Oxford: Clarendon Press, 1988) and also in the author's *Moral Absolutes* (New York and Bern: Peter Lang, 1989).

Chapter 16.   Empathy, Shared Experience, and Other Minds

1. Charles Sanders Peirce, *Collected Papers*, ed. Charles Hartshorne et al., 8 vols. (Cambridge, MA: Harvard University Press, 1931–58), vol. 1, sec. 81 (orig. pub. 1896); cf. vol. 7, sec. 220.

2. Ibid., vol. 6, sec. 530 (orig. pub. 1901).

Chapter 17.   Philosophy as an Inexact Science

1. See Olaf Helmer and Nicholas Rescher, "On the Epistemology of the Inexact Sciences," *Management Science* 6 (1959): 25–52.

2. For a vivid illustration of this phenomenon, see Robert K. Shope, *An Analysis of Knowing: A Decade of Research* (Princeton: Princeton University Press, 1983).

3. See Plato's dialogues, especially the *Theaetetus*. For further reading see F. M. Cornford, *Plato's Theory of Knowledge* (London: Routledge & Kegan Paul, 1935); Michael Huemer, *Epistemology: Contemporary Readings* (London and New York: Routledge, 2002), which reprints the Gettier article "Is Justified True Belief Knowledge?"; P. K. Moser, D. H. Mulder, and J. D. Trout, *The Theory of Knowledge* (Oxford: Oxford University Press, 1998); W. G. Runciman, *Plato's Later Epistemology* (Cambridge: Cambridge University Press, 1962); Ernest Sosa, Jaegwon Kim, and Matthew McGrath, eds., *Epistemology: An Anthology*, 2nd ed. (Oxford: Blackwell, 2008); and N. P. White, *Plato on Knowledge and Reality* (Indianapolis: Hackett, 1976).

Chapter 18.   Philosophy's Involvement with Transcendental Issues

1. Aristotle, *Nicomachean Ethics* 1094b, my translation.

BIBLIOGRAPHY

Included are works of interest for the issues discussed as well as works explicitly cited. A few easily accessible classical works with edition-independent references have been omitted.

Ammon, K., and S. C. Gandevia. "Transcendental Magnetic Stimulation Can Influence the Selection for Motor Programmes." *Journal of Neurology, Neurosurgery, and Psychiatry* 53 (1990): 705–7.

Ashworth, J. E. *Language and Logic in the Post-Medieval Period.* Boston: Reidel, 1974.

Balaguer, M. *Free Will as an Open Scientific Problem.* Cambridge, MA: MIT Press, 2009.

Basil-Neto, J. P., A. Pascual-Leone, J. Valls-Solé, L. G. Cohen, and M. Hallett. "Focal Transcranial Magnetic Stimulation and Response Bias in a Forced-Choice Task." *Journal of Neurology, Neurosurgery and Psychiatry* 55 (1992): 964–66.

Billicsich, Friedrich. *Das Problem des Übels in der Philosophie des Abendlandes.* 3 vols. Wien: A. Sexl, 1952–59.

Bodanis, David. *Einstein's Greatest Mistake.* Boston: Little, Brown and Co., 2016.

Boulding, Kenneth. "The Menace of Methusalah." *Journal of the Washington Academy of Sciences* 55, no. 7 (March 1965): 171–79.

Brown, Laurie M., ed. *Feynman's Thesis: A New Approach to Quantum Theory.* Hackensack, NJ: World Scientific, 2005.

Burley, Walter. *Treatise on Obligation.* Translated in part in N. Kretzmann and E. Stump, eds., *The Cambridge Translations of Medieval Philosophical Texts,* vol. 1, *Logic and Philosophy of Language.* Cambridge: Cambridge University Press, 1988.

Calaprice, Alice, ed. *The Expanded Quotable Einstein*. Princeton: Princeton University Press, 2000.

Chisholm, Roderick M. "The Defeat of Good and Evil." *Proceedings and Addresses of the American Philosophical Association* 42 (1968–69): 26–38.

———. "Law Statements and Counterfactual Inferences." *Analysis* 15 (1955): 97–105.

Chlup, Radek. *Proclus: An Introduction*. Cambridge: Cambridge University Press, 2016.

Churchland, Paul. *Brain-wise: Studies in Neurophilosophy*. Cambridge, MA: MIT Press, 2002.

Clark, Ronald W. *Einstein: The Life and Times*. New York: World Publishing Company, 1971.

Cornford, F. M. *Plato's Theory of Knowledge*. London: Routledge & Kegan Paul, 1935.

Davis, J. H., and H. L. Poe. *Chance and Dance: The Evolution of Design*. West Conshohocken, PA: Templeton Foundation, 2008.

Dawkins, Robert. *The Blind Watchmaker: Why the Evidence of Evolution Reveals a Universe without Design*. New York: Norton Publishing Co., 1986.

Delgado, José Manuel Rodríguez. *Physical Control of the Mind; Toward a Psychocivilized Society*. New York: Harper & Row, 1969.

Dembski, William A. *The Design Inference: Eliminating Chance through Small Probabilities*. Cambridge: Cambridge University Press, 1998.

———. *Intelligent Design: The Bridge between Science and Theology*. Downers Grove, IL: InterVarsity Press, 1999.

———. *Mere Creation: Science, Faith, and Intelligent Design*. Downers Grove, IL: InterVarsity Press, 1998.

Dennett, Daniel C. *Elbow Room: The Varieties of Free Will Worth Wanting*. Cambridge, MA: MIT Press, 1984.

———. "I Could Not Have Done Otherwise—So What." *Journal of Philosophy* 81 (1984): 553–65.

Dilthey, Wilhelm. *Weltanschauungslehre. Gesammelte Schriften*, vol. 8. Stuttgart: Teubner; Göttingen: Vandenhoeck & Ruprecht, 1961.

Dongen, Jeroen van. *Einstein's Unification*. Cambridge: Cambridge University Press, 2010.

Downie, R. S., and Elizabeth Telfer. *Respect for Persons*. London: Allen & Unwin, 1969.

Eddington, Arthur. *The Nature of the Physical World*. New York: Macmillan; Cambridge: Cambridge University Press, 1929.

Edelman, G. M. *The Remembered Present.* New York: Basic Books, 1989.

Einstein, Albert. *Ideas and Opinions.* New York: Bonanza, 1954.

———. "On Generalized Theory of Gravitation." *Scientific American* 182 (1950): 13–17.

Feltz, Bernard. "Plasticité neuronale et libre arbitri." *Révue Philosophique de Louvain* 111 (2013): 27–52.

Flew, R. N. *The Idea of Perfection in Christian Theology.* London: Oxford University Press, 1934.

Foss, M. *The Idea of Perfection in the Western World.* Princeton: Princeton University Press, 1946.

Gale, Richard M. *On the Nature and Existence of God.* Cambridge: Cambridge University Press, 1991.

Gazzaniga, Michael S. *Nature's Mind: The Biological Roots of Thinking, Emotions, Sexuality, Language, and Intelligence.* New York: Basic Books, 1992.

Goldstein, Rebecca. *Incompleteness: The Proof and Paradox of Kurt Gödel.* New York: W. W. Norton, 2005.

Haeckel, Ernst. *Die Welträtsel.* Leipzig: A. Kröner, 1899.

Haggard, Patrick, and Valerian Chambon. "Sense of Agency." *Current Biology* 22, no. 10 (2012).

Haggard, Patrick, and M. Eimer. "On the Relation between Brain Potentials and the Awareness of Voluntary Movements." *Experimental Brain Research* 126 (1999): 128–33.

Heller, Michael. *Ultimate Explanations of the Universe.* Trans. Teresa Baluk-Ulewiczowa. Berlin: Springer, 2009.

Helmer, Olaf, and Nicholas Rescher. "On the Epistemology of the Inexact Sciences." *Management Science* 6 (1959): 25–52.

Hick, John. *Philosophy of Religion.* 4th ed. Englewood Cliffs, NJ: Prentice-Hall, 1990.

Hobart, R. E. (= Dickinson S. Miller). "Free Will as Involving Determinism and Inconceivable without It." *Mind* 43 (1934): 1–27.

Huemer, Michael. "An Enquiry Concerning the Principles of Morals." In *Enquiries Concerning Human Understanding and Concerning the Principles of Morals*, ed. L. A. Selby-Bigge. Oxford: Clarendon Press, 1985.

———. *Epistemology: Contemporary Readings.* London and New York: Routledge, 2002.

———. "Of Suicide." In *Essays: Moral, Political and Literary*, ed. Eugene F. Miller. Indianapolis: Hackett, 1985.

Jourdan, P. E. B. *The Principle of Least Action.* Chicago: Carus, 1913.

Kane, Robert. *The Significance of Free Will.* New York: Oxford University Press, 1996.

Knebel, Sven K. "Necessitas moralis ad optimum." *Studia Leibnitiana* 23 (1991): 3–24 and 78–92, and 24 (1992): 182–251.

Lanczos, Carnetris. *The Variation Principle of Mechanics.* New York: Dover, 1986.

Larrimore, Mark, ed. *The Problem of Evil.* Oxford: Blackwell, 2001.

Leibniz, G. W. *Philosophical Papers and Letters.* Trans. and ed. L. E. Loemker. Dordrecht: Reidel, 1969.

Leslie, John. "Anthropic Principle, World Ensemble, Design." *American Philosophical Quarterly* 19 (1982): 141–51.

———. "Efforts to Explain All Existence." *Mind* 87 (1978): 181–97.

———. "The Theory that the World Exists Because It Should." *American Philosophical Quarterly* 7 (1970): 286–98.

———. *Universes.* London and New York: Routledge, 1989.

———. *Value and Existence.* Oxford: Clarendon Press, 1979.

———. "The World's Necessary Existence." *International Journal for Philosophy of Religion* 18 (1980): 207–23.

Leslie, John, and Robert L. Kuhne, eds. *The Mystery of Existence: Why Is There Anything At All?* Oxford: Wiley-Blackwell, 2013.

Libet, Benjamin. *Mind-Time: The Temporal Factor in Consciousness.* Cambridge, MA: Harvard University Press, 2004.

———. "Unconscious Cerebral Initiative and the Role of Conscious Will in Voluntary Action." *Behavioral and Brain Sciences* 8 (1985): 529–66.

———. "The Unconscious Initiatives of a Free Voluntary Act." *Brain* 106 (1983): 623–42.

Lorenz, Stefan. *De mundo optimo.* Studia Leibnitiana Supplementa 31. Stuttgart: Steiner Verlag, 1997.

McMullin, Ernan, ed. *Evolution and Creation.* Notre Dame: University of Notre Dame Press, 1985.

Mihailescu, Calin-Andrei, and Walid Hamarneh, eds. *Fiction Updated: Theories of Fictionality, Narratology, and Poetics.* Toronto: University of Toronto Press, 1977.

Morris, Herbert. "Persons and Punishment." *The Monist* 52 (1968): 475–501.

Moser, P. K., D. H. Mulder, and J. D. Trout. *The Theory of Knowledge.* Oxford: Oxford University Press, 1998.

Nagel, Tom. *The View from Nowhere.* Oxford: Oxford University Press, 1986.

Norton, John. "Nature Is the Realization of the Simplest Conceivable Mathematical Ideas: Einstein and the Canon of Mathematical Simplicity." *Studies in the History and Philosophy of Modern Physics* 31 (2000): 135–70.

Numbers, Ronald L. *The Creationists: From Scientific Creationism to Intelligent Design.* Cambridge, MA: Harvard University Press, 2006.

Peirce, Charles S. *Collected Papers.* Ed. Charles Hartshorne et al., 8 vols. Cambridge, MA: Harvard University Press, 1931–58.

Pennock, Robert T. *Tower of Babel: The Evidence against the New Creationism.* Cambridge, MA: MIT Press, 1998.

———, ed. *Intelligent Design Creationism and Its Critics: Philosophical, Theological, and Scientific Perspectives.* Cambridge, MA: MIT Press, 2001.

Pepper, Stephen C. *World Hypotheses: A Study in Evidence.* Berkeley and Los Angeles: University of California Press, 1942.

Pereboom, Derk. *Living Without Free Will.* Cambridge: Cambridge University Press, 2001.

Perkins, R. K., Jr. "An Atheistic Argument from the Improvability of the Universe." *Nous* 17 (1983): 239–50.

Plantinga, Alvin. *God, Freedom, and Evil.* New Haven: Harper Torch Books, 1974.

———. *The Nature of Necessity.* Oxford: Clarendon Press, 1974.

Prantl, Carl. *Geschichte der Logik im Abendlande.* 4 vols. Graz: Akademische Druck- und Verlagsanstalt, 1955.

Prichard, H. A. "Does Moral Philosophy Rest on a Mistake?" *Mind* 21 (1912): 21–37.

Pruss, Alexander R. "The Hume-Edwards Principle and the Cosmological Argument." *International Journal for Philosophy of Religion* 434 (1988): 149–65.

———. *The Principle of Sufficient Reason: A Reassessment.* New York: Cambridge University Press, 2006.

Quine, W. V. "On What There Is." *Review of Metaphysics* 2 (1948): 21–38. Reprinted in W. V. Quine, *From a Logical Point of View*, 1–19. Cambridge, MA: Harvard University Press, 1953.

Ratzsch, Del. *Nature, Design, and Science: The Status of Design in Natural Science.* Albany: State University of New York Press, 2001.

Reichenbach, Bruce. *Evil and a Good God.* New York: Fordham University Press, 1982.

Reid, Thomas. *Essays on the Intellectual and Active Powers of Man.* Edinburgh: J. Bell, 1785; American ed., Philadelphia: William Young, 1793.

Rescher, Nicholas. *Axiogenesis: An Essay on Metaphysical Optimalism.* Lanham, MD: Lexington Books, 2010.

———. *Conditionals.* Cambridge, MA: MIT Press, 2007.

———. *Explaining Existence.* Frankfurt: ONTOS Verlag, 2012.

———. "Leibniz and Possible Worlds." *Studia Leibnitiana* 28 (1995): 129–62.

———. *The Logic of Commands.* London: Routledge, 1969.

————. *Moral Absolutes*. New York and Bern: Peter Lang, 1989.

————. *Nature and Understanding*. Oxford: Clarendon Press, 2000.

————. *Productive Evolution*. Frankfurt: ONTOS Verlag, 2011.

————. "Randomness and Reason." *Symposion: Journal of the Romanian Academy of Science* 2 (2015): 11–18.

————. *Rationality*. Oxford: Clarendon Press, 1988.

————. *The Riddle of Existence*. Lanham, MD: University Press of America, 1984.

————. *A Theory of Possibility*. Oxford: Blackwell, 1975.

————. *A Useful Inheritance: Evolutionary Epistemology in Philosophical Perceptive*. Savage, MD: Rowman & Littlefield, 1989.

Rescher, Nicholas, and R. Brandom. *The Logic of Inconsistency*. Oxford: Blackwell, 1980.

Rescher, Nicholas, and Estelle Burris. *Free Will: An Extensive Bibliography*. Frankfurt: ONTOS Verlag, 2010.

Rowe, William L. *The Cosmological Argument*. Princeton: Princeton University Press, 1975.

————. "Two Criticisms of the Cosmological Argument." *The Monist* 54 (1970). Reprinted in *Philosophy of Religion: Selective Readings*, 2nd ed., ed. W. L. Rowe and W. Wainwright, 142–56. New York: Harcourt Brace Jovanovich, 1989.

Runciman, W. G. *Plato's Later Epistemology*. Cambridge: Cambridge University Press, 1962.

Ruse, Michael. *The Evolution-Creation Struggle*. Cambridge, MA: Harvard University Press, 2000.

Russell, Bertrand. *Our Knowledge of the External World*. London: Allen & Unwin, 1922.

————. *Religion and Science*. London: Oxford University Press, 1935.

Rüstow, Alexander. *Der Lügner: Theorie, Geschichte und Auflösung*. Leipzig: B. G. Treubner, 1910. Reprint, New York & London: Garland Publishing Co., 1987.

Selby-Bigge, L. A., ed. *British Moralists*. Vol. 1. Oxford: Clarendon Press, 1897.

Shope, Robert K. *An Analysis of Knowing: A Decade of Research*. Princeton: Princeton University Press, 1983.

Skinner, B. F. *Beyond Freedom and Dignity*. New York: Vintage Books, 1971.

Sober, Elliot. *Philosophy of Biology*. 2nd ed. Boulder, CO: Westview Press, 2000.

Sommerfeld, Arnold. *Electrodynamics: Lectures in Theoretical Physics*. Vol. 3. Trans. E. G. Ramberg. New York: Academic Press, 1964. German original, *Vorlesungen über theoretische Physik*. Wiesbaden: Klemm Verlag, 1945.

Sosa, Ernest, Jaegwon Kim, and Matthew McGrath, eds. *Epistemology: An Anthology*. 2nd ed. Oxford: Blackwell, 2008.

Tatarkiewicz, W. *On Perfection*. Warsaw: Warsaw University Press, 1992.

Tennant, F. R. *Philosophical Theology*. 2 vols. Cambridge: Cambridge University Press, 1928.

van Inwagen, Peter. *An Essay on Free Will*. Oxford: Oxford University Press, 1983.

Watson, Gary, ed. *Free Will*. New York: Oxford University Press, 1983.

Weatherford, Roy. *The Implications of Determinism*. London and New York: Routledge, 1991.

Wegner, Daniel. *The Illusion of Conscious Will*. Cambridge, MA: MIT Press, 2002.

White, N. P. *Plato on Knowledge and Reality*. Indianapolis: Hackett, 1976.

Wippel, John F., ed. *The Ultimate Why Questions: Why Is There Anything at All?* Washington, DC: Catholic University of American Press, 1911.

Wolf, Susan. "Sanity and the Metaphysics of Responsibility." In *Responsibility, Character and Emotions: New Essays in Moral Psychology*, ed. Ferdinand David Schoeman, 46–62. Cambridge: Cambridge University Press, 1987. Reprinted in *Free Will*, ed. Robert Kane, 147ff. Malden, MA: Blackwell, 2002.

INDEX

Alfonso X, king of Castile, 113
Anselm, Saint, 244n26
Aquinas. *See* Thomas Aquinas, Saint
Aristotle, 9, 20, 43, 207, 215, 226,
    238nn1, 2, 248n1 (ch18)
Ashworth, J. E., 239n6

Bentham, Jeremy, 205
Bergson, Henri, 230
Berkeley, George, 26
Billicsich, Friedrich, 242n2
Bodanis, David, 238n6
Bohm, David, 53, 237n2 (ch5)
Boulding, Kenneth, 243n17
Brandom, Robert, 241n12
Buridan, John, 62
Burley, Walter, 116–17, 243n14
Burris, Estelle, 246n4 (ch13)

Calaprice, Alice, 238n4 (ch5),
    242n1
Chisholm, Roderick M., 240n2,
    242n8
Chlup, Radek, 240n3 (ch8)
Chrysippus, 238n3
Cicero, 238nn1, 2
Clark, Ronald W., 237n1 (ch5)
Cornford, F. M., 248n3

Darwin, Charles, 169
Davis, J. H., 243n11
Dawkins, Robert, 239n2
Dembski, William A., 239n2,
    243n11
Democritus, 26
Dennett, Daniel C., 160, 245n1
    (ch13)
Descartes, René, 30, 60, 150
Dilthey, Wilhelm, 23, 24, 237n1
    (ch2)
Dongen, Jeroen van, 237n2 (ch5)
Downie, R. S., 246n4 (ch14)
Doyle, Arthur Conan, 236n5

Eddington, Arthur, 35–36, 37, 237n2
    (ch3)
Edwards, Paul, 10–12
Einstein, Albert, 19, 33–34, 53–56,
    237n1 (ch5), 242n1
Epimenides, 62
Eubulides, 62, 238n2
Flew, R. N., 244n22
Foss, M., 244n22

Gale, Richard M., 236n1
Gettier, Edmund, 217, 248n3
Goldstein, Rebecca, 237n1 (ch5)

Hamarneh, Walid, 240n5
Heller, Michael, 240n4 (ch8), 244n24
Helmer, Olaf, 248n1 (ch17)
Hick, John, 242n7
Hobart, R. E. (Dickinson S. Miller), 245n3
Huemer, Michael, 248n3
Hume, David, 10–12, 114, 185, 242n6, 247nn8, 9
Hutcheson, Francis, 246n7

Jacobs, W. W., 120
James, William, 176, 234
Jaspers, Karl, 237n3 (ch2)

Kant, Immanuel, 18, 35, 130, 184–85, 192, 207, 215, 218, 246nn3, 6
Kim, Jaegwon, 248n3
Knebel, Sven K., 244n27
Kretzmann, Norman, 243n14

Laertius, Diogenes, 238n3
La Mettrie, J. O. de, 26
Larrimore, Mark, 241n2
Leibniz, G. W., 9, 13, 16–17, 19, 26, 91, 112–13, 114, 129, 130–31, 132, 166, 220, 236n3, 242n13, 244n28
Lewis, Clarence Irving, 52
Lewis, David, 106
Lorenz, E. N., 118, 243n15
Lorenz, Stefan, 244n27

McGrath, Matthew, 248n3
McMullin, Ernan, 243n11
Mihailescu, Calin-Andrei, 249n5
Miller, Eugene F., 247n9
Morris, Herbert, 246n4 (ch14)
Moser, Paul K., 248n3
Mulder, Dwayne H., 248n3
Müller-Freienfels, Richard, 237n3 (ch2)

Norton, John, 238n5 (ch5)
Numbers, Ronald L., 239n2

Pascal, Blaise, 231
Paul, Saint, 238n3
Paul of Venice, 62–63, 238n4 (ch6), 239n7
Paulsen, Friedrich, 237n3 (ch2)
Peirce, Charles Sanders, 198, 248n1 (ch16)
Pennock, Robert T., 239n2, 243n11
Pepper, Stephen C., 237n2 (ch2)
Perkins, R. K., Jr., 242n9
Phietas of Cos, 238n3
Plantinga, Alvin, 114, 241nn7, 8, 242n8
Plato, 18, 26, 35, 113, 127, 185, 244n20, 248n3
Plotinus, 244n21
Poe, H. L., 243n11
Prantl, Carl, 238nn1, 2, 4, 5 (ch6), 239nn6, 7
Prichard, H. A., 180, 246n2
Pruss, Alexander R., 236n1, 239n1 (ch7)

Quine, W. V., 110, 241n11

Ratzsch, Del, 239n2, 243n11
Rawls, John, 238n7, 243n12
Reichenbach, Bruce, 121, 244n19
Rescher, Nicholas, 241n12, 243n13, 246n4 (ch13), 248n1 (ch17)
Rowe, William L., 236n1
Runciman, W. G., 248n3
Ruse, Michael, 243n11
Russell, Bertrand, 35, 113, 114–15, 217, 237nn1, 2 (ch3), 242n4, 243n10
Rüstow, Alexander, 238n3
Ryle, Gilbert, 150

Schaffner, Kenneth, 237n3 (ch5)
Scotus, Duns, 244n22
Selby-Bigge, L. A., 246n7, 247n8
Sellars, Wilfrid, 237n2 (ch3)
Shope, Robert K., 248n2 (ch17)
Sober, Elliot, 243n11
Socrates, 7, 185
Sommerfeld, Arnold, 237n3 (ch5)
Sosa, Ernest, 248n3
Spinoza, 13, 129, 244nn24, 26
Stump, E., 243n14

Tatarkiewicz, W., 244n22
Telfer, Elizabeth, 246n4 (ch14)

Tennant, F. R., 244n18
Theophrastus, 238n3
Thomas Aquinas, Saint, 128, 239n1
    (ch8), 244nn22, 23
Thompson, D'Arcy Wentworth, 87
Trout, J. D., 248n3

Voltaire, 113–14, 130–31

Wainwright, W., 236n1
White, N. P., 248n3
Whitehead, A. N., 26

Zeno, 160–61

NICHOLAS RESCHER is Distinguished University Professor of Philosophy at the University of Pittsburgh. He is the author of 175 books, including *Objectivity: The Obligations of Impersonal Reason* (University of Notre Dame Press, 1997).

www.ingramcontent.com/pod-product-compliance
Lightning Source LLC
Chambersburg PA
CBHW070400100426
42812CB00005B/1582